Finding Pete

Finding Pete

Rediscovering the Brother I Lost in Vietnam

Jill Hunting

WESLEYAN UNIVERSITY PRESS

Middletown, Connecticut

Published by Wesleyan University Press,
Middletown, CT 06459
www.wesleyan.edu/wespress
© 2009 by Jill Hunting
Printed in United States of America
5 4 3 2 1

Library of Congress Cataloging-in-Publication Data
Hunting, Jill, 1950–
Finding Pete: rediscovering the brother I lost in Vietnam / Jill Hunting.
  p. cm.
Includes bibliographical references and index.
ISBN 978-0-8195-6923-3 (cloth: alk. paper)
1. Hunting, Peter, 1941–1965—Death and burial. 2. Hunting, Peter,
1941–1965—Correspondence. 3. Hunting, Jill, 1950—Family.
4. Brothers and sisters—United States—Case studies. 5. Loss
(Psychology)—Case studies. 6. Civilians in war—Vietnam—
Biography. 7. International Voluntary Services—Biography. 8. Vietnam
War, 1961–1975—Biography. 9. Vietnam War, 1961–1975—Casualties.
10. Vietnam War, 1961–1975—United States. I. Title.
CT275.H75568H86   2009
959.704'30922—dc22
[B]   2009018233

Wesleyan University Press is a member of the Green Press Initiative.
The paper used in this book meets their minimum requirement for
recycled paper.

For Cis and Hol

Sea of Clouds

The time has come to brave the sea of clouds,
To bear away though aching young and hardly made,
Rolled down in dark and brooding seas.

Soon gone from sight, our faces lost in waves,
Our cries no longer heard,
We finally slip into a wind-blurred far away.

Till we are gone—a small and slanted line
To bravely cut that endless edge,
Where dark and boiling clouds wedge down
To meet the sea.

—Kirtland Mead, 1965

Composed by a college friend of Pete Hunting and enclosed
with a sympathy letter to his parents. Used with permission
of Kirtland Mead.

CONTENTS

Illustrations follow pages 80 and 224

AUTHOR'S NOTE

On November 12, 1965, two days before one of the first major battles of the war in Vietnam, my only brother, Pete, was killed there. I had just turned fifteen.

Pete's death was widely reported, but it so traumatized my family that we didn't discuss what had happened to him. Before long, we stopped talking about him at all.

Between July 1963—when my brother arrived in Southeast Asia as a civilian volunteer with a little-known nongovernmental organization called International Voluntary Services, or IVS—and November 1965, he wrote dozens of letters home. As a teenager, I didn't pay close attention to them, but I was aware that Pete routinely mentioned names I heard on the news, such as Diem, Lodge, Rusk, Ky, Westmoreland, and McNamara.

Pete was twenty-four when he was killed. When I reached that age, I longed to learn more about the young man I had known only from the vantage point of a little sister. I asked my mother if I could read his letters again. She told me they had all been destroyed in a basement flood. My connection with Pete was lost forever—or so I thought.

In 2004, sixty-four letters surfaced. Those letters led me to others, and eventually I had 175. Only by reading them and talking with many kind, generous individuals who remembered Pete did I come to know once again my wonderful big brother. I know him better now, in fact, than when he was alive.

Many people have suffered a loss like mine: someone we loved died in a war zone. Thousands, perhaps millions, of us waited for someone who did not return from a faraway land. We have struggled, with various degrees of success, to integrate our loss. Life has not stopped for us, even if we went forward with a chamber deep within sealed up. Some of us have not told our closest friends or spouse about a person we once mourned, or still mourn.

In my case, thirteen years passed between Pete's death and the weekend my sisters and I got together for the first time just to talk about him. It was twenty years before I met his closest friends in IVS, and twenty-five years before I went with one of them to Vietnam. Thirty-two years went by before my family helped create a memorial to Pete in the form of a trail that winds through the Connecticut woods he explored as a boy.

None of these turning points, meaningful as they were, matched the significance of discovering my brother's letters. What they meant to me, where they led me, and how they changed me is the substance of *Finding Pete*. Two days into my fifteenth year, I lost my brother and the freedom to talk about him. This is the story of what I found and how I found it.

Finding Pete is a work of nonfiction. Real names are used for all but four individuals, who have been given another name to protect their privacy. No characters or conversations have been invented, with one exception: In the final chapter, I reconstructed Pete's last day on the basis of data gathered from many sources. Because certain facts are lost to time, however, I filled in some details, consistent with what I learned.

Minor changes of spelling, grammar, and punctuation have been made to some letters quoted in the book.

In some quarters, "Vietnam War" is considered U.S.-centric, while elsewhere it is accepted as standard usage. The term is used in this book.

In the narrative, the spelling of Vietnamese place names conforms to those in *Webster's Collegiate Dictionary, 11th Edition*. In quoted material, *Viet-Nam* and *Viet Nam* are sometimes used instead of *Vietnam*.

The U.S. Agency for International Development, or USAID, is a foreign assistance agency of the U.S. government, situated within the State Department. In its field mission in Vietnam, USAID was known as USOM. In his letters and journal, Pete did not always distinguish between USAID and USOM, and for this reason "U.S. Agency for International Development," "USAID," "AID," "U.S. Operations Mission," and "USOM" are used interchangeably.

Usage of "Vietcong" and "VC" (referring to Vietnamese insurgents and considered by some to be derogatory) and "National Liberation Front" and "NLF" (the organization of the insurgency) follows that of my brother and his peers.

"MAAG" and "MACV" were the designations for U.S. military commands in Vietnam. MAAG, the Military Assistance Advisory Group, was formed in 1955 and later subsumed under the Military Assistance Command–Vietnam, or MACV. My brother's correspondence made no clear-cut distinction between the terms, and his usage of the acronyms has been preserved.

On second reference to Pete's friends whom I know personally, I have used their first names except when it is clearer to use surnames.

I have not included a list of my conversations and correspondence that informed the writing of this book. I am indebted to the many people who spoke with me about my brother and Vietnam.

Portions of the book first appeared in different form in "A Lost Brother's Lost Words," published by the *Washington Post Magazine.*

Finding Pete

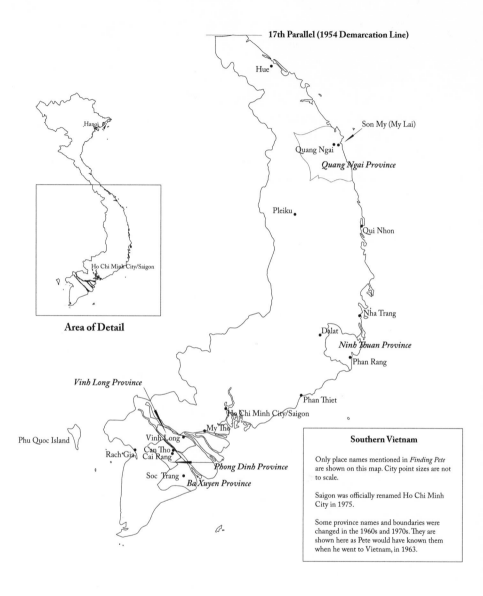

17th Parallel (1954 Demarcation Line)

Hanoi

Hue

Son My (My Lai)

Quang Ngai

Quang Ngai Province

Pleiku

Qui Nhon

Area of Detail

Nha Trang

Dalat

Ninh Thuan Province

Phan Rang

Vinh Long Province

Phan Thiet

Ho Chi Minh City/Saigon

Ho Chi Minh City/Saigon

My Tho

Phu Quoc Island

Vinh Long

Rach Gia

Can Tho
Cai Rang

Phong Dinh Province

Soc Trang

Ba Xuyen Province

Southern Vietnam

Only place names mentioned in *Finding Pete* are shown on this map. City point sizes are not to scale.

Saigon was officially renamed Ho Chi Minh City in 1975.

Some province names and boundaries were changed in the 1960s and 1970s. They are shown here as Pete would have known them when he went to Vietnam, in 1963.

Prologue

"This is a good map," my Vietnamese guide says. "We can find this place. We will make a ceremony."

I have just shown him a map with an X where Pete, my brother, was killed.

Before I left home I had exchanged e-mails with a Vietnam veteran whose Web site included old maps of Southeast Asia. He had helped me pinpoint the military coordinates I obtained from the National Archives and Records Administration: Vietnam ws 820 036. One map of the Lower Mekong Delta was a clutter of hatch marks, village names, and small blue squares inside larger black ones, so I asked for help finding the coordinates. He sent me a map with a big red X. It was a mile and a quarter south of Cai Rang on National Highway 4.

I had stared at the map. *So that's where it happened.*

Now it is September of 2006 and I'm traveling in Vietnam with four men. Two are Americans. One of them founded an organization that builds libraries in Southeast Asia, and the other is a donor. The two Vietnamese are a driver and our guide and interpreter, whose name is Song. His dignified bearing and formal manners, and the way he sits with his legs crossed knee-upon-knee, remind me of European men. He owns a tour company and has taken many returning GIs to the places where they fought or their buddies died.

We stop at a little shop and buy a package of fifty incense sticks, a plastic cigarette lighter, and a long bouquet of white freesia wrapped in newspaper and cellophane.

Nine o'clock in the morning and it's already hot. Our minivan crosses the Lower Mekong on a ferry and bumps off the ramp onto a two-lane road lined with concrete houses and shops. Most have a tin-roofed porch and one or two white plastic chairs in the shade. We pass a Tiger Beer sign and a small table covered with sunglasses in neat rows. Internet Game Online. Aquafina. Petimex Gas. Pepsi. Massage. Mobilfone.

The road is dusty and our windows are closed. Where the shops bunch up, the road narrows, and truck and car traffic slows. Bicycles and mopeds overtake us. Beside our van a man stands on his porch, holding a coppery rooster by its legs. With his free hand, he dips a paper towel into a bucket of water and carefully wipes the bird. It squawks and wriggles free. After a few seconds' chase, the man catches the rooster by the feet and places it in a cage.

"At night, the Vietcong dug holes in the road," Song says. "Maybe they buried a land mine, or maybe they only dug a hole. You didn't know if there was a mine, so you had to stop."

I think about the duty officer's log I had obtained. It said there were no skid marks, indicating that Pete's vehicle had slowed to a stop.

"Forty years ago there were no shops here. Only rice fields and bushes and family tombs."

Signs for Tay Long coffee and Vitaly, the bottled water, vie for space with thickets of twelve-foot-tall bamboo and coconut palms, their green globes hanging high overhead in clusters. This would be an ideal place for vc to hide, Song says. "When someone stops, a sniper shoots him. TOK-koooo. That's the sound an AK-47 makes. TOK-koooo. I remember this sound."

My mind travels to the army medical officer's report I had found. It didn't mention a type of gun or bullets, only "multiple GSW." *Multiple gunshot wounds.*

I write in my notebook: Banana trees with clusters of green fruit. Bamboo. Coconut. High grass. An ideal place for an ambush.

We've picked up speed again and the asphalt has widened to about sixty feet. The road would have been half as wide back then, Song says. "We are close to the place."

My eyes sweep the road. I have imagined this scene for so many years, I'm hyperalert to colors and shapes and sounds. *Pete has only a few minutes left.*

Song says that even when he was armed, he feared places like this. "After I left the air force, I was still afraid I would be shot by vc. A few miles from a place like this and you are in the middle of nowhere."

He asks what year my brother was born.

"Nineteen forty-one."

"The year of the snake," he says. "My brother was born the same year. He spent seven and a half years in a reeducation camp."

He asks about Pete's and my birth order, and I tell him Pete was the eldest and I was the youngest, of four children. He says there is an old Vietnamese saying that parents make their best effort at the beginning and the end. The first and last are the most brilliant, he says. For the first time today, I laugh.

Song gestures to the driver and we pull over. I step down from the van, balancing my notebook, the freesia, the *Book of Common Prayer* I've brought along, and a yellow rose from the vase in my Saigon hotel room. Song has chosen a stopping place with a twenty-foot expanse of vegetation—hard to find on this commercial thoroughfare. We could be ten feet from where Pete was killed, or fifty, or a hundred yards.

The passing traffic rumbles. Horns squeak loudly and nasally. Although Song says there is no road rage in Vietnam, drivers here honk in a constant conversation. "Meeeep! Meep-meep!"

We will pay our respects to Pete the Vietnamese way. Song explains that first we will light the incense. Then we will place the flowers and incense on the ground. He will say something in the Buddhist tradition, then I will say something in mine.

I unwrap the flowers and hand the lighter and newspaper to Song. He rolls the paper tight, clicks once, holds flame to paper until it catches, and lights the incense. With his shoe he presses the last of the burning newspaper into the earth. He hands me half of the sticks. Smoke blows across my face.

"We hold the incense like this," he says. We clasp the bundles between our palms, touch our ten fingertips and the heels of our hands together, and pull them toward our chest. "To your heart," he says. With our backs to the road we bow slowly, three times. In my peripheral vision I see that a few Vietnamese have stopped to watch. They observe us for a minute or two before continuing on foot or riding away on their bikes.

The flowers I'm holding are almost three feet long and I'm balancing them in an ungainly elbow tuck under one arm, while also clutching the incense and holding my hands to my heart. *Am I doing this right?* Even though I'm not big on rituals I want to observe this custom respectfully, knowing that Vietnamese venerate their dead with profound devotion. And while I have honored Pete in my heart for forty years, I'm ready to remember him with this new, more out-ward form of expression.

Sweet smoke drifts into my nostrils and eyes. Song nods to me, a silent signal that we will now give half of our incense to Chuck and Jim.

I lay the flowers in the weeds. Song kneels beside me and we plant our smok-ing incense sticks in the ground. Chuck and Jim plant theirs. We step back up to the roadside and bow. Cars, trucks, bicycle taxis, and motorcycles are passing within a few feet of us. I can feel the rush of air on my neck as they go by. Song speaks.

"You were a good man, Pete Hunting. You came here to help. I came here to pay respect to your soul. I understand that you came to Vietnam with a good purpose, to help the people. There was a misunderstanding and you died. I deeply regret that. We came to see the place where you were killed. You have done many good things. May you rest in peace, wherever and forever."

No one can hear me over the din of the traffic, but I read aloud from the prayer book, about God's unnumbered mercies and the shortness and uncer-tainty of life.

Three men are standing very close to us, looking from the incense and flow-ers to our faces. They can tell that we are honoring someone, or, as Song says, they see our reverence. Two continue on their way. One man lingers. His face and arms are the color of a hazelnut. After we have stood in silence for a few minutes, he asks who we are. Song tells him, then translates what the man has said: An American was killed down the road. His mother told him about it many times when he was a little boy.

With his lit cigarette the man points to a sign with the word "COM." There was a fork in the road, he tells Song. A long time ago. That's where they killed the American, right there.

I search Song's face. *Can we really have found the very place?*

We walk to the sign, about fifty yards away.

The man is forty-two. In 1965, he was one year old. His mother always warned him not to go where the American was killed. Everyone in the sur-rounding villages knew about it.

"*Ghe lam.*"

"Very dangerous," Song translates. "His father told him this place was very, very dangerous."

The man gestures to indicate the area around us. "The American was killed here," he says. "There used to be a fork in the road."

Looking at me, he asks, "Did he come to build a bridge?"

"He came to teach English," I say. It was the simplest answer. Pete had also dug wells, laid brick, built windmills, and translated hygiene pamphlets into Vietnamese.

I slip my pen into my pants pocket and walk a few steps down a footpath that leads to a two-story turquoise house. The path bends left and continues around the house, then disappears. In a clearing, a little boy in a red T-shirt watches me from beside a clothesline pinned with pants and tops. Where the turquoise house now sits, a narrow road concealed by elephant grass and bamboo once led to a village, and death lay in wait for Pete.

Song looks farther down the highway. "From there, they could see him coming. They could see he was an American. You said he was tall and had blond hair. It was easy to see him."

Ghe lam.

Very dangerous.

ONE

The Brunt of It

In the Mekong Delta, a 24-year-old American civilian aid worker, Peter Hunting of Oklahoma City, was killed in a guerilla ambush today. Officials said that Hunting was led to his death by two Vietnamese, apparently Vietcong agents, who had posed as his friends.

—Excerpt from the transcript of the CBS *Evening News with Walter Cronkite*, Friday, November 12, 1965, 6:30–7:00 P.M., eastern standard time

Every morning before high school, my sister Holly and I put on our makeup and fixed our hair leaning over two maroon sinks in front of a large mirror in the bathroom. Holly was two years older, and I tried to copy the way she teased and combed her hair and applied liquid eyeliner in a straight line. As a sophomore I was just learning these skills, and in Oklahoma City and our crowd they were important.

Outside our little enclave was a hallway and a black telephone, the only one in our house. My parents believed the telephone was for business. It was definitely not there for teenagers to indulge in rehashing the day's events with friends. All conversations were to be limited to three minutes, and to enforce this regulation my father had placed an egg timer on the shelf where the phone rested. When the last grain of sand dropped through the little hourglass, time was up. Holly and I got around this by keeping our voices down and inverting the timer when we heard Dad coming. Naturally, there was no chair in the hallway and the phone had a short cord.

The telephone rang around seven o'clock on the morning of Friday, November 12, 1965. There was a football game that night, and Holly and I were already dressed in our Pep Club uniforms. We went to a large public high school, and our football team, the Putnam City Pirates, was one of the best in the state. Football games were important social occasions even if, like me, you knew nothing about sports.

The caller, a man, asked to speak with my father. Years later I was astonished to learn that Holly recalled answering the phone, while I distinctly remembered taking the call and summoning Dad. He and Mom were in their bedroom. Dad came out and must have signaled to us to go into my room. From just a few feet away, behind the closed door, we stood listening to his voice. He spoke quietly and seriously. We couldn't hear what he was saying, but it was clear from his grave tone that something bad had happened. He hung up the phone and returned in silence to his bedroom.

I thought someone must have died, but who? Was it my grandmother in Connecticut? My other sister, Carol, who was married and lived in St. Louis? I knew there was a war in Vietnam, but it didn't enter my mind that the bad news concerned my only brother, Pete.

Then we heard a terrifying shriek coming from my parents' bedroom. It was my mother. Not knowing what was happening was as frightening to me as the sound of her cry.

Holly and I waited for what seemed like a long time before Dad returned to us. He explained that Pete had been killed in a land mine explosion. I had never heard of a land mine, but somehow I understood that it was a kind of bomb and Pete had driven over it.

Many years later I found the notes my father had jotted during the phone call. He had grabbed a pencil and the nearest piece of paper, which happened to be the Aircraft Owners and Pilots Association monthly forecast for domestic flight routes. Bearing down so hard that the pencil lead left a rut, he wrote two names, John Hughes and Don Luce, and the words "Peter killed Land Mine Kan Tu."

It was the saddest piece of paper I had ever seen: the deep creases his hand had carved, the phonetic rendering of the city Can Tho as "Kan Tu." Dad was an excellent speller. No one could beat him at Scrabble except, occasionally, Mom. He would never have misspelled a word unless it was a proper noun he didn't know, and even then, under ordinary circumstances, he would have asked how to spell it. He must have carried that paper into the bedroom when he told my mother. Did it shake in his hand?

A stream of my parents' friends began to arrive at the house. There were phone calls to and from our relatives, many in Connecticut and a few in New York, Illinois, and Indiana. Casseroles and desserts appeared and were set out on a large table at the end of the living room. I looked at the food but didn't feel hungry. Some of it went into a freestanding freezer in the garage. I recall a pineapple upside-down cake wrapped loosely in foil, which remained there for months, maybe years.

It was still morning when someone turned on the radio and we heard a man announce our personal tragedy to the world. Driving in the Mekong Delta, the voice said, Peter Morse Hunting, a twenty-four-year-old civilian with International Voluntary Services (ivs), had been killed when his vehicle hit a land mine. "Thank God he died instantly," someone in the room said.

My parents kept their composure as, throughout the day, adults came and went. Friends and neighbors stood in the kitchen or sat helplessly in the living room. At one point, to avoid their searching stares, I buried my head in Holly's lap and cried. My parents were not demonstrative and there was no hugging, nor did they take us aside to talk with us. Holly and I were on our own to figure out how to behave or fill the long hours of that day, and I suppose my parents were, too.

Just two days earlier, I had turned fifteen. Smaller and less developed than most of the girls in my class, I was barely an adolescent. In early childhood I had been scrawny. Whenever my mother recited a line from the Mother Goose rhyme "Monday's Child," which she seemed to think described me—"the child that is born on the Sabbath day is bonny and blithe and good and gay"—Pete would make a joke and change the word "bonny" to "boney." As an adult I learned that I was born on a Friday and wondered if my mother had ever understood me.

My three siblings and I were born in two sets. Pete and my sister Carol, whom we called Cis, were eighteen months apart. A six-year gap followed, then came Holly and, two years later, me. We thought of ourselves as two pairs, but not two alliances. Mom avoided singling any of us out and usually praised us as a unit. "You kids are special!" she would say when she was proud of us. She placed a high value on loyalty and taught us not to criticize each other. Once when Cis, eight years older than I, was getting ready for a date, I noticed that her slip was showing. I whispered my observation to Mom. She said not to tell Cis, as if it were a criticism and not something she would want to know.

Before we moved to Oklahoma, my brother, sisters, and I had been 4-H members in Dexter, Missouri. One day the leader gave a lesson on grooming. We were supposed to decide who in the group had the cleanest fingernails. I carefully considered each of the nominees' hands before I voted. After the meeting Pete scolded me because I hadn't voted for Holly. "You *always* vote for your sister," he said.

He had shown the same loyalty to Cis on her first day of high school, where the custom was for upperclassmen to initiate freshmen by scribbling on their faces with lipstick. Before Pete and Cis left home to walk to school, he took a tube of the scarlet color Mom always wore and gently wrote on Cis's cheeks and forehead so the other kids would leave her alone.

Cis was a newlywed of three months when Pete was killed. Dad called her husband, Frank, at work. He immediately went home to break the news to Cis and could hardly get the words out before he began weeping. They went for a walk in the park. Fresh snow muffled every sound, and the world was still and beautiful. One day years later, Cis was driving alone when she found herself inexplicably overcome with grief. Then she realized that it was a day of quiet, fresh snow—like the one when she learned Pete had been killed.

A couple who lived next door to us were driving home from Dallas that day. Mrs. Storment had gotten into the car, laid the *Dallas Times Herald* on her lap without looking at it, and set her purse on top. She and her husband talked all the way to Oklahoma City. After four hours, they turned onto our street and saw lines of parked cars. Only then did Mrs. Storment look down at the newspaper and see the story about Pete.

Newspapers across the country carried the story, as did radio stations. Gloria Johnson, who had known Pete as a fellow volunteer in Vietnam, had returned to the United States and was living in Corvallis, Oregon. "The words from the radio brought me out of a dead sleep," she remembers. "They were something like, 'Peter Hunting, of International Voluntary Services, was ambushed when he passed a military convoy.' I was shocked and saddened. We all thought that we were invincible—that no VC would want to kill us. We were the good guys, after all. Didn't even carry a gun. I was amazed when a grenade was set for me in a small town in which I lived, on a path that I routinely took. That was a very big clue that we weren't any more popular than the military—at least to the vc."

Another teammate, William Meyers, had also returned from his tour with ivs and was recruiting for the organization on college campuses. News of Pete's death reached his alma mater, Wesleyan University in Middletown, Connecticut, while Willi was meeting with students there.

The next day, in Boston, a young nurse who had dated Pete during college and for a time expected to marry him received a phone call from her mother: "Sue, have you seen the *New York Times?*" Unable to tell her daughter what she had just read, Mrs. Patterson insisted, "Go find a copy of the *Times.*" Sue hurried out to find a paper and saw Pete's photograph and, beneath it, the headline "Vietcong's Ambush of U.S. Aid Worker Laid to 2 'Friends.' "

Within hours of the phone call to our home, the Associated Press and United Press International were reporting that Pete was not killed by a land mine. First, we had struggled to believe that he was dead. It was almost impossible to take in that he had been the victim of a deliberate and brutal attack.

From Saigon, the Associated Press reported that a military convoy had found Pete's body alongside his bullet-riddled vehicle. He had been shot through the head five times. Ten more rounds had been fired into his body. Two passengers who were seen with him had presumably escaped injury and left with the Vietcong. According to the wire story,

> Hunting had departed with the two Vietnamese from the Delta city of Vinh Long. They were on their way to Can Tho, 20 miles away and about 100 miles south of Saigon. . . .
>
> The guerrillas opened fire on the convoy, but quickly broke contact when the troops returned the fire.
>
> The International Voluntary Service [*sic*] is a private, nonprofit organization under contract to the United States aid mission in South Vietnam. It employs about 60 people specializing in agriculture, education and public health.[1]

A story in the *Oklahoma City Times* opened with the Associated Press account and continued with locally reported information. My father was identified as an examination specialist with the Federal Aviation Administration. He had been informed of his son's death by telephone, the story said. He expected to learn more when the caller, who was not identified, had more information. The article continued:

> In July the younger Hunting began his second two-year tour in Viet Nam after spending a two-month leave at home.
>
> He spent his first two years working with youths in flood relief and English teaching programs.
>
> In a recent letter, he wrote: "The Vietnamese have long felt that Saigon, the government and the Vietnamese educated classes were progressing without concern for the agricultural countryside."
>
> Hunting's latest mission was to help bridge the gap between governmental and agricultural growth.[2]

At some point my parents turned their attention to arrangements for services in Connecticut, where our family roots were and where we spent nearly every summer. We would fly to New Haven, and in the meantime my Uncle Jim would receive Pete's body. Memorial and graveside services would take place in Woodbridge, where Mom's immediate family lived. My parents had lived there, too, in the early years of their marriage. Pete and Cis had spent their childhoods in one of the houses on the farm that had been in my family for generations.

Bill and Tiny Waite, who had been members of my parents' wedding party, had also lived in a house on the farm. Now Bill Waite was a music professor at Yale. Some of the students and faculty there were protesting America's deepening involvement in Vietnam. Senator Barry Goldwater, a conservative Republican who had lost the previous year's presidential election to Lyndon Johnson, had just spoken in favor of U.S. foreign policy at St. Luke's Episcopal Church in New Haven.

On November 17 the *Yale Daily News* published a letter from Professor Waite. Referring to Pete by his first name only (presumably because his death was widely reported), he began by stating that he had known Pete since the day he was born. He remembered the boy who had built "highly improbable soapbox racing cars" and grown into "a builder of human lives and dignity." Praising Pete's work with Vietnamese peasants, Waite denounced the Vietcong as destroyers of builders and leaders. Then, as if to scorn those in the Yale community who would not dirty their hands or risk their lives to volunteer in Vietnam, he expressed the hope that some on campus would mourn Pete's passing. The letter concluded by noting pointedly that Pete was a direct descendant of "another builder," one of Yale's founders.[3]

At least two members of my family learned about Pete's death from Walter Cronkite. My great-aunt and great-uncle, who had not yet received a call from the family, watched the CBS *Evening News* in shock from their home in Florida. Aunt Miriam wrote to another relative that Cronkite "announced Pete's death with so much dignity and evident feeling that after the first unbelieving moments we felt that it might have been a good way to hear it." My family did not turn on the television that evening, and I did not find out about the broadcast until many years later.

Just a few months before, when Pete visited the family in Connecticut between tours in Vietnam, many of our relatives were eager to hear his opinion of the escalating war and how it was affecting his work. "Do you go armed?" Aunt Miriam asked. Pete replied that, no, the sight of a gun was an excuse for someone to shoot you.

I was full of questions I didn't think I could ask. I wondered who the two Vietnamese were, why they had betrayed my brother, and how anyone could have wanted to kill him. I overheard my parents telling other adults that Pete had said he was sometimes followed by Vietcong. There were whispers that he may have been so well liked by his Vietnamese friends and colleagues that the Vietcong considered him a threat. A *Christian Science Monitor* clipping I found many years later supported this notion. Above the headline "Cheerful greeting" was a photograph of Pete in his jeep, with a large group of children waving at him in the background. The caption stated that IVS's efforts to improve the U.S. image were apparently too successful, because Pete had been ambushed the previous week.

That an IVS volunteer's very acceptance could have placed him in danger is given credence by John Balaban, a former IVSer, in his Vietnam memoir, *Remembering Heaven's Face*. In 1967, two years after Pete's death, forty-nine team members signed an open letter to President Johnson denouncing the war as "an overwhelming atrocity." The letter was published on the front page of the *New York Times* and hand-carried by an IVS volunteer to Communist North Vietnam's embassy in Phnom Penh, Cambodia. Balaban recalled a Vietnamese official's chilling response to the letter: "By doing good works, you are doing wrong, for you confuse the people about the aim of the American imperialists."[4] Balaban's friends in South Vietnam told him that the protest letter had convinced them of IVS's good intentions; one admitted that, until then, they had thought he was with the CIA.

Another team member, Carl Stockton, said that one of the greatest struggles of IVS was to convince Vietnamese that the group's motives were altruistic. There was a basic assumption, he said, that Westerners were "complicit and therefore not to be trusted."

IVS volunteers in Vietnam accepted risk as a part of life. The view expressed by Larry Laverentz, who at one time shared a house with Pete, was common among the unmarried men on the team: "You had freedom and independence. You're a single guy, you have no family, you can take risks. You got used to it." Bill Betts, who worked in malaria eradication, recorded thirty different attempts on his life that he never mentioned to anyone while he was in Vietnam. Another volunteer, Bob Biggers, hoped his IVS team leader wouldn't think he sounded cowardly when he informed him, "Today the V.C. attempted to assassinate me."[5]

Because news reports said that Pete had been led to his death and I heard nothing to the contrary at home, I didn't question this story. My parents didn't discuss what had happened, and all I knew was what I observed and overheard. I had been told more times than I could count that children should be seen and not heard. I kept my curiosity to myself.

In my passage from adolescence to adulthood, losing my brother would be the still point around which my world turned as I reached the milestones of applying to college, addressing wedding invitations, and sending out birth announcements—all without the fullness of sharing them with the brother I never forgot. The feelings of bewilderment and insecurity I experienced on that traumatic November day in 1965 would revisit me for years to come as I faced life decisions. At a pivotal developmental stage, I did not learn how to ask questions about what mattered most to me. I had no voice with which to explore important issues. As the youngest of four children I was already observant. With Pete's death and the family silence that enveloped it, I also became cautious.

Although I did not talk about Pete, I thought about him a lot. I didn't know much about his life in Vietnam. It wasn't until his letters surfaced in 2004 and I studied them that I fully understood what he had been doing.

When I think now about my big brother, a host of memories settle around me. I can still see him as a teenager diligently tinkering with George, his old red motor scooter, the greasy parts lying in pieces on the floor of the carport. Then I'm hugging his waist and the wind is blowing my hair after he has gotten the Cushman running and we're taking it out for a spin. I felt special when he let me hang out with him.

To this day, I can hear the unpleasant honking of his tuba. I can still picture his messy bedroom and smell his sour gym socks and the sweet glue he used to build model airplanes. I remember how small I felt the time he asked me why I wouldn't play with the girl across the street. I made up an excuse, but he saw through it. "Who are you?" he asked. "Queen Elizabeth?"

Pete was fourteen when the curiosity and confidence that in time would lead him to Vietnam were captured by a photographer from the *St. Louis Post-Dispatch*. The picture, taken at the Boy Scout Jamboree in Stoddard County, Missouri, shows a yard-long king snake "showing affection for Pete Hunting," who nonchalantly eyes the snake while holding it a few inches from his face. He was photographed again for the paper as a high school sophomore when he built and flew a seven-foot box kite. A few years earlier, Pete demonstrated similar ingenuity, along with his ever-present sense of humor, after our family had moved from posh Lake Forest, Illinois, to southeastern Missouri. He carved a letter to a former teacher at the Lake Forest Country Day School on a rough-hewn piece of wood and somehow persuaded the Dexter post office to mail it.

He left for college in 1959. I missed him so much that a month after he started at Wesleyan, he wrote to Mom and Dad, "Better tell Jill to quit crying. This could get ridiculous. I appreciate her thinking about me and writing, but how old is she now, anyway?"

To save money, he hitchhiked home on vacations, thumbing his way from Connecticut to Missouri, then to Oklahoma when we moved there after his freshman year. He wore a tie and taped a "References" sign to his suitcase, hoping some driver would give him an opportunity to produce the tongue-in-cheek letters he had put his friends up to writing.

When Pete was around, I just knew something amusing or interesting was going to happen. He was affectionate and fun loving. One of his friends described him as a person who took his work seriously, but not himself.

He loved playing jokes, and he played them on me. My grandfather had a camp in Maine, a rustic, rambling old place so remote that we had to cover the last stretch by dinghy, in shifts. One time I'll never forget, it was dark when we pulled up to the dock. Pete had gotten there first. When I scrambled up out of the boat, he was waiting for me. He came roaring and springing at me in the pitch-blackness from behind a stuffed bear cub he had dragged out of the great room.

Sometimes he took things a little too far. There was the time he pulled the legs off a daddy longlegs one by one to see what would happen, and if the dot would hop. He knew I had severe asthma, but I remember him pinning me down and tickling me as I wheezed and gasped for breath.

It didn't occur to me that these childhood memories would have to be enough for a lifetime or that, when I saw Pete in the summer of 1965, it would be the last time I would ever see him. Things like the wood carving he'd made of an old man, a pair of earrings he gave me, and a flippant letter from college — "Write me, knothead, okay? Just kidding, you're not a knothead very much. I was being brotherly" — would become my treasured possessions.

Soon after Pete was killed, my family stopped talking about him. My father, my sisters, and I learned that to mention Pete's name, let alone his violent death, would be to set off my mother's tidal-force grief. We were all shocked and sad, but the enormity of Mom's emotion and her abandonment to it, especially after she had been a model of decorum, was fearsome.

My mother's grief was so intense that how the rest of us felt seemed unimportant, even irrelevant. I can understand her better now, but back then her behavior was confusing and off-putting. We tacitly accepted that it was just easier not to talk about Pete. His death and everything else about him became my mother's personal possessions — possessions she was not willing to share.

At fifteen, I didn't know that the way my family coped was unhealthy. It would be years before I learned that there was another way and that, by some standards, my mother's conduct was self-indulgent. Maternal love is exalted in many cultures, but in the Buddhist tradition, the suffering of a grieving mother is not idealized; to the contrary, it is considered the antithesis of the spiritual ideals of detachment and dispassion. The ancient Greek writer Plutarch suggested that excessive sorrow was a form of impropriety. Writing to his wife after the death of their daughter, he said that a virtuous woman must fight against "the incontinence of her soul."

My mother seemed to feel that no one understood her suffering. She may have been right. But I would like to think that if she had been able to turn the force of her emotion on nurturing and being nurtured by my family during our most difficult time, she might have brought us together instead of silencing and dividing us.

Although the grief of a sibling sometimes goes unacknowledged, as my sisters' and mine was, it is profound. In her Vietnam memoir, *When Heaven and Earth Changed Places*, Le Ly Hayslip put it well when she said of losing her brother, "No matter how many men you love, or how many men love you, no bond is thicker than the blood which passes through the umbilicus to brothers and sisters."[6] Usually, brothers and sisters outlive their parents and their loss stays with them longer.

Silence in the face of grief made it harder for me to bear, but eventually my curiosity and determination won out. I would venture beyond the confines of my family with just one question: What happened to Pete?

TWO

"Kiss the Sisses Good-bye"

Late in the afternoon of June 2, 1963, through the viewfinder of his movie camera, my father slowly panned across the lawn behind Olin Library on the campus of Wesleyan University. He also took in the brownstone chapel covered with ivy, families strolling on the sidewalk behind College Row, and rows of chairs set up for the evening's one hundred thirty-first commencement exercises.

Dad had received his bachelor's and master's degrees from Boston University, but he had begun his undergraduate studies here. He had lots of stories. My favorite was that he had earned money by baking beans and selling them in the dorm. Mom had started college at Smith. She transferred to Wheaton after the dean of students suggested that a year somewhere else, without the social distractions of the other colleges near Northampton, might be profitable. Wheaton would teach her to study. Mother did not return to Smith and she may not have learned to study, because she didn't graduate. After Wheaton, she moved back in with her parents. She took classes at the Yale music school until the following December, when she and my father were married. Pete was born in June.

The four years at Wesleyan had not been easy for Pete. Coming from southeastern Missouri, where his summer jobs had included working on a farm, he felt different from his more sophisticated and, in many cases, prep-schooled classmates. At times he was homesick. He struggled to keep up, explaining in a letter his freshman year that he was "not as fast as the other boys." Pete had been accepted by Wesleyan only after being wait-listed, with four applicants in line ahead of him. Yale, where my mother's male ancestors had gone in an unbroken line since 1701, had turned him down.

During his first two years he withdrew from physics and nearly failed calculus and French. The dean placed him on academic probation after the fall semester of junior year. Probation carried "the stern warning that we will expect considerable improvement by June," Dean Mark Barlow wrote. Pete pulled his grades up slightly, and Barlow sent a note to my parents saying that Pete had "just simply stubbed his toe this past semester, and has learned considerably from it." In four years, he earned just two As, one in physical education and the other in advanced Chinese.

The graduating class of 1963 processed to the stage behind the library. The tassel on Pete's mortarboard bobbed against his cheek as he turned to look at Dad, flashing a tolerant, embarrassed half-smile recognized by all parents. Blond, blue-eyed, and six feet tall, Pete crossed the platform with a long stride, reached for his diploma, and shook hands with the president. Then he took the steps quickly, opening the black leather case on the way down as if to make sure the thing was really in there. A little while later, he plopped his mortarboard on my head and I mugged for the camera.

That spring, Pete had played Frisbee in front of the Alpha Delta Phi house with a fraternity brother, David Biddle, who recalled how excited Pete was about going to Vietnam. Another Alpha Delt, Pete's roommate Bill Owens, remembered a number of discussions in which Pete debated whether to take a government job or attend graduate school in Michigan or California. Whether either school had accepted Pete is unknown. He had scored in the fifty-third percentile, a mediocre fifty-four, on the Graduate Record Examination advanced test in his major, government. He may have thought that practical experience on the ground in Vietnam would improve his academic prospects. In his application to International Voluntary Services he wrote, "I want to acquire some teaching experience. I want time to think, and acquire a 'feel' for the area's people and culture—all in preparation for graduate school. I would rather serve my country through organizations such as IVS than the military."

"We all thought he would go to graduate school," Bill Owens recalled, "but I think he wanted more direct language experience." One day Pete showed him what he had received in the mail. It was an offer from the Central Intelligence Agency. The letterhead was folded in an unusual way that hid the masthead and agency name. "The offer would have been very language-intensive, but probably less people-oriented than the ivs job he finally accepted," Owens said. Pete laughed off the cia letter. He was "very enthusiastic" about joining ivs.

By April of his senior year, he had begun counting the days to graduation. ivs had sent a formidable list of immunizations he needed. He imagined "running the gauntlet with my undershorts at my knees, getting the needles in all four areas every two seconds, emerging . . . with old, worn, bent hypodermic needles they didn't bother removing when they missed." He had also taken "a few liberating steps backward" from a nursing student he had been dating, Sue Patterson. Her attitude about the future was less casual than his, he said, and he felt relieved to be making plans on his own. His rpm's were running high, he wrote in a letter home. With only fifty-six days left at Wesleyan, he was "as restless as an octopus in a pan of hot water."

Some of Pete's fellow students had concerns about his decision. One was Bruce Kirmmse. A class behind Pete, Kirmmse remembered "a tallish, lean, rather quiet, serious, idealistic young man with owlish clear-rimmed glasses. Soft-spoken and determined." Wesleyan was "very international-oriented in those days," and many students were watching the situation in Vietnam. Kirmmse and his friends were skeptical about going there "to do 'good' in what seemed to be an inescapably no-good situation," he said. "But Pete was determined to go there and do good peacefully. I think he was the first person I knew personally who died in Vietnam. Not many from our age group and social class at Wesleyan died over there."

Stephen Rankin also questioned Pete's decision. Like Kirmmse, a class behind Pete, he was already thinking seriously about what to do after graduation. His interest in international affairs had led him at one point to consider a career with the State Department. But the Bay of Pigs invasion in 1961 and the Cuban Missile Crisis in October 1962 had caused him to doubt that he could support U.S. foreign policy. By 1963, he recalled, many at Wesleyan were aware of increasing military involvement in South Vietnam and support for the regime of President Ngo Dinh Diem.

Rankin came to know Pete over meals at eqv, another fraternity on campus. Wesleyan had no dormitory dining halls, and students took their meals at eating clubs. Although Pete was an Alpha Delt, he joined EQV's eating club in the fall of his senior year. It had a reputation as a more intellectual and political house than Pete's, where the atmosphere was more literary and easygoing. Rankin recalled that Stuart Byron, who later became a New York film critic, made an eloquent speech proposing that Pete be admitted. His interests had changed, Byron stated, and Pete was now seeking a more stimulating environment. Pete did not want to join the fraternity, only to take his meals there for a few months. Rankin wondered what kind of unorthodox character Byron had turned up. He thought this Pete Hunting must have either unusual strength of character or diplomatic skills to risk the opprobrium of his own fraternity brothers by joining another club. "I was very pleased that my expectations of eccentric behavior were disappointed," he said. "Pete seemed mature, well grounded, good humored, and approachable. I greatly admired the easy rapport that he established with the many different personality types that EQV attracted."

The two had many conversations over lunch and dinner. Rankin came to seek out a place near Pete wherever he happened to be sitting. "He had that great knack of making you feel good about yourself, even when the feedback from others was predominantly negative," he remembered.

When Pete said he was going to Vietnam, Rankin was astounded. They all knew that the situation in Vietnam was getting worse. More than once he asked Pete whether he would not be putting himself at risk. Pete admitted that he would be, but displayed an "almost serene confidence and optimism that good communications and well-managed projects would command popular support."

John Sommer was another member of the Wesleyan class of 1963 who joined IVS that year. Graduating with honors, he had applied to the Peace Corps, but IVS's offer came first. Rankin observed in Sommer the same "radical serenity" and confidence. He and Pete seemed to share a belief that they could make a contribution.

The CIA was recruiting at Wesleyan in the 1960s, but it wasn't until after Pete's death that his classmates wondered if there had been a connection with IVS. There was the job offer he had shown his roommate. The real questions began, however, with the story that two Vietnamese had led Pete to his death. Reporting by Cronkite, the wire services, the *New York Times*—and later the propaganda machine JUSPAO, the Joint U.S. Public Affairs Office—all fueled the intrigue.

When one of Pete's classmates saw his name on a plaque at the entrance of the U.S. Agency for International Development (USAID) in the 1970s, he may have inferred, as did people who had not heard of IVS, that Pete really worked for the government. Although he did not, IVS had USAID contracts for its work in Vietnam. The small voluntary organization strived to maintain its autonomy, but the relationship inevitably aroused suspicion. IVS volunteers fought an uphill battle trying to convince Vietnamese friends, co-workers, and students that IVS was independent.

My father had tried to discourage Pete from going to Vietnam. As an FAA examiner, he had given a helicopter check ride to an army officer who had recently returned from Southeast Asia. Captain Art Boudreau told Dad it was too dangerous for Pete to go there. The left hand didn't know what the right hand was doing, he insisted. "I knew what was going on and I had a premonition that we were going to lose. I pleaded with your dad not to let Pete go. It was really suicide to be out in the countryside. Your dad was very well informed and had some serious conversations with your brother, but he wouldn't listen to him. Pete was stubborn about it."

If my parents had reservations about Pete's going to Vietnam, I was not aware of them. Even if they were against it, I am certain they would not have tried to stop Pete. They placed a high value on independence and on doing the right thing, whatever the risk.

After commencement weekend at Wesleyan, my father returned to work in Oklahoma City. We had moved there in the summer of 1960, when Dad took a job with the FAA in the Examination and Records Division as a writer of flight manuals and pilot exams. That fall, Cis entered Swarthmore College. Holly and I started junior high and elementary school in Oklahoma.

I adjusted to fifth grade about as smoothly as Pete had to Wesleyan. That year, I wrote to him that I had failed the first quarter of resources and science class. I described the "very affectinate [sic]" stray cat we had adopted and named Valentino. I hatched a plan to pick Pete up the next summer at my grandmother's house in Woodbridge, some twenty miles from Wesleyan, on our way to Maine. Meeting at Nana's house would be more fun, I said, but we could also pick him up at college. This was "just brain-work," I explained, "but it never hurts anybody else when you're only dreaming, does it?" Pete dubbed me "the correspondent of the family, by George." I said I would try to write more often. He complained that my sisters, meanwhile, hadn't "filled their quotas." He asked my parents to crack the whip over their heads.

Mother, Holly, and I spent the summer of 1963, as we spent a portion of almost every summer, at Round Hill Farm. Nana's house was a large saltbox colonial built in the 1700s. Her father-in-law, a New Haven surgeon and professor at Yale, had bought it when one of his sons contracted tuberculosis. The place in the country had restored the boy to health. It had a tonic effect on all of us.

We associated Round Hill with stability, security, and good times. Except for having to remember not to say "y'all" in front of my Connecticut cousins, I hadn't a care in the world there. Some years we stayed next door to Nana's house in my Uncle Jim's cottage. That summer in my little room there, I read *To Kill a Mockingbird* and *The Ugly American*. Outside my window grew pink flowers called bleeding hearts. The spicy sweetness of boxwood perfumed the air.

For two hundred years the house had sat mostly unchanged on a small rise bordered by a stone wall and quiet lane. Venerable "husband and wife" matching pine trees framed the front door. A small waterfall in back produced a soothing rush day and night, year round. When we weren't staying with our uncle, Holly and I shared one of the front bedrooms. Squirrels in the trees sometimes awakened us by tossing pinecones against the windows. We usually arrived at the farm in the dark, and looking out the windows that next morning guaranteed a thrill. There was the swimming pool, waiting for us.

The front yard sloped down to a pool of enormous proportions. Its impressive size belied the fact that it was really a cement pond. My grandparents had tried to tame the seeping lawn, first by planting water lilies and then turning the marsh into a goldfish pond. As a last resort, they created a brook-fed swimming pool.

I was only two when my family moved to Illinois, so I never knew my grandfather Popeye. In time I would learn that the aircraft-parts manufacturing company he founded and his liking for large swimming pools (he had been on the Yale swim team) were connecting points between Pete and the young woman who might have become my sister-in-law, had he lived.

Holly and I spent carefree days poolside and across the lane on the tennis court. Despite years of lessons I was not a good tennis player, but the poison ivy that encroached on the court from all sides was an incentive to keep the ball in bounds. My mother and her friends sat on blankets by the pool and played bridge in their swimsuits, while my grandmother watched the action from her rocking chair on the porch. She loved us from afar, whether we were just across the lane, down by the pool, or away in Oklahoma. She wrote letters to us faithfully and often tucked in an arrangement of pressed wildflowers glued onto paper. Nana was not physically demonstrative, but I knew by the way she greeted me after each long absence, taking my face in her hands, how glad she was to see me. Her hospitality was well worth our long pilgrimages from the Midwest. My mother drove the fifteen hundred miles herself. I can still see the set of her jaw, her head held high as she gripped the steering wheel of our station wagon, determined as a ship's figurehead, bearing us back East to our roots.

Pete spent many of his college vacations at the farm. Although he complained of dim lighting and the lack of an available desk in Nana's house, he studied or went to parties in New Haven or painted my uncle's house. Uncle Jim was handsome and young looking, and the two of them occasionally double-dated.

Between Pete's graduation and his departure for the IVS orientation in Washington, he drove to Highland Park, Illinois, to attend the wedding of a friend, and back again. In the interval, something shocking happened in Vietnam. A Buddhist monk, Thich Quang Duc, burned himself alive in a busy intersection of Saigon to protest the repressive policies of the Catholic, U.S.-backed President Diem. David Halberstam of the *New York Times* was an eyewitness to this first of many public self-immolations. So far, U.S. military advisers, but not yet combat troops, had been committed to the conflict in Vietnam. Many Americans were unaware of how desperate the situation there was becoming. Some did not know where the country was. A neighbor of John Sommer's in New Jersey wished him off, when he left to begin his IVS tour, with, "Have a good time in Africa."[1]

When the horrific photograph of Thich Quang Duc in flames appeared in newspapers around the world, Americans took note, but without the foreknowledge that our country was venturing into a quagmire where it would remain for twelve years. In fact, many were thinking less about the future than about ancient history. The next day, June 12, the movie *Cleopatra* premiered in New York. It would gross more than any other movie of 1963, forty-eight million dollars, a little less than one-tenth the total amount of U.S. aid to South Vietnam that year.

Pete was up at six o'clock on the morning of June 20, 1963. "Kiss the sisses good-bye," he wrote in his journal that night. He flew from Bradley Airport, near Hartford, to Washington, D.C., to begin a weeklong orientation program. On first impression, his IVS teammates seemed serious and dedicated, but uninteresting. Although he observed no "studied neuroses," the group seemed to lack the "zest and feeling of self-potential" of the "rich and consuming personalities" with whom he had spent the past four years.

The orientation began with introductions and slideshows. A conference with A. Russell Stevenson, the executive director of IVS, followed. On the way to the meeting, Pete realized that all the buttons were falling off his sport coat. When he arrived at Dr. Stevenson's office, he discovered that he had forgotten the expense receipts he was to submit for reimbursement.

Pete found the first lectures on Southeast Asian politics dull and was quick to compare them unfavorably with his Wesleyan classes. He felt frustrated by the lack of substance and was at a loss to know even what questions to ask. The session ended with Pete suggesting to one of the few women in the group, Anne Hensley, that they go out for a beer. The idea snowballed and soon all twenty-one of the new recruits were barhopping. "Bull sessions ensued."

The next day's lectures and discussions, about diseases, sexual relations, and health tips, were livelier. In a letter to his nursing-student girlfriend, Sue Patterson, Pete—who was an inveterate kidder and, on top of that, fresh out of college on an all-male campus—teased, "We've got some beautiful gorgeous girls along, and what's more, Washington is full of secretaries that wear these tight, revealing things." Although he had stepped back from their relationship, Pete would write to Sue for another year and a half.

The new recruits received copies of the "IVS Handbook," a thin green binder with the title hand-scrawled on the cover. Inside were thirty-five mimeographed typewritten pages and maps of South Vietnam and Saigon. Chapters covered recreation, security, and Vietnamese customs, along with procedures for claiming expenses, shopping at the PX (or post exchange, a military store), and hiring domestic help.

The handbook also included an introduction to Vietnam's modern history. The country had been divided at the seventeenth parallel, it stated, by agreement of the French and Communists at the Geneva Conference in July 1954.

North of the demarcation line was a "monolithic dictatorship," the Democratic Republic of Vietnam. The "legitimate" government of South Vietnam was derived from a 1948 agreement between France and Bao Dai, the last emperor of Vietnam. Bao Dai had appointed Ngo Dinh Diem prime minister in June 1954, and a referendum the next year had "overwhelmingly" awarded Diem the presidency.

Pete had studied Asian history at Wesleyan. While the handbook's slant on Vietnam's history may not have matched the views of his skeptical college friends, Pete's course notes and journal entries gave no indication of his political sympathies as he left for Asia.

Along with dividing Vietnam into North and South, the 1954 Geneva Accords stipulated that free elections would determine a single president and reunify the country by 1956. The United States endorsed but did not sign the agreement and sent a counterinsurgency team to Vietnam. Its mission was to undermine the popularity of the Vietminh, the insurgent nationalists who, during World War II, had successfully resisted Japanese occupation, with U.S. support. Subsequently, they had thrown off French colonial rule. The Vietminh and their leader, Ho Chi Minh, were heroes, especially among the rural Vietnamese, who far outnumbered the urban, French-educated and -trained populace. It is generally conceded that Ho Chi Minh would have won the election by a landslide. The free elections were never held.

After Diem, a celibate Catholic, was installed as president of South Vietnam, he named one of his five brothers, Ngo Dinh Nhu, head of the secret police. The Vietminh had killed one Ngo brother. Another, Ngo Dinh Thuc, was a Catholic archbishop.

Working behind the scenes in these years was an intelligence officer and former advertising executive whom Ambassador Richard Holbrooke—who arrived in Vietnam as a junior foreign service officer within weeks of Pete—has called "perhaps the most famous American operative in Southeast Asia," Edward Lansdale.[2] Widely acknowledged as the model for Graham Greene's "quiet American," Colonel and later General Lansdale helped build support for and dismantle opposition to the Diem presidency. He advised Diem on political matters and defied American decision makers when they withheld support for the regime.[3]

Early IVSers knew Lansdale as an affable host at pig barbecues, to which he invited the volunteers as fellow members of Saigon's small American community in the late 1950s. According to Don Luce, who first went to Vietnam as an IVS volunteer in 1958, Lansdale represented one wing of the U.S. counter-insurgency effort—composed of those who believed that distributing plows and fertilizer was the way to succeed in Vietnam, rather than kicking down doors and terrorizing people. Luce declined Lansdale's invitations, knowing of his CIA affiliation.[4]

The "IVS Handbook" portrayed the Diem government as effective in controlling challenges from several oppositional factions, including disaffected elements of the military. Diem, the handbook explained,

> has looked primarily to the United States for foreign political and diplomatic support and for the military and economic assistance without which the present degree of stability could not have been achieved. Continued United States support for the government contributed to its ability to deal with rebellious elements and has probably helped to create public confidence in the viability of the regime.[5]

Before long, Pete and the other new members of the IVS team would see for themselves how effectively Diem and Nhu dealt with rebellious elements such as Buddhists and how much confidence the people placed in the regime.

Economic development was the key to defeating the northern Communists, the "IVS Handbook" stated. The government of South Vietnam was in a race with the North to earn the loyalty of the people. To win this race, it would have "to counter the impression of dynamic progress in the North so assiduously spread by the Communists."[6] The South would also have to offer the promise of economic advancement. Without help, the country could not become self-supporting. It could not "shoulder alone the cost of military and police needed to protect the people from Communist aggression and subversion."[7] In the long term, the country would need to be less dependent on foreign aid and develop a viable economy of its own. Until then, and to reach this goal, assistance from the United States was crucial for nation building. This is where the idealistic young men and women of IVS entered the picture.

The genesis of IVS was a meeting in 1953 of fourteen Americans from diverse backgrounds in religion, government, agriculture, and social services. The question that brought them together was how best to assist developing countries. The outcome of their meeting was the creation of a private, nonsectarian, nongovernmental organization (NGO) they named International Voluntary Services.

IVS's charter stated that its aim was "to utilize the services of volunteers on an organized basis to combat hunger, poverty, disease, and illiteracy in the underdeveloped areas of the world, and thereby further the peace, happiness, and prosperity of the people."[8] One early volunteer, Ray Borton, told me that the first IVSers were typically individuals who wanted to help overseas but did not want to be missionaries.

The fledgling NGO sent its first volunteers to Egypt and Iraq to help with livestock and poultry improvement projects. In 1956 six agricultural workers went to two villages in South Vietnam to assist some 860,000 refugees from the North. Many of the refugees were Catholics who had moved south to flee the Communists, thereby providing a political base for Diem in what was a predominantly Buddhist culture. IVSers helped the transplanted families clear land for crops and obtain farm animals and seed. These early efforts were to become the model for future teams. Soon the Ministry of Agriculture asked for assistance in other regions. IVS responded by sending more volunteers.[9]

In 1962 IVS sent its first English teachers to Vietnam. The following year, more teachers were added, seven of whom were quickly diverted to a new hamlet education program. These seven, including Pete, taught English, helped identify hamlets likely to support a school and then helped to build the schools, and worked with the people to develop sustainable projects that could generate enough income to fund teachers' salaries.

Also in 1962, President Diem adopted the Strategic Hamlet Program.[10] Its fundamental purpose was to provide services and security for the rural population and to deprive the insurgents of support where it was strongest. The plan was modeled on a program Lansdale had developed in Malaysia. His protégé Rufus Phillips worked closely with Diem to establish the program in South Vietnam.[11]

Smaller than a village, a hamlet was considered "strategic" after it had met three criteria: its boundary had been fortified against Vietcong intrusions with fencing and a moat or mound between the fence and a command post or pillbox; it had elected a council of leaders and chief; and it had organized an armed self-defense unit capable of summoning the civil militia or army at any hour.

Having fulfilled these requirements, the people of a hamlet could choose a self-help project for which they would receive government funding. Projects might include building a school, a clinic, a church, or a well. The idea was that if the rural population could, with assistance, improve their lot and their children's future, they would resist the Vietcong because they would have something to defend—if necessary, with their lives. The Vietcong, thus deprived of food and other means of support at the hamlet level, would be forced out of the jungle and into a conventional war—the kind of war that U.S. advisers best understood how to train and equip South Vietnamese forces to fight.

In 1961, the year before the Strategic Hamlet Program was adopted, Rufus Phillips had gone to South Vietnam to analyze how the USAID mission could support a program to undermine and help defeat the insurgents. After Phillips submitted his official report, he was appointed to develop the program.

The new program was administered by the Office of Rural Affairs. Although IVS operated outside the structure of the U.S. government, the NGO received a contract to work with Rural Affairs in Vietnam. Rufus Phillips's associate, Bert Fraleigh, described how the relationship with IVS came about:

> In our earlier study visit, Rufe and I had been very impressed by the work of the young men and women in International Voluntary Services (IVS), an American voluntary agency partially funded by USOM [the U.S. Operations Mission, the "field" arm of USAID] that was doing Peace Corps–like work (before there was a Peace Corps). All IVS activities were in rural areas of South Vietnam. Many of the IVS volunteers were Vietnamese language speakers with several years' experience in the countryside. . . . I thought of deputizing some of them to be USOM Rural Affairs [provincial representatives], and [USOM acting director] Fippin agreed, so I called on their team chief, Don Luce. . . . He called me the next evening and said that he had clearance from his U.S. headquarters and that he could give me the names of ten prospective volunteers. . . .
>
> It was heartwarming to talk with the IVS people and to observe their maturity, enthusiasm, intelligence, and knowledge of South Vietnam. . . . Although their IVS pay was only eighty dollars per month (about one-tenth of the salary for an American in USOM), they seemed much more interested in and motivated for the job ahead.[12]

When Pete arrived in Vietnam in 1963, the combined agriculture and education teams of IVS numbered sixty-nine men and women in twenty-eight locations. Don Luce was the in-country director, with the title of chief-of-party. An agriculture graduate from Vermont, Luce had gone to Vietnam with IVS in 1958. He had held the top post there since 1960. Some of the volunteers, including himself, were at first afraid they would not be able to handle the problems they encountered. On delivering one new recruit to his assignment, Luce was asked, "You aren't leaving me here alone, are you?" Another asked a teammate as they left for Vietnam, "Aren't any adults going with us?"[13]

If Pete questioned his ability to work effectively, he didn't let on in his letters. Like many of his peers, he emulated the confident, jocular, energetic President John F. Kennedy, whose inaugural address inspired a generation with these words:

Let the word go forth that the torch has been passed to a new generation of Americans. . . . To those peoples in the huts and villages of half the globe struggling to break the bonds of mass misery, we pledge our best efforts to help them help themselves, for whatever period is required—not because the Communists may be doing it, not because we seek their votes, but because it is right. . . . And so, my fellow Americans: ask not what your country can do for you—ask what you can do for your country.[14]

IVS found its volunteers in the ranks of college students who took up Kennedy's challenge. It drew likewise from young people whose families, like mine, valued honest labor and service to others. Agriculture graduates were sought because many of them had grown up on farms. Their experience would presumably be an asset in their work with Vietnamese farmers.

In these young volunteers, the Office of Rural Affairs also found the personnel it needed to build up Vietnam and carry out an agenda of weakening the Vietcong's appeal among South Vietnam's vast poor, uneducated, rural population.

Out of respect for the Vietnamese, or in some cases primarily because IVS required it, the volunteers learned their hosts' language and shared their standard of living. "The communist principles were to live together, work together, and enjoy the results together. That's also what IVS did," said Dang Nguyen, one of the group's Vietnamese interpreters in the early 1960s. Dang was once asked to mediate between a volunteer and his landlady, who wanted to raise the rent. He explained to her, "These IVS people are young, and fresh out of school. They are not making much money. They have come to Vietnam to help you and me, not to make money." When she heard this, she was surprised and changed her mind about raising the rent.[15]

Early in 1961, when John Kennedy took office, the U.S. military presence in Vietnam was advisory; that is, American advisers worked with the South Vietnamese ostensibly in a training and support role. Lansdale sent a memo to Kennedy stressing that the situation was critical and required emergency action. The president called a high-level meeting to discuss the memo. Military aid was increased, as was the number of advisers. Still more advisers followed, until by mid-1962 the number had risen from the original seven hundred to twelve thousand.[16] Although Congress would never formally declare war on Vietnam, the stakes increased steadily in the early 1960s. IVSers were eyewitnesses to U.S. foreign policy in the making.

A group of U.S. representatives visited Vietnam just before Kennedy's inauguration to study the use of foreign aid in Southeast Asia. Their subsequent report to Congress noted "the discovery of a group of young American college graduates, living alongside the Vietnamese and teaching basic agriculture."[17] The "discovered" were IVS volunteers. The report contributed to the establishment of the Peace Corps, based in part on the IVS model, by presidential executive order in March 1961.

Unlike the Peace Corps, however, IVS functioned as a private agency with its own board and staff. The largest volunteer NGO ever to serve in Vietnam, IVS prized and fought for its independence until it finally closed its doors in 2002, after forty years. In hindsight it seems remarkable that an organization so underfunded and altruistic survived for so long.

Pete and his teammates reached Vietnam on July 5, 1963. The week before, President Kennedy had declared his support for the citizens of a divided Berlin at the infamous Wall, and Henry Cabot Lodge had been appointed U.S. ambassador to South Vietnam.

The new IVSers settled in at My Tho, a city in the Mekong Delta, for several weeks of language training. Pete quickly rose to the top of his class. He felt that his Chinese studies at Wesleyan had given him an edge.

On the layover in Hong Kong, he had tried out his Chinese language skills on a boy who knew just enough English to say hello. Pete startled him by answering in Chinese. A crowd gathered to look and listen. "It felt wonderful to be fluent enough to talk with him, show him and the people around us two that there were Americans who were interested enough—young ones, and interested in a positive way—in China," he wrote in his journal.

It was Pete's first trip out of the United States and he saw, for the first time, crowded slums and people sleeping and dying in the streets. But he was not shocked, unlike some members of the team who came from more sheltered backgrounds. One "bird of a girl" fretted about the poverty and her helplessness to do anything about it. "If she was somewhat good-looking," Pete admitted, "one might be able to forgive that sort of thing." He admired pretty girls. He was, as one of his closest friends put it, "all male."

The next day, he met an American student who spoke Mandarin. They made their way to Hong Kong's shipyards. Pete inquired about the cost of having a boat built, admired the view of Victoria Harbor from the docks, and imagined the life here of author André Malraux in the 1930s.

"At last in Vietnam," Pete wrote from My Tho. His early impressions of the country would become the constants of his letters for the next two and a half years: Vietnam and the Vietnamese were infinitely fascinating. Everything seemed like something out of a novel. Signs of war were everywhere; barbed wire and a pillbox fortified every bridge. Downtown My Tho was a cluster of bicycles and markets and open-air barbershops. Food stalls lined the banks of the muddy river. U.S. advisers had named the place Fruit Juice Row, and Pete composed a song about it: "Went down to My Tho's Fruit Juice Row / There were lilies in the snow / And every corner had a peddler lad / With a fruit juice stand in tow." The words seemed to be what the lyrics of an army song should sound like, he thought, even if they didn't truly express his feelings about the place.

Mornings were taken up with language class. Afternoons were free, leaving the team to "sit around and sweat at each other, or go bike riding, or sit under the rain spout when it rains, or talk to the neighbors." In the evenings, Vietnamese dropped by for instruction in English. Pete took on five female students so shy it was "like pulling tusks out of a walrus."

Homesick GIs stopped by, along with USOM personnel and the American major in charge. The population of the province was "50 percent VC," the major claimed. Although the American advisers had arrived in My Tho a year earlier, Pete complained that they still didn't know what street they lived on.

Columns of tanks and armored personnel carriers rumbled past in the early morning, sometimes pausing directly in front of the IVS quarters to broadcast their radio commands at high volume. At night the sound of exploding flak interrupted sleep.

Pete acquired some young friends:

Kids swarm all around you. I told one that I had a cat in my pocket. At first he couldn't believe I was speaking Vietnamese. He thought I was speaking English that sounded an awful lot like the Vietnamese equivalent of "I have a cat in my pocket." Then I pulled out this little cat puppet mounted on a block of wood, with a button underneath that you press here and there to make the cat move. Well, the kid went wild. . . . I gave a little puppet show to the boy and his friends, and they had never seen anything like it. Over here, the children are very creative when they're little, playing with sticks and spools and things.

After a few weeks studying Vietnamese, the IVSers received their work assignments. Pete learned he would be pouring cement, teaching English to provincial officials, and giving science demonstrations in connection with the Strategic Hamlet Program. "Supposedly, the government of Vietnam considers it the most important program going," he wrote.

Pete's post would be Phan Rang, a city on South Vietnam's central coast and the capital of Ninh Thuan Province. It was the country's most arid region and, because of the paucity of good farmland, one of its poorest. With his "stationmate," a member of the IVS agricultural team, he would share a house and a cook, a jeep and a driver.

He earned his first blisters in country when the team took a break from studies to help build a bicycle parking lot in Can Tho, a city in the Mekong Delta. The "primeval" local construction methods shocked him. Workers carried dry cement in tiny buckets and poured it, still dry, into the footing. Then they mixed in the water.

In the off hours Pete learned to play Vietnamese folk songs on his guitar. He found them melancholy and didn't understand the words, but he liked the tunes and noticed that the Vietnamese took obvious pride in them. Children heard the singing and yelled their approval: *"Hai lam!"*

The "IVS Handbook" cautioned new recruits against using American customs as a rulebook for judging other cultures. "The Vietnamese are very sincere and open-hearted," the handbook explained. "They love to smile and they will show their affection by telling you how much they like you."[18] Pete's experience corroborated this. The girls were "the biggest swooners you've ever seen. Charming is hardly the word, and it's not flirting that they're doing. I don't know what it is."

He figured it out soon enough and took up flirting Vietnamese style. He learned that a boy showed affection for a girl by speaking of pairs—the beauty of the moon and the clouds or the happiness of two doves. To one Vietnamese girl, he pointed out the happiness of identical blisters on his thumbs. Another day, working in his shorts, he asked a girl which one of his two sunburned knees she preferred. It was innocent fun. Some of his new Vietnamese friends thought he and John Sommer were so polite, in fact, they must be rich.

It was exciting to Pete to be learning new customs and trying to make himself understood in a new tongue. All too soon, to be an American and to be understood by Vietnamese people would become a matter of life and death.

THREE

Sand between My Toes

Ask anyone what Oklahoma City is like and the first thing they will say is, it's flat. If they appreciate the place, they might add that you can see for miles and the sunsets are spectacular.

The city is situated on a broad plain. It receives only about thirty-two inches of rain a year, making its skies among the sunniest of those in any U.S. city. Flying weather is often ideal. In an average year, Oklahoma City has three hundred fifty good days for flying.

Although it's the bright blue skies and intense coral sundowns I picture when I think of my home from the age of ten to eighteen, and again in my late twenties, other people associate it with violent weather. They have good reason. Oklahoma is the most tornado prone of all fifty states. Oklahoma City, the state's capital and geographical center, is struck by more tornadoes per year than any other city.

Tornadoes are violent and unpredictable. They can occur at any time of day and in any month. Typically, they inflict their worst damage between four and eight o'clock in the evening. The month of May is the most unnerving if you're afraid of extreme weather. In my family, we weren't.

When the local TV meteorologists broke into regular programming to report on the movement of funnel clouds, my father and I would stand on the front porch and observe the swift-moving clouds as they traveled past our house in the direction of nearby Lake Hefner. When a tornado watch was upgraded to a warning and the TV set began emitting harsh beeps, my mother would once in a while suggest we come inside. But none of us overreacted, and only once did Mom plead with us to take cover under the dining room table. It was fun to stand outside with Dad, watching the sky turn yellowish-green and black, like an old bruise. He was steady. What most people called a storm, he merely called "weather." Without being conceited, my father was sure of himself and his knowledge of the air. He didn't put his confidence into words, but what I observed in him inspired a feeling of security. To this day, if I'm trying to get to sleep, I picture myself beside Dad in the cockpit of a single-engine Cessna enshrouded in clouds and him intently monitoring the instruments.

He was a pilot's pilot. He discovered his first love when his future father-in-law took him up in an old Steerman biplane. Dad learned to fly in the army, then became a schoolteacher. During summers off from his job at the Lake Forest Country Day School, Dad dusted crops for Green Giant over the vast farmlands of Illinois. Crop dusters had a high accident rate, but my father was a natural. So suited was he to flying that in 1953 he left his job teaching the heirs to meat-packing fortunes and children of Cook County politicians to instruct cadets at an air base in southeastern Missouri. By then he was a father of four.

My brother, sisters, and I grew up hearing my dad and his pilot friends tell stories of derring-do around our dinner table. To me they seemed interminable, and it was only after I left home that I realized my father seemed adventurous and colorful to others. His flying students, whom I remember as handsome and charming to a man, all visited our house at least once, when they had finished their flight training and my parents gave a party for them. Dad would make a big batch of spaghetti or pizzas from scratch, entertaining us by flamboyantly spinning the dough in the air. Many of the young men were of other nationalities or races, so my siblings and I were exposed to interesting people from all over the world. My parents invited all of Dad's students, including non-whites, and raised some eyebrows for it.

Our house outside of Dexter, Missouri, sat on a hill surrounded by twelve acres of woods. When the new road was being cleared and I was about four, I was sitting on a felled tree and watching the grown-ups while I chewed on a piece of what I thought was white meat. Pete asked what I was doing. I pointed to the stringy, beige, exposed insides of the tree, which looked and tasted just like my mother's roast turkey. Dad was the cook in the family.

He had a good voice and directed the choir at the air base chapel, which meant that we had to get to church on time. One Sunday morning, Holly and I were playing outside in our church dresses when we saw a snake. Our property had a lot of snakes, including copperheads. There wasn't time that morning for Dad to do anything but stuff the creature into a gallon peanut butter jar, screw the metal lid on, and poke air holes in the top. As he backed the station wagon out of the carport, I eyed the jar on a shelf. The snake flicked its tongue at us, its dark, patterned skin pressed fat and fleshy against the glass. I knew my father would take it deep into the woods later and release it. Where and how he did that, on his own and out of sight, he didn't say.

It was from this home in Dexter that Pete went to Wesleyan. Cis followed him east a year later when she left for Swarthmore. Then the air base closed and my father took the job in Oklahoma City with the FAA. Holly and I were sad to leave our house in the woods. When my mother told us we were going to move, she said we should not tell anyone. Without comprehending what it would be like to leave our home and friends, or knowing whether we would like where we were going, we did as were told. In those days it was not unusual for parents to make major decisions irrespective of their children's feelings. My mother and father assumed that Holly and I would adjust, and we did.

Runways and airport control towers had been a part of my life ever since early childhood. As a little girl, I had slept in the air base tower under layers of signal flags. I had grown up waiting in airports while my father filed flight plans or the weather improved. But on the day we left Oklahoma City for Pete's memorial service in Connecticut, not even the familiarity of an airport offered solace.

We took off from the FAA Aeronautical Center adjacent to Will Rogers Airport. Our flight path might have taken us over the Canadian River, where Pete had worked on a bridge construction crew one summer during college. Beneath the bridge a band of pink sand separates the river from its banks, which are lined with cottonwoods and willows, ashes and elms, and bur, shumard, and chinkapin oaks. The Canadian is not for swimming. Not only is it shallow, but the riverbed is full of quicksand.

Pete's job on the bridge-building crew had paid well, but the work was sweaty and backbreaking. I can still picture him when he came home at the end of the day, utterly exhausted and his clothes covered with red mud. When he first arrived in Vietnam and helped build a bicycle parking lot in Can Tho, he said he hadn't worked so hard since that summer in Oklahoma. "Lots of good, tough calluses to show the hamlet chiefs," he wrote.

My family, except for Cis, who traveled to Connecticut from her home in St. Louis, flew on a government-owned cargo plane. How we packed and got to the airport is a complete blank in my memory, like many other details of those first days of shock and grief. Someone Dad worked with had gotten permission for us to fly at taxpayers' expense. We were the only passengers.

Mom and Dad sat up front, where they could talk with the pilots. Holly and I sat at the back of the airplane. Our seats faced aft and looked directly onto pin-ups of nude women. We had been in the air for some time when one of the crewmen came over and pulled down the pictures, looking terribly embarrassed. I remember his apology because the long flight was otherwise quiet and lonely.

It was evening when we landed in New Haven. Uncle Jim met us and took us to Mory's, the Yale restaurant named in the Whiffenpoof Song. The room was dark and the anonymity was comfortable. After dinner we drove out to the farm.

The next day, my parents went to Bradley Airport to meet the plane that was bringing Pete's body. After a few hours, they returned. Pete had not been on the airplane. They made one or even two more trips to the airport before enduring the awful grief of watching their son arrive in a coffin.

In 1994, when I was in Connecticut on a business trip, I went to the farm to visit my aunt and uncle, who lived next door to one another. Living in California, I didn't get back East very often, so I had arranged to have dinner with them and spend the night. We talked about old times. We chuckled at their memories of Pete as a young boy learning to ski, gathering the courage to push off and glide down the gentle slope in front of my grandmother's house. Pete had spent his first twelve years on the farm, when my parents lived in the little house that was now Uncle Jim's. My aunt and uncle had watched him grow up and had grown close to him again during his college years.

Perhaps it was triggered by a story they told me or the easiness of our conversation, or I may have realized I would not have this opportunity again. In any case, when a question popped into my head, I blurted it out: Who had identified Pete's body? I had wondered for many years if or how my parents knew it was really Pete we had buried.

Uncle Jim's face turned gray. He was reserved, but he was also a loving uncle. He could have conveniently evaded my question, but instead he answered, "Your mother did." She had insisted on going alone to the funeral home, he said. She had refused to let him go, or even my father.

I wondered if she could not bear to have anyone witness her grief. Or had she thought they were not as strong as she was? Could she have been angry with them? Did she believe that Pete was somehow hers?

While my parents were planning the memorial service in Woodbridge, the subject of Vietnam was fomenting discussion just a few miles south, on the Yale campus. On November 16 the *Yale Daily News* published a graduate's account of his recent encounter with the Vietcong. He had been a passenger in the vehicle of two French students when they were stopped. The two students did all the talking except for one word the young man uttered in response to a question: *Oui.* He thought it had saved his life. Two days later, the *News* reported that a group of Yale students were forming a delegation to attend the March on Washington for Peace, nine days away. Among the speakers would be Martin Luther King, Jr., and Dr. Benjamin Spock, two outspoken opponents of the war.

On November 19, a formal service for Pete was held at the Congregational church in Woodbridge. There, in the small town where my brother had spent his boyhood and that had been his second home during college, the minister gave thanks for the qualities we loved in him, including "the way he carried his vision of a better world . . . into effective action," his "freedom from vanity and self-importance, and his glad, easy way, and for the example of his love and courage, and of his work."

The reason I know what was said is that I have a copy of the service. All I remember about it is arriving at the church under weeping skies and seeing a lot of people I didn't know.

Cis remembers that Mom was worried about the potential awkwardness of two women Pete had dated meeting each other. One of them, Sue, remembers not that, but the aloofness she perceived in the IVS staff members who had come up from Washington. These men included the organization's executive director, Arthur Z. Gardiner, who had never met Pete; the personnel officer, John Hughes; and Tom Luche, one of the first IVS volunteers sent to Vietnam. Willi Meyers was also there. He and Pete had gone to Vietnam in the same group and were good friends. Now a recruiter for IVS, Willi would soon return to Vietnam to assume Pete's duties in the Mekong Delta.[1]

Pete was buried in a family plot in a cemetery facing West Rock, a sheer cliff northwest of New Haven. We placed wildflowers from the farm on his casket.

I am sorry to say that when my mother handed some of the flowers to me to place on the casket, I was thinking only of myself. With what I regard now as appalling pettiness, I resented her for expecting me to take part in a rite, one more in a series of rites, for which I was unprepared. I was close to Pete and had not been reluctant to express affection for him, and placing flowers on his coffin was my mother's gesture and not mine. Mine-and-not-mine was to become a theme of our family story.

At fifteen, I was too young to know that children can take part in mourning rituals and find them meaningful if adults respect their feelings. The adults around me expected silence and gave silence. Not knowing where to look for comforting guidance, I stared at the casket and the immense hole over which it was suspended.

Holly and I were both in the cast of *The Music Man* that year. When we returned from Connecticut and before we started back to classes, we went to a rehearsal. Several of my friends who were also in the cast saw me come through a door to the auditorium and gathered around me. My appearance made a strong impression on Nancy Kerby, who still vividly remembers that I was wearing a plaid jumper and "looked just so, so sad."

After the dress rehearsal a couple of nights later, a boy in Holly's class who played the lead character, Harold Hill, invited me to go out for a hamburger. He was the student body president and I was in awe of him. At fifteen, I had never been out on a date and wasn't sure I should go without my mother's permission. Holly said it would be all right and I should do it. Off we went to the Split-T, a popular restaurant, six of us in the car.

Later, on the way home, we had stopped at a large intersection and were entering it after the signal changed when we were hit head-on. Not all cars were equipped with seat belts in those days, and the four of us in the back seat were not buckled in. I flew forward and hit the windshield with such force that it cracked. A second before my head met the glass, I "heard" a voice—not an audible voice—say, "Put your hand up!" I raised my left hand to my forehead. Two bones in my hand broke.

The driver of the other car and I were taken to the hospital by ambulance. As emergency technicians hoisted the stretcher I was on into the ambulance, one asked whom he should call. I told him our telephone number and said, "Just don't ask for my mother." I was afraid the news would be too much for her after Pete's death. She had been anticipating the call, however. Holly had come home and said she had driven by a big accident. My mother, who had a sixth sense, knew that I was involved.

In the emergency room a doctor stitched my head wound and wrapped my broken hand in a cast. He gave my mother pills for my double concussion and told her to wake me every two hours. The next day, loaded with drugs, I was back on stage for the final performance. When I returned to school, I learned a rumor had circulated that I'd been killed.

When the wound on my forehead became a vertical scar, my history teacher started calling me Slot. He was the wrestling coach and a macho guy, but he showed a kindness I have never forgotten. He thought up one reason after another to issue hall passes to a friend and me. He would send us to the office to see if there was anything in his faculty mailbox. He handed us change and asked us to bring him a Coke from the vending machine. I didn't realize it at the time, but letting me out of class was his way of giving a break to a girl who had just lost her brother and survived a head-on collision.

In a letter I found many years later, Dad had written to one of our relatives about how things were going at home. Besides my being in an accident, our two Dalmatians had "done a thorough job" on a toy poodle up the street and my parents had bought the neighbors a new puppy. Dad's plane had ruptured a fuel line aloft, but he smelled it and "got down quickly." Trying to make light of a difficult situation, he said he might hide awhile in the closet, where a poisonous spider would probably bite him.

His grief over Pete's death was not obvious. The only time I heard him speak of it was one afternoon when the two of us were in the car and he was pulled over for speeding. As he handed over his driver's license, he said simply, "I'm sorry, officer. I didn't have my mind on my driving. I've just lost my son in Vietnam." The policeman sent us on our way.

My mother was different. She lost her temper more easily than before, and Dad, Holly, and I kept out of her way to avoid setting her off. We tiptoed, figuratively and literally, around the house. She couldn't sleep at night, and her nerves were so badly frayed that my father muted the ring of the telephone by inserting a piece of foam where the hammer struck the bell.

When I came home from school, I could count on finding Mom in the living room, always in the same chair, hunched over a pad of graph paper. Who knows how long she might have been sitting there, lost in drawing house plans. An ashtray on the table beside her would be full of cigarette butts with red lipstick prints. In her right hand she held a pencil, usually a stubby one. She drew house plans prolifically, obsessively on her green graph paper. For the remaining two and a half years that I lived under my parents' roof, she generated house plans by the hundreds, each one no more than a few inches across, as if by drawing the perfect floor plan she could restore order to her fractured psyche.

Sometimes as I walked up to the house after school, I could hear her at the piano. Her beautiful playing was a concert for one, however. As soon as she became aware of someone coming, the music would stop. But for a minute I could occasionally catch the rippling notes of "May Night" or the jazzy rhythm of "Manhattan Serenade."

My mother's depression took up a lot of space in the house, which had always felt a size too small for us. The living room, dining room, and kitchen were one L-shaped room, so that all of the common living space was exposed. Our Oriental rug was too large for the living room and had to be turned under along one side. We had too much furniture for the space. My parents' bedroom was so crowded that the only way to get from one door to the other, on opposite walls, was to make your way along a single lane between bureaus, shelves, and tables that were heaped with newspapers and magazines. In the living room were still more shelves, crammed with books upon books. The piano sat in one corner, and over it hung a guitar and a cello on the wall. Sitting on the piano bench with the instruments looming overhead produced a sensation of something vaguely precarious and impending.

After Pete was killed, the living room became a shrine to him. Our household with four children had once been lively, but now it was restrained. My mother put photographs and drawings of Pete around the living room, including a pencil sketch dated August 6, 1965, and signed Tay-Do. It had been found in Pete's vehicle. There were brownish spots on the paper, which someone said were bloodstains.

When anyone but my closest friends came to the house, I felt embarrassed by the display. It seemed so raw and loud, even though it was understood we did not talk about Pete.

My family was more comfortable with secrecy than most. My mother's great-grandfather, William Huntington Russell, founded Skull and Bones, the secret society at Yale. I have wondered, half seriously, if we had a genetic predisposition to secrecy, or whether it was a New England Yankee trait or merely a family eccentricity.

I had heard stories about my ancestor General Russell, but I knew hardly anything about Skull and Bones until after my college years. Only once did I hear it mentioned in the family. On that occasion, someone made a humorous reference to the society in the presence of a Bonesman relative. The tradition is supposedly that a member of Skull and Bones leaves the room if the name is mentioned. In this case, the relative just laughed. Even so, another family member didn't think it was funny and demanded that we change the subject.

What I did know about my famous ancestor was that he founded a military academy in New Haven and organized the Connecticut militia for the Civil War. More than three hundred of his graduates served in the Union army. He harbored escaped slaves in the school and, as the family lore goes, told his students never to tell anyone about the mysterious sounds they heard. I imagined the creaking of doors late at night, footfall on squeaky stairs, and pots clanging in the kitchen as meals were hastily prepared for weary travelers.

Skull and Bones's roster reads like a Who's Who of the American upper class. Although my great-great-grandfather's name is associated with this elite group, he was better known in his day as an Abolitionist. John Brown was his personal friend and a frequent guest in the Russell home. In his will Brown named my ancestor a trustee of his estate.

General Russell was born in Middletown, Connecticut, where Wesleyan

University was established in 1831. Three of his ancestors had been pastors of the First Congregational Church there for a continuous period of 118 years. He was a descendant of Noadiah Russell, one of the ten Congregational ministers who founded Yale in 1701. To attend classes there, my great-great is said to have walked the twenty-six miles to New Haven "owing to financial necessity" and to have taken up teaching for the same reason.[2] In 1833 he graduated at the head of his class. One explanation has it that General Russell founded Skull and Bones to redress the injustice of Phi Beta Kappa denying membership to a deserving classmate.

My mother was proud of her ancestry. She could be imperious, and even toward us children she maintained a certain reserve, as a photograph of our family taken during my childhood illustrates. She stands near us without touching anyone, her arms folded across her chest.

At the same time, she had a very generous and outgoing side. She had an unusual capacity for warmth that won her many friends throughout her long life. In college, her dorm room was such a gathering place that she was nicknamed Madame de Rambouillet, after the hostess of a seventeenth-century literary salon in France. During my teenage years, when Holly's friends or mine stopped by the house and we were not there, they would stay and talk with my mother. She never lost her reserve or forgot her New England roots, but she loved the friendliness of the people of Oklahoma.

Both my mother and father were strict parents, but the house rules were hers. Words my friends used with nary a thought never passed my lips at home — racial epithets were unthinkable under any circumstances, but so too were profanity, barnyard language, and references to bodily functions. Body parts, with the exception of extremities, were largely off limits. I remember my mother telling Pete not to use the informal "thanks" but "thank you," although she eventually let up on that one. Still, she was not a prude. Her rules seemed to be based less on propriety than on class consciousness. One's station was revealed by one's speech and conduct. To me, rules such as not waving to a friend from the car seemed ridiculously old-fashioned and ill suited to the open spirit in Oklahoma. A lady doesn't wave, Mom said. She nods.

She was emotionally intense and, as Dad would say, given to hyperbole. It wasn't enough for her to describe her father as an honest businessman; he was "the only man in New Haven who could get a bank loan during the Depression." She didn't just love her country, she "passionately adored" it. "Always," "never," "ever," and "only" were among her prime vocabulary words. Temperamentally, I was more like my father. For as long as I can remember, I regarded my mother somewhat warily.

My family told a story about my emotional declaration of independence. I was three or four when one day I asked my father's permission for something. As many fathers of his era would have replied, he told me, "Ask your mother." I said I didn't want to ask her, because she didn't know what the other side of the moon looked like and she didn't know how sand felt between my toes. We were not allowed to talk back to our parents, but I had invoked a poem by a favorite family author, "Sand-Between-the-Toes" by A. A. Milne, and my father thought it was funny. Even that young, I had measured a certain distance between my mother and me.

In the aftermath of Pete's death, the distance between us increased. On one occasion she misplaced her pen. She accused my father and me of taking it to make her think she was crazy. I remember looking at him helplessly. In truth, she was a little crazy.

She was in tears many times during my remaining high school years. Her mind was often elsewhere. Once, it was her turn to provide a ride home for my friends and me after the rehearsal for a school play. We waited a long time for Mom before I called to see if she was on her way. She said she was coming. More time passed and my friends grew impatient. When I called again, she said she had gotten up from a nap when I called the first time, but she had forgotten what she was doing and, instead of getting dressed, went back to bed.

In April 1966, six months after Pete's death, my parents received a letter from Vice President Hubert Humphrey inviting our family to Washington. He had recently returned from South Vietnam. In a ceremony at the presidential palace, Premier Ky had given him a medal awarded posthumously to Pete. Humphrey would deem it a privilege, he said, to present the medal in his office, with ivs officials present.

Humphrey was one of several U.S. politicians who in the early 1960s sought out ivsers for their opinions. He visited the ivs house in Saigon and considered the young men and women—sometimes to their chagrin—part of the

American mission in Vietnam. It was thus more than a formality for Humphrey to extend an invitation to the family of the only ivs volunteer to have been killed.

On April 27, we were escorted into the vice president's office at the White House. Humphrey entered the room and welcomed us. With obvious emotion and moist eyes, he eulogized Pete. The mood was extremely somber. My parents, sisters, and I fought back tears, as a journalist present observed. He added:

> Mr. and Mrs. Hunting withstood the poignant moment, his right hand clasping her left, while Humphrey said, "Peter represented the best of this country as a volunteer for peace, for the love of mankind. . . . But no medal can take the place of your son. . . . He didn't mind the danger of going to remote villages. His was the kind of work that America is known for. The way we treat people is the way we treat God."[3]

After the medal presentation we were standing for photographs when U.S. Senators Fred Harris and Mike Monroney of Oklahoma rushed into the room. Humphrey apologized for inviting them late. I remember that the two men wore wide grins oddly unbefitting the occasion.

The ceremony was over, but Humphrey lingered with us for almost an hour. The mood lifted and he began telling us about the lowly status of the office he held. Speaking animatedly, he illustrated his point by showing us various cast-offs in the room. There was a chandelier that had been banished from Theodore Roosevelt's earshot after the tinkling glass kept the president awake one summer night. A mirror on the wall had been the focal point of a rift between President James Madison and the Congress, and now served as a reminder of the separation of powers. Humphrey said that nothing original was ever purchased for the vice president's office. Finally, he recommended that we have lunch in the Senate dining room. I remember his enthusiasm for the bean soup, and because he urged us to order it, we did.

At that time, Humphrey was taking criticism for being overly loyal to President Johnson and too hawkish. Some thought he should be staking out his own positions if he wanted to win the White House in 1968, and complained that he was preoccupied with ceremonies. Carl Rowan, the syndicated columnist, defended Humphrey. Referring to the medal presentation and to Pete, he doubted that voters would think much of a candidate who was too busy to present a post-humous medal to a young man who had died working for peace.[4]

The morning after the ceremony, Cis and I walked from the hotel where we were staying to a department store. I bought a floor-length yellow gown to wear to the junior–senior prom. I was straddling two worlds, that of a fifteen-year-old Oklahoma sophomore just getting interested in boys, and the sad, confusing, go-it-alone environment of my home.

FOUR

"Just Heard over the Radio"

As his language class in My Tho came to a close, Pete found out more about his work assignment in Phan Rang. He would be teaching English and assisting with hamlet self-help projects, such as digging wells. He would be a contact in the field for the "prov rep," or provincial representative, assigned to the area. The prov reps represented the U.S. Office of Rural Affairs. They controlled the purse strings, he noted in his journal.

The job would allow for some imagination. Pete looked forward to "lots of living in the villages," he wrote, and even wearing native dress. He would do "a lot of sleeping in the hamlets themselves" and get to know the local people. He would eat and drink the same food as they did, including a "really powerful distilled-oil sort of stuff"—the Vietnamese condiment *nuoc mam*, made from fish.

If Pete was aware that the Vietcong were systematically assassinating hamlet chiefs and schoolteachers, and that a group of ivs volunteers working at the agricultural station at Nha Ho, near Phan Rang, had moved to the city for safety, his letters and journal did not mention it.

Shortly before Pete left the United States, South Vietnamese troops had killed nine Buddhist demonstrators in the university city of Hue who were protesting the Diem regime. What were called the "Buddhist incidents" had been reported in American newspapers, and Margo Bradley, whom Pete had dated and would correspond with for the duration of his time in Vietnam, had evidently asked about them in a letter. The incidents had been terrible, he told her, but newspapers in the States exaggerated the situation. Few Americans, or at least few reporters, went that far north, he said, because there were not enough air-conditioned bars and swimming pools for them.[1]

As the IVSers were preparing to head out to the provinces, new Vietnamese friends gave a party for them. Dancing with torches, the men dramatized Vietnam's long history of wars for independence, and the women performed a line dance depicting the planting and harvesting of rice. A group of women gave Pete a lacquered cigarette box as a going-away gift. "I can never understand how I am always getting involved—innocently, yet—with so many girls," he wondered in his journal.

The team members spent several days in Saigon, staying at the IVS house. The "IVS Handbook" warned newcomers not to let cab drivers take advantage of them. "Most of the drivers will try to overcharge you," it stated. An inexperienced volunteer could easily pay double the going rate. "If the driver thinks you are fresh in the country he may ask for 150 [piasters] instead of 15 coming in from the airport. Be careful!"[2]

Young men could also be taken in by Saigon's working women. Pete went barhopping with teammate Bill Laakonen two nights in a row. "Those bar girls have been waiting for just the right guy to come along," he wrote. "[They] look into your eyes with *true love*. You're number one all over town." The women flirted, rubbing the hair on Pete's arms and asking him to sleep with them. "The thing is, [talking with bar girls] is an excellent opportunity to practice your Vietnamese," he told Sue. That was why he went to bars. For the language practice.

In mid-August Pete flew to the coastal resort of Nha Trang, the closest city to Phan Rang with an airport, and met the U.S. Operations Mission man for the province where he would be working. When he wasn't required to follow the chief-of-party, Don Luce, around "at the drop of the hat," Pete went to the beach—a long, white-sand crescent he described as "South Pacific all over again. The fishing sailboats are anchored twenty-five yards offshore with their painted eyes pointing to sea, warding off the sea monsters." He discovered a little French place named François' that made one think one was in Marseilles. The place was legendary for its local lobster and for entertaining both American and South Vietnamese clientele, including, late at night, Vietcong.[3]

The "ag" teammate with whom Pete would share a house was Chuck Fields, a Tennessee native whose specialties were chickens and pigs, and their attendant parasites. Chuck joined Pete and Don Luce in Nha Trang. The three of them tried to get through to a hamlet but were stopped by military police, who were out in force and blocking the roads. A Buddhist nun had immolated herself the day before, and Pete and his companions witnessed the police spraying orderly demonstrators with water and tear gas. The three IVSers left by a side road and headed south for Phan Rang.

It was his first view of rugged Ninh Thuan Province, which would be home for the next two years. "Beautiful country," he wrote. "Flat, but with mountains on the plain. Barren almost. Ocean close. Old temples." It reminded him of photographs he had seen of the Oklahoma Badlands. Ancient temples of the Cham people who had settled here hundreds of years ago were perched atop steep, rocky mountains. On the plain, hamlets baked in the sun, and charcoal farmers, whose grubby livelihood consisted of burning wood to produce cooking fuel, squatted outside their thatched huts. Pete liked it better here than down in the delta, where "everything [was] water, rice, people, and banana trees."

The next day they visited John Witmer and Larry Laverentz in Qui Nhon. They went on a picnic with seventeen children, all crammed into a single vehicle. Larry told a story about another IVS volunteer, Bob Dubyne, who was living in a province where conditions were such that he had to padlock his outhouse to keep the neighbors from using it.

With the others, Pete sorted corn for pigs and visited a leper colony.[4] Another day they drove to Dalat, which Pete described as "the Allegheny wonderland of Vietnam." The road up into the mountains was paved but only three or four yards wide, and "curvy and twisty, with rock on one side and space on the other. . . . Exciting driving, since you're always in suspense, not knowing when some madman of a bus driver will come plummeting down at you." Children standing in front of grass huts called out, *"Ong my!"* — "Mr. American!" — as they passed.

Pete was starting to think about McDonald's hamburgers. Before leaving home, he thought he knew the difference between comfort and "the fundamentals of living, but man — when you get here, you really get a subjective feeling for the extent of luxury as you knew it in the U.S." And yet he wasn't uncomfortable in Vietnam. If people back home assumed living conditions were primitive or dangerous, they were neither, he said. In fact, he was enjoying himself,

> riding along in the jeep perched atop the spare tire mounted on the tailgate. I like to ride back there for the breeze. . . . Well, I was sitting there, bounding along, singing a song to myself and thinking how rich a tremolo one could put into one's song while riding a jeep over these bumpy roads.

If he sounded a bit like Edward Bear in *Winnie-the-Pooh*, it was because the book was one of Pete's favorites. His other two favorite books, as he stated on his IVS application, were *India: The Most Dangerous Decade*, by Selig S. Harrison, and *Syntactic Structures*, by the linguist Noam Chomsky.

After two months in country, Pete was settling in at Phan Rang. IVS required all volunteers to submit reports about their projects. The write-ups formed the basis of newsletters mailed to supporters and family members. Although Pete wrote mostly private letters, volunteers were given the option of writing a newsletter that the IVS headquarters, in Washington, would send to a list of relatives and friends. The newsletters kept people back home informed and probably helped stave off homesickness. Larry Laverentz recalled two pieces of advice given to new volunteers about writing their newsletters: keep them short, and don't write about diarrhea.

Pete wrote his first newsletter on September 3, 1963:

> For the last couple of weeks I've been tooling around the country on various business; now the body finds itself deposited on home base, at least for a couple of days. My stationmate and I went up to observe some pigs . . . (pause for dramatic effect) . . . that have been brought to the country, compliments of your taxes—an improved variety.
>
> Chuck's a very competent animal husbandry technician, and is about to start a pig project in our region. Not being anything of an authority on pigs, I didn't know what to look for, but noticed some differences in pigment and that's about all. Nevertheless, I must admit catching a whiff of enthusiasm for the organization's work in the field, even while trying to maintain a detached air. . . .

As some might already know, I'm assigned to the Strategic Hamlet education program. There are seven of us boys scattered around Vietnam, having just completed a month of intensive language training. In addition to the seven of us, there is the regular corps of USAID Rural Affairs men; we're an on-the-spot supplement, so to speak.

As our job is described on paper, we go into the hamlets, discuss teaching methods with the hamlet teachers who have the equivalent of a normal-school training. We provide films and other materials needed by the teachers, through IVS contact with the United States Operations mission (USOM). USOM is the field organization of USAID. We assist in hamlet self-help programs by providing materials and pointers if needed, if possible. Most important, we make friends and try to gain the confidence of these people in order to better assist them in approaching their problems in a more scientific manner. It has been said that one might think "organizational ability" was a trait of Americans. In this respect, we're trying to work ourselves out of our jobs, and succeed. There are already a number of former IVS agricultural stations which are now completely operated by Vietnamese technicians.

. . . One notices that in some areas the Vietnamese have put their low-watt street lights high up in the air, thinking this will provide light to a greater area. However, one dimly recalls some theory of physics learned in the 12th grade that says light waves decrease in strength equal to the distance squared. As we've always known, the light directly under a street lamp is always stronger, and as you walk away, the light becomes increasingly dim. The light 10 feet away from a bulb is only ¼ as strong as the light 5 feet away; and there's a point when the light is no help at all, although there *is* light, technically speaking. Well, in some places they'll put the light so high off the ground that the only illuminated spot is a circle of light 10 feet in diameter directly under the bulb—all else will be shadow, with the next lamppost 40 feet down the street.

In such a case, one would point out such and such was the theory, and demonstrate its truth, which is sometimes rather difficult even with simple theories. In the case of street lamps, though (1) probably the government couldn't afford to change its posts to a shorter variety, and (2) one wouldn't have time to either gain the confidence of the administrator in charge, or demonstrate the truth of the theory. And over here, confidence and friendship are as important in the process of persuasion as technical know-how. In summary, we'll be doing everything from that which is described on paper to drilling wells, to pouring cement, to planting coconut trees, to distributing roosters.

. . . The only drawback is your exuberance—you have to learn to slow down and do things at their pace. Consequently, one is liable to have a lot of spare time between projects.

Right now, while I'm waiting for the formalities of my assignment to get sorted out, I use my spare time for reading some books I never got a chance to read in school. . . .

I've also drawn a plan for a homemade air-cooler. The kind with the vented box and water dripping down. I'm going to freeze up my bedroom when we move into the new station house next week.

After the air cooler, I'm going to build a light plane—note air of confidence—if the Chief of Province lets me. I'll fly over this lovely terrain and buzz fishing boats. . . . I will have left my mark on Vietnam, although I'm hoping for bigger things. I can hardly wait to finish it. I built a few model airplanes and know a little about aerodynamics; enough to get myself killed, you'll say . . . ha. I can do it if all these skeptics don't embarrass me to death first. . . .

Speaking of these skeptical people in this vein, you should have been with me the other day: I went down to the local Vietnamese lumberyard, my interpreter close behind. I'd filled him in on number one project, i.e., the plane, and he was well indoctrinated. He's a good bit older than myself, but didn't say anything, being a fatalistic chap, I think. Well, we got there, and the owner became a little mystified and irked when I started looking at this one particular piece of wood. (I was thinking of whittling a propeller . . . you laugh, perhaps.) He was wondering about my being so critical of this one cotton-picking board, and envisioning one whole day being taken up, bickering with some recently weaned youth of America over the quality of his boards; but he didn't say anything—just watched.

"What's he going to build?" he asked interpreter Kim, in Vietnamese, with much consternation. "An airplane," explained Kim, without so much as a flutter of eyelid, dead serious. Because Kim is quite a bit older than myself, and therefore expected to know and judge things with great wisdom a la Confucius, the owner would have been relieved had Kim communicated some fatherly indulgence, or perhaps scorn. But no, he gave it to him straight; deadpan; poker face; with great gravity, as though some lad of a youth could be expected to accomplish such a thing. . . .

P.S. You all are probably wondering about what the security's like and all the other exciting things you read in papers, stateside. Well, I haven't been shot, yet. In this province, the Province Chief has everything well under control—it's the most secure province in the country. And whenever we do any traveling, we ask the local U.S. Military Advisers, and they clear their throats and say, "Yes, we have everything well under control—it's the most secure province in the country, you know."

The other day we were coming back from Dalat, myself driving, when a man appeared from the side of the road and motioned us to stop. I downshifted, but was ready for anything, not knowing the guy. As we pulled even with him, a second chap leaps from behind the bush with a submachine gun in his hands. I applied my foot to the top of the carburetor, sank down behind the dashboard out of sight, and took evasive action. . . . Something inside the body was searing, white hot—now I know where my fear gland is located. We found out later that the two chaps were only civil guardsmen out on patrol. No sweat.

Pete was eager to get to work—too eager. Four days after he arrived in Phan Rang, he introduced himself to the top education official in Ninh Thuan Province. They hit it off immediately, but things didn't go as well the next day when he met the chief of the province. The Vietnamese authorities had not been alerted to Pete's arrival. The province chief was angry. He claimed he "did not know *what* kind of agents were in his province," Pete said.

To make matters worse, the Military Assistance Advisory Group adviser, one Major Cook, had not received a letter of introduction either. He delivered a withering lecture that Pete described in a letter to John Sommer:

The Prov. Chief and MAAG's Major Cook were in an uproar, balls-wise. Flame and smoke all that day! I left for Saigon two days later in an angry sweat, for the purpose of getting my protocol straight.

It seems that a major figure in Vietnamese education channels, connected with our work, was arrested; and on top of *that*, USOM fucked up by not sending out letters. Consequently I am shifting my ass from chair to chair, alternating study of Vietnamese with Steinbeck and perhaps masturbation. Thap Cham doesn't have much else to offer. Next week we move into Phan Rang proper. . . . Every once in a while I go into the MAAG compound for excitement, to get my ass scorched by some new, novel, and imaginatively conceived method. . . .

The latest angle the major has thought up is that I will be duplicating everything "they" have done. I was impudent enough to ask (1) whether "they" meant the Army or perhaps the Special Forces, and (2) what this work *was* that I'd be duplicating. He fumed that I'd be duplicating the work that HE, as a private citizen *and* major of the *U.S. Army* (thumping of chest) had been doing for the last *eight* months; as though he had a monopoly on good deeds, Boy Scout behavior patterns, and dollhouse activity. . . .

You *dared* get associated with Buddhist monks? Christ! You know, that's what's feeding this CIA neurosis they've contracted of late. Besides needing a scapegoat. . . .

Aside from the occasional bouts with officialdom and sitting around, I also accompanied my stationmate, Chuck Fields, up to Qui Nhon, and sat on my ass *there*, too. We went up to observe pigs. I think perhaps there ought to be a better word for this sort of thing, given the fact that English is supposed to be such a richly descriptive language. . . . Particularly interesting was the way they inoculated pigs, which I'd never seen before: they pick up the beast by the hind legs, exposing its sensitive parts. Then they take a lethal-looking hypodermic and ram it in about 2½ inches away from the pig's ass hole. Needless to say, the pig will have a very self-conscious look about him after undergoing treatment.

The relationship with Chuck, his stationmate, wasn't going well either. Chuck criticized Pete's Vietnamese pronunciation. Proud of his grasp of tones, Pete defended himself until one day the discussion deteriorated into an argument. The sore feelings hung in the air for days. Pete also sensed that Chuck disapproved of his eating so much, and smoking. In return, he didn't like Chuck needling their maid. A week later, however, Pete wrote that the relationship had improved "one hell of a lot."

They moved into a new house. Pete named it God's Half Acre, after the name of a novel about a writer who moves into a convalescent home to gather local color for his book. (Pete may have been wrong about the title and meant, instead, *God's Little Acre*, a story of Georgia sharecroppers.) The yard was strewn with old furniture and parts for a water pump. Inside, Pete's room was furnished with a desk and a packing crate for a chair. The dining room consisted of a table and one left-behind book, described by Pete as a "lusty account of the Roman games," called *Those About to Die*.

Because telephone service was spotty and ivs members usually had to place calls from a post office, the ivs team kept in touch by writing letters and visiting each other's stations. In September, ag teammate Bob Dubyne came down to Phan Rang from his station in Ban Me Thuot. A farmer was having trouble with wild pigs eating his corn and had asked for help.

Pete and Bob borrowed two guns from the civil militia. They bought Cokes and french fries in town, loaded mattresses and mosquito nets into a jeep, and made camp in the dusty road to wait for the pigs. It was a moonless night so dark they couldn't see the end of their rifles. Two hours later, the Vietnamese men waiting with them heard the sound of munching. They lit torches and tried to drive the pigs in the direction of Pete and Bob, but the pigs got away. Later, Pete guessed that Major Cook would soil his pants if he knew what they had done.

He and Bob lit cigarettes and imagined Vietcong "sighting on them and shooting their heads off." They ate their french fries, "chewed the wad with the civil guardsmen," counted their bullets, and listened to the night sounds. Someone had brought a radio, and they tuned in Voice of America and a Bartok violin concerto. To make it easier to see in the dark, Pete squashed a lightning bug onto the back of his rifle's forward sight. Finally they called it a night, resolving to try again when they had better guns and a spotlight.

It was autumn, and in a letter to Sue, Pete described how he imagined Wesleyan coming back to life as the students returned to fix up their rooms.

Around this time, a young Brown University graduate named Richard Holbrooke had just volunteered for a sensitive assignment. Holbrooke was a new foreign service officer and had arrived in Vietnam only a few months earlier. Learning that a province chief in the Lower Mekong Delta required handling with kid gloves and did not get along with the Rural Affairs man, Holbrooke offered to take the prov rep's place. "Like I said," he would say years later of his youthful confidence, "I was twenty-two."[5] The prov rep Holbrooke replaced, Bob Friedman, moved to Phan Rang.

On September 9, at the urging of Secretary of State Dean Rusk and with the backing of President Kennedy, Ambassador Henry Cabot Lodge informed President Diem that his brother Nhu should make himself scarce for a few months. Nhu had been criticized on the floor of Congress and at the United Nations for his harsh handling of the Buddhist opposition. Diem was told that, unless Nhu was restrained, Congress might not vote favorably on appropriations to South Vietnam. Diem objected, and eventually Lodge adopted a position of silence.[6]

A different approach from that of Lodge—who, according to Rural Affairs Director Rufus Phillips, could not help "his inbred, imperious manner" and had no personal rapport with Diem[7]—was put forward late in the summer of 1963. Edward Lansdale, now a major general, suggested to Harvard economist John Kenneth Galbraith that the two Ngo brothers could be separated. Such a move was bound to make Diem more cooperative if it were done without either Diem or Nhu losing face. Lansdale suggested that Galbraith use his influence to obtain Nhu a teaching position. Incensed, Galbraith replied, "We don't do that at Harvard."[8]

Also in the fall of 1963 President Kennedy sent his defense secretary, Robert McNamara, and General Maxwell Taylor to South Vietnam on a fact-finding mission. Pete noted in his journal that they had come through the province for an inspection. They returned to Washington optimistic about the Strategic Hamlet Program and the military outlook, but pessimistic about the Diem government.

By the end of September, after almost three months in Vietnam, Pete had received no mail from home. He wondered if his letters were being censored.

ivsers were expected to try to fit in and make friends wherever they were stationed. The "ivs Handbook" explained that a volunteer's location and attitude would determine the kind of recreation available to him or her. "In many situations, you will have to find new ways to entertain yourself," the handbook said, "but this is usually not much of a problem once you have become acclimated and involved in the community life."[9]

Pete was adapting and enjoying his new surroundings, but he admitted that he missed American desserts. On September 22, he asked in a letter home:

Say, how do you make pie crust, and what's the basic formula for making the filling using berries or fruits, or lemon meringue? Could you send over a recipe or two on how to make a cake when you don't have instant cake mix, also? And a recipe for cookies of some sort? All we have for dessert over here is fruit, fruit, fruit.

He and Chuck attempted to cook a "bachelor cake." It was the same as an ordinary cake, but it contained the additional ingredients of cigarette ashes, fly specs, and charcoal and was noticeably lopsided, with a fallen center. Their oven had been too hot and burned the outside of the cake after only three minutes. Desserts were better at the home of an American missionary couple who lived nearby, where the wife made cakes and cookies. Pete and Chuck sometimes played Scrabble or Monopoly with them. Other evenings, they watched movies at the MAAG compound, or Pete studied Chinese or traded English for Vietnamese lessons with the hamlet education chief.

On free days, he sometimes made the fifty-mile drive up the coast for lobster at François'. The American major in Nha Trang was more affable than his counterpart in Phan Rang. Pete guessed it was because his wife had come with him. She wore tight clothes and complained with affected naïveté about the uproar of frogs mating in her fishpond. "Ah," Pete speculated, "the nightly orgies that must go on behind the walls of *that* home."

The drive home from Nha Trang was beautiful, he wrote in his journal:

The low-flying fleecy clouds stood out against the black overcast of the higher storm clouds. . . . Looking at the ridgeline we could see the fleecy fingers of these clouds spilling over the top and down our side. Wind was coming at us. Then it began raining. A very thick-falling rain, everything half covered in the mist. . . . At one bridge we had to stop and wait for a bicyclist to pass. He smiled and said in very distinct though fractured English, "I'm sorry." Such wonderful, friendly people.

He drove to the mountain resort city of Dalat to visit John Sommer. The road ascended through villages of the Montagnard—French for "mountain people," a name Westerners applied to several different indigenous groups. The Montagnard men wore loincloths. The women went bare breasted, Pete told Sue after she asked what women in Vietnam were like. The girls were uninhibited in some ways, he said, but looking at a topless Montagnard woman was "like seeing the back of somebody's head. As much erotic appeal, I mean. Anyway," he added graphically, "their breasts are always soft and lopsided and uneven and sagging, with big ugly nipples."

Next door to the ivs house in Dalat was a villa owned by Madame Nhu, the powerful sister-in-law of President Diem. The previous Christmas, the ivs team had gathered in Dalat and were roasting hot dogs when someone joked that they should ask their glamorous neighbor to join them. She happened to be in residence and, after being told she was invited, sent word that she would attend. Thirty minutes later she appeared, wearing long evening gloves with her traditional Vietnamese-style gown, an *ao dai*. As she roasted her hot dog, she asked the young Americans what they called this activity. "She did not seem to have the word 'barbecue' in her vocabulary at that time," volunteer Harvey Neese remembered.[10] Not long afterward, Madame Nhu made headlines around the world by referring to the Buddhist self-immolations as "barbecues."

The horrifying suicide protests continued, and the young men and women of ivs were not spared the horror. On October 27, 1963, an ivser in Saigon was returning from church when she saw policemen hosing away the ashes of a Buddhist monk.[11]

Several of Pete's teammates visited him that fall in Phan Rang. He showed them the market, a Cham temple outside of town, and the beach at Ninh Chu. He took Vaughn Stapleton, a team leader, to meet the bombastic Major Cook and discuss with him the need for irrigation windmills in the province. In this most arid region of Vietnam, farmers needed water for their parched crops. The Rural Affairs manual contained plans for building a windmill to drive a water pump, but before the project could be undertaken, Major Cook's consent was required. Stapleton suggested trying it and Cook agreed.

Another team leader, Mike Chilton, and the ivs executive director, Dr. Stevenson, also stopped in when they were checking on the organization's stations throughout South Vietnam. Pete introduced them to the assistant province chief, who received them nervously. Mr. Phuong had trained as an actor and spoke slightly dramatic broken English. He produced a bottle of champagne and gave it to a servant to pour for his guests. When the cork exploded loudly and half of the wine spilled onto the floor, Phuong aimed a torrent of anger at the servant. Mike "split his gut laughing."

When Pete wasn't entertaining his teammates or launching self-help projects in villages, he was building his air conditioner and getting acquainted with the local barber. For a quarter he could have his hair cut and his forehead, nose, ears, and upper back shaved; to finish things off, the barber would give him a massage and apply "plenty of perfume." He bought a pair of trousers from the local tailor and asked him to sew a V-shaped insert into the crotch "to correct for wrinkles and tightness when walking or squatting." Hearing of this, Pete's Vietnamese male friends thought it was very funny. They were slender, with thin legs, and didn't need the extra room.

By now, everyone knew Pete's name, which they pronounced "Ong Peck." He called one boy Chattanooga. The young man wore the nickname with pride.

Pete finally had begun to receive mail. He replied to a letter from Holly and me, assuring us that, no, bombs were not dropping around him. Most of the trouble in Vietnam was concocted, he told us, in the minds of newspaper reporters:

> You never see them outside a bar as far as I know. The Vietnamese are doing well, but from the sounds of things in the States, you wouldn't know it. Myself, I'm in the safest province of Vietnam. No worse and a lot better than a person's odds who drives in the U.S.

On November 1, 1963, Pete wrapped Christmas presents and recovered from an evening with Don Luce and the local Rural Affairs man, Bob Friedman. The chief of the fishing village had presented Don with a gift of smoked fish after a smokehouse project there had been successfully completed. The three had washed down the fish with five bottles of wine. A cool breeze had brought the hint, and later the relief, of rain.

Pete packed up a few weavings he had bought from a Cham family in a nearby hamlet, explaining in a note that the Cham were a semi-tribal minority group. The beautiful, brightly colored blankets were dry-clean-only, he warned—anticipating that my mother would launder one in the washing machine and ruin it.

He turned on a radio he had recently picked up second-hand. The first time he had tried it out, he'd had to repair it with scraps of wire. He had just tuned in a broadcast of music from Saigon when suddenly the radio went silent. Broken again, he thought.

Half an hour later, former IVSers Harvey Neese and Jim Green, now USAID employees, rushed into the house. There had been a coup d'état in Saigon. They turned on the radio again and heard BBC reporting heavy fighting and artillery fire in the center of the city. Troops loyal to Diem had surrounded the presidential palace and were awaiting an attack by his rivals.

Chuck arrived with word that three machine guns were mounted on the local army compound wall. The entrance gates were closed.

They waited for more news, eating dinner with the radio positioned in the center of the table. An army captain hurried in to recommend that everyone remain indoors. He said that Dalat had been placed under curfew and Diem's brother Nhu had taken charge of Phan Rang.

In fact, Diem and Nhu had been captured. South Vietnamese military officers had taken control of the government, and troops supporting them had surrounded the palace.

Throughout the evening Pete and the others absorbed the unfolding events. At 7:30 P.M., civil servants were ordered to return to work as usual. By eight o'clock, all ministers of the Diem government were being "invited" to register with the new government within twenty-four hours. In truth, they were being rounded up.

As Pete listened, he reflected on a recent visit to Dalat when he had shot an arrow from a Montagnard bow into "the Queen Bee's" flower garden. He couldn't resist punning that he had "gotten his barb in."

By morning the palace had been taken, and eventually it was learned that Diem and Nhu had been executed. Within days, Diem's picture had been torn down in Phan Rang. Otherwise, the only noticeable effects of the coup "besides enthusiasm," Pete noted, were that gasoline was being rationed and a nine o'clock curfew had been imposed.

Two weeks after the coup, the IVS office in Washington sent a report to the parents of team members in Vietnam. It included eyewitness accounts of two volunteers. Gloria Johnson described the tension on the day of the coup and the present mood:

I was caught at the military airport at 1 P.M. . . . We heard shooting, saw planes dipping and rolling in the air drawing fire from below, but didn't know for sure what was happening until an hour later. Turned out that they took the airport first, then moved downtown.

Returned to IVS about 6:30 P.M. . . . I was glad to be in Saigon, to have the experience of witnessing the coup. It's frightening, and a little exciting too.

On Saturday, Saigon was a shambles. The coup was over and it was obvious that the battle was a tough one. Several government buildings were badly damaged by fire and shelling [including] downtown establishments owned by Mme. Nhu.

. . . Of course there has been a lot of excitement. No one has talked of anything else; rumors are a dime a dozen—you wouldn't believe how many rumors there are! Dancing has resumed in the nightclubs downtown. Vietnamese people are jubilant and are 100 percent friendlier to Americans. Americans are happy, too, to say the least.

As I write this, we're not sure what will happen, but we're expecting things to be brighter in the future than they have been in the past. The feeling in the air is not one of tension, but a controlled release of the accumulated tensions of months, and people are smiling, singing, and laughing. There's really more of a festive, holiday feeling than six Christmases could produce.[12]

Forest Gerdes managed to keep two dental appointments during the overthrow:

The Independence Day holiday had begun Monday, so I was in the capital taking advantage of it to have dental work done. . . .

I was still at the dentist's office about 3:00 when the first messages from the newly captured radio station were broadcast by the revolutionary council. During the first day of broadcasts, we didn't know how much reporting about the coup's progress we dared believe, but it became obvious by early Saturday morning that success was probable. We were almost afraid to cheer it, lest our cheers prove premature.

By seven o'clock Friday night, all previously captured students and monks had been released from prison. At 6:05 A.M. the President capitulated.

Of course Americans were asked to stay off the streets during the coup, but I managed to sneak out to keep another dental appointment on Saturday and look along the way. The people were gathered around radios in shops along the streets, smiling hopefully, smugly, jubilantly. . . .

I have never seen the Vietnamese people in a more spontaneously gay mood than downtown after the coup. Old women were scurrying to bring the soldiers food and water, the children climbed all over the tanks on street corners, and younger ladies gave away cigarettes. The Buddhists are still collecting money to buy gifts for the soldiers and the pagodas are jammed with praying thankful. The prestige of an Army uniform has risen fifty per cent and the sight of an American has never brought more friendly smiles. (Many Vietnamese believe we sponsored the coup.) . . .

When night fell, and the noise continued, we tuned into the Voice of America. Once again, we knew its value, as the hours-old news of what was happening five miles away was reported to us from Washington, D.C., relayed through the Philippines![13]

The young volunteers' optimism must have quelled parental anxieties. A few days after the letter from ivs headquarters reached my parents in Oklahoma City, my mother used the back of the envelope to jot a prosaic note: "Hair. 10 A.M. Thursday."

It was late autumn, and Pete's thoughts traveled occasionally to Wesleyan. He recalled the lengthening nights in Middletown, and the falling leaves and cold gusts of wind. He listened to Sinatra love songs on the radio and told Sue he wished they could be together.

She wanted to start a hope chest. He replied that there was a reason they were called "hope" and not "certainty" chests, but agreed to help her with one if she didn't make him nervous by talking about it too much. He seemed different, she said. He wondered why.

Sometime in November 1963, Pete abandoned his plans for building a light airplane. Though he had found a company in Oregon that would sell him a seventy-two-horsepower aircraft engine, he thought it cost too much.

He turned to a new scheme: he had found a boatyard that would build him a sailboat for about 170 dollars. He hoped that after his two years with ivs were up, one of his teammates would help him sail it to Europe.

He asked my mother to organize a fund-raiser to build classrooms in his province—classrooms in addition to those jointly funded by USAID and the South Vietnamese government. Adding a room to one of the old and over-crowded schools would cost only 274 dollars. The province could use nineteen more classrooms, but Pete would be happy with three or four. With Diem gone, he hoped that Americans would have more confidence in the work of IVS. If Mom would put on a Vietnamese dinner, he offered to send all the *nuoc mam* she needed. Nothing came of these suggestions. Pete had always been full of ideas. Perhaps my mother had grown used to his enthusiasms. She may not have known how to begin organizing a fund-raiser, and she had never been much of a cook.

Late that month, Pete began a letter to Margo. The radio was playing in the background. What came next was almost too shocking to put into words:

My God. Just heard over the radio about President Kennedy's assassination. Not very much news. How terrible. Just a sick, angry feeling.

As if the news had disoriented him, he turned to other subjects. He reflected on life in the States: gas stations on every corner, restaurants that sold pie and ice cream, Thanksgiving coming. The IVS office in Saigon had sent a turkey and suggested that he and Chuck invite Vietnamese guests for dinner and explain the American holiday and its traditions. The turkey was so small, he said, that he could eat it all by himself.

He apparently took a break and then resumed his letter. He returned to the subject of the assassination:

Every time I think about Kennedy it makes me feel sick, as though it had been somebody in my own family. Makes me really hate racists. All our Vietnamese friends have stopped us on the street to say they were sorry to hear it, too. Doesn't it just make you sick to think of it?

FIVE

"A Peaceful Sleep Forever"

Kim Nguyen stepped out of a taxi in front of the IVS house in Saigon and smoothed the long panels of her *ao dai*—the fitted tunic with slacks underneath worn by Vietnamese women of all ages. Kim was eighteen, with straight black hair cut short.

Her father, who held a high position with the post office, had sent Kim to a good school. One day a notice went up on the bulletin board there. Someone was looking for a secretary who could speak English and take shorthand. Kim got the job and went to work for Don Luce. By November 1965, only thirty-four years old, he had been chief-of-party for five years.

The IVS headquarters was located near Tan Son Nhut Airport on a livestock experiment station owned by the South Vietnamese Agriculture Ministry. It was a modest two-story concrete structure connected by a breezeway to an older, French-era residence. In the newer building were a small men's dormitory and a large living room where the volunteers gathered occasionally for meetings or parties. The upper floor of the older building housed the few women on the team. Downstairs were a kitchen, a dining room, and two offices. Kim and Don shared the smaller office. A few administrative staffers shared the larger room with their Vietnamese typist and an interpreter.

When Kim entered the building, not a person was in sight. She looked in the kitchen and saw several of the young Americans huddled and speaking in whispers. Their faces were grim and worried. *Something is wrong,* she thought.

She walked into her office, looking for Don. He wasn't there. She walked to the doorway of the other office and saw Mai, the typist, sitting alone. *What is wrong?*

Mai said she didn't know if it was true, but she had just heard that Pete Hunting had been killed.

A few minutes later, Don found Kim and took her aside. "He looked very soft," she remembers. The room was silent. His eyes were red.

Don said he had bad news. Pete had been on his way somewhere and was killed in a mine explosion.

"Oh, my God! Did I hear it right?" she asked. She was numb. She could not believe it.

Kim had not known Pete well, but she had seen him on the occasions when he stopped by the ivs house. She had thought him very good looking. He had always wished her a good morning. "A lot of the other guys would chitchat, but Pete—he had things to do," she said. "He would just stop in and then go right back to work." He was purposeful.

For the rest of the day, Kim struggled to do anything. Don asked her to type a list of Pete's belongings. It was just one page, but she kept making mistakes and it took three hours. Don told her the list was for Pete's mother. There was also a short letter, which began, "It is with deep regret . . ."

For a long time the atmosphere of the ivs house was one of sorrow. People who once had been loud in the office were now quiet.

Gene Stoltzfus, a Mennonite pacifist from Minnesota, was Pete's closest friend on the ivs team. Just two days before Pete was killed, he had taken Gene to the Saigon airport for a flight to Nha Trang, where he lived.

After learning of Pete's death, Gene returned to Saigon and helped arrange a memorial service at the International Protestant Church.

Among many who attended the service on November 16 was Charles Mann, director of the U.S. Operations Mission in Vietnam. A few days before, his deputy had sent my father a telegram assuring him that Pete had been "in front lines of war to help win the hearts and minds of the Vietnamese people."[1]

At the service, some of Pete's Vietnamese friends sang his favorite folk songs, which they had taught him. Don Luce spoke for the team:

Pete Hunting was a friend to all those with whom he associated. He will be greatly missed.

He came to help and felt deeply the problems of the Vietnamese people. He worked because there was work to do. There are wells he dug in the villages of the Cham people near Phan Rang; ideas were changed and new thoughts introduced by his long hours in and out of the classroom with the youth of this country; clothes and food were distributed through his efforts to refugees from the Viet Cong in Cai Be. The simple things like supporting a boy through high school with his own living allowance, carrying a farmer to market, selling a Cham woman's blankets were part of Pete's daily life.

He came with a much higher motivation than materialism. Pete came to Vietnam and returned for a second tour because he wanted to get close to people . . . to help make life easier for others. Most important of all is the greater understanding Pete gave us all of the things he felt important . . . brotherhood, service to man, and the need for peace.

The contributions Pete Hunting made, his courage, his kindness, and his great sacrifice will remain. He was a man of his word who will be remembered by people of many walks of life—the Cham farmer, the Vietnamese school teacher, the NVS [National Voluntary Service] youth leader, the USOM representative, and his fellow IVSers.

At the time of his death, Pete carried this verse in his wallet. I think he would like all of us to share it:

> By the way of Bethlehem lead us, O Lord, to newness of life;
> By the innocence of the Christ child renew our simple trust;
> By the tenderness of Mary deliver us from cruelty and hardness of hearts;
> By the patience of Joseph save us from all rash judgment and ill-tempered action;
> By the shepherds' watch open our eyes to the signs of thy coming;
> By the wise men's journey keep our searching spirits from fainting;
> By the music of the heavenly choir put to shame the clamor of the earth;
> By the shining of a star guide our feet into the way of peace. Amen.[2]

The loss of Pete Hunting has affected us all deeply. He was a personal friend as well as an inspiration to all. I pray that we will be given the strength to continue as Pete would want us to.

Many of Pete's teammates wrote to my parents. Bob McNeff said he would miss Pete "beyond words." He recalled Pete's dedication, and the trust and respect he had earned among Vietnamese colleagues and friends. After the service, Bob collected the ribbons from a dozen wreaths and mailed them to my parents.

Jim Linn was one of the volunteers on Pete's team after he was promoted to a supervisory role. For three months Jim and Pete had lived next to each other. Jim was "so thoroughly upset" that he felt compelled to write to my parents. "It was solely through my observations of Pete in his daily living that I was convinced that the IVS team leader position could be meaningful and productive," he said. "I am sure that he cannot be replaced—no one could work as effectively and honestly as he did." Jim was later promoted to team leader himself.

He wrote again a few weeks later. He had recently seen a Cham couple who knew Pete up in Ninh Thuan. Pete had helped them, and others in their hamlet, to sell the weavings that were their sole source of income. The couple had asked Jim to send a special blanket to Pete's parents "to convey both their sympathy and their pride in having had such a good and valued friend." He enclosed a letter from the husband and translated it: "He will always be in my heart as a friend whom I shall forever be fond of. I will never be able to forget him. . . . I send urgent prayers to the heavens above, asking that you be protected and that you will receive peace and good health for you and your family."

Because my parents did not share the letters they received with my sisters and me, I was not aware of the number of people who felt as if they, too, had lost a brother. One Vietnamese man said, "I can only say that we felt like we had lost someone very dear, a brother. He was always friendly, helpful, and optimistic. As all Asian peoples, we believe in fate. I must say that fate is not always fair, but we cannot do anything about it. Pete Hunting has gone but his name will remain forever in his friends' mind and heart."

A high school principal wrote that his staff and students were deeply grieved:

We can hardly believe such a tragic event. Pete has gone forever! You lost a beloved son; the United States lost a dignified citizen; we, the teaching staff, lost a colleague of good will; our students lost a kind and devoted teacher; Vietnamese people lost a clement benefactor.

How can you forget such a good-natured young man who had more than once set foot on this poor land on a sacred humanitarian mission? Pete's days were already numbered, but still his image remains in those he lived with, and with the places where he passed. Pete died but his work is still being carried forward. We can't help being moved when thinking of a youth who had left his prosperous country with magnificent cities and skyscrapers to engage himself in this remote strip of land and mingle himself with the Vietnamese peasants. Many a time, Pete was seen among the Cham, helping them dig wells, build houses and do various agricultural jobs. And it is in the scope of education that we know Pete best. What Pete did at our school remains as cherished memories for us.

We would like to end the letter with our most sincere condolences to your family and relatives. God bless Pete and consolate him in the other world.

An elementary school teacher told my parents about the mobile science laboratory Pete had developed a few months earlier. "We made acquaintance with a young and gentle American," he wrote. It was the first time that the school had worked so closely with an American. Pete had spared neither time nor money, paying for much of the lab equipment himself. The teachers had noticed his disappointment when other Americans did not share his enthusiasm for the new science lessons.

Before moving to the delta, Pete had spent an evening with the teacher and two new IVSers. They had shared "a friendly Vietnamese dinner in the full moonlight at a popular restaurant in the outskirts of Saigon," the teacher wrote. Pete had taught the new recruits some Vietnamese customs. He had promised the teacher they would meet again whenever he was in Saigon. After he moved south, they had missed him. The letter continued:

Because he dared to accept his risky duty in touring the countryside, because he was well aware that the enemy was waiting for him at his every step to help us develop the education of the Vietnamese youth, foreseeing his lethal fate as a constant companion and an ultimate reward, he really possessed his life and made it full of sense. Peter's life was too short! But his souvenir will always be alive in our hearts.

My parents also heard from American government employees in Vietnam, such as Paul London, an assistant provincial representative. London lived in Ba Xuyen Province, where Pete had driven past the verdant rice fields on his last day, and wrote:

> Being in Vietnam is one of the best opportunities to see Americans as they should be . . . but of all the fine people I've met here it is honest to say that Peter was the one I liked best to think of as representative of America. Certainly he was the most sensitive and the one I expected to profit most from this experience. He took trouble to speak Vietnamese well and it was appreciated. . . . I would have been very pleased if I could have influenced him to join the State Department.

Frank G. Wisner II was a second secretary at the U.S. Embassy. At the time of Pete's death, he was in Mississippi for the funeral of his father, a high-ranking CIA official. Upon his return to Saigon, he learned the "heartbreaking news" and wrote to my parents, "I was proud to be one of Peter's greatest admirers. His exuberance, imagination, consideration, effectiveness, and bravery made a deep impression on me during the months we knew each other . . . I shall miss Peter *very* much."

In the following months, Wisner would come to my parents' aid by expediting the return of Pete's personal effects. As a federal employee, my father was no stranger to bureaucracy, but he grew frustrated when the promised shipment failed to arrive, despite one assurance after another. Wisner had offered to help in any way he could, and my father eventually turned to him for assistance. Wisner got things moving.[3]

President Lyndon Johnson was informed of Pete's death by his national security adviser, McGeorge Bundy, on December 18, 1965. Bundy's memo included a report from USOM Director Charles Mann stating that Pete had been ambushed and murdered. "Consideration might be given to award a posthumous decoration," he suggested.

The following day, in Oklahoma City, the *Sunday Oklahoman* reported that a flood of sympathy letters and telegrams had been pouring into our home from strangers and friends around the world.[4] Meanwhile, in Saigon, Don Luce had been collecting condolence letters and telegrams received at the IVS house. He sent them to my parents in a dark-green lacquered box with golden bamboo painted on the cover, a beautiful example of Vietnamese craftsmanship.

Pete had worked closely with a volunteer in a youth program who wrote:

Nobody could anticipate such a cruel thing would happen to such a nice man. This is not the first time an American died on this thankless land for the service of Vietnamese people, but it is just unbearable to us. . . .

Would you, his eldest brother in ivs team, please be kind enough to let us share this great common loss and sorrow.

Finally, let us hope this is the only case that ivs has to undergo, a very special case, happened through mistakes, as Pete often joked that there was nothing special in Phan Rang but himself.

A Buddhist student leader wrote that Pete's contribution to youth activities and social improvement had been "so great that it is still alive in our mind forever. On behalf of the Buddhist students, I send to you our mourning, and I want to let you know that we all share your suffering and loss."

Another student leader struggled to believe what had happened to his friend:

The news of Peter's death reached me one gloomy afternoon two days ago. Could I believe in my ears? How could such a bitter thing happen? As a close friend of Peter, I was severely shocked, but what can compare with the sorrow you have to bear.

. . . I still remember the day [we] transported water pumps to Suoi-Gieng hamlet to help peasants save hundreds of acres of rice fields from a certain death due to the drought. The rice fields were saved but who could imagine death would come to Peter a few months after.

Braving danger, ignoring promising careers in the states, he came to Vietnam to help us reconstruct our wretched countryside and soothe wounds of a divided country. Now our energetic Peter gone. His life was sacrificed for his humanitarian ideal, what could be more noble?

We bow our heads before your son's death. Your mourning is also ours, as we consider Peter our brother sharing our ideals of serving the underprivileged and deprived. This letter is to let you know that although thousands of miles are between us, our hearts are with you in your bereavement in this moment.

The executive committee of a Vietnamese volunteer organization founded on the IVS model addressed the Vietcong's attack and Pete's legacy:

> The news that your son was assassinated while carrying out his altruistic mission down in the Mekong delta was just like a stab in our own hearts. It was something that we could hardly believe. How could that happen to our nice friend who had come from a distant and prosperous country with just an aim to help us fight misery and ignorance.
>
> If Peter's death was due to a mistake on the part of our enemy, it was a regrettable mistake causing a great loss to all country people of Vietnam. If it was the result of a deliberate act, it was then a blunt murder worth to be condemned by all.
>
> Peter passed away from this world but his works realizing love of humanity will remain everlasting in rural Vietnam. As for us, we have engraved in our memory his radiant look and open smile while expressing his determination to help poor Vietnamese peasants. . . .

Don also forwarded the letters sent by Pete's former teammates who had completed their terms of service and left Vietnam. Some expressed, along with shock, a concern that the killing of a team member would damage IVS.[5] The organization's record had been "blemished, but hopefully not permanently scarred," Mike Chilton and Kirk Dimmit wrote. "We can take comfort and pride in knowing that Pete will be kindly remembered by his many Vietnamese friends and counterparts through the fine examples he set as an IVS worker."

From Hong Kong, Phyllis and David Colyer wrote to say they hoped the incident would not threaten IVS's future and believed Pete would not want it to:

> It is our hope that Pete's death will not sway IVS from carrying on the work Pete returned to Vietnam to do; work which we feel is perhaps even more urgently needed now than before.
>
> Not being present in Vietnam now and not knowing the particular facts and details involved in this tragedy, we cannot evaluate or presume to judge what IVSers there should do. But for ourselves, we would like to say that we stand in continued support of IVS Vietnam and hope that the volunteer work which has proved effective in the past and which still may be carried out in relative safety will be continued. We believe that

had Pete narrowly missed or survived the ambush, he would have still continued his work in South Vietnam.

Gloria Johnson had served on the IVS administrative staff in Saigon. She wondered if the account she had heard was true and, if it was, how IVS could carry on:

I have just heard the news about Peter's death on the radio. It has said that he was led into an ambush by two supposed friends—Vietnamese. . . . What a terrible thing, especially if this report about the friends is true. Peter's parents must feel terrible; I surely hope they didn't object to his being there in the first place. And the IVSers must be stunned—I know I am now, and would have been when in Viet-Nam, too.

I suspect you'll be in for a hard time of it now, not only with internal problems this will create in the team and their feelings about Viet-Nam, but with reactions from parents, from AID, from all sorts of other people who might be concerned, including the IVS Board of Directors. I am so sorry about it—so sorry.

When you have time, I'd be interested in hearing what really happened. I just put almost no confidence in the reports I read and hear here. . . .

How will IVS be able to trust anybody now, if Peter was led into this by friends? How much difference the death of a person in Viet-Nam is if you know that person. The impact of 1,000 deaths of soldiers is not as shocking to me as the one of Peter Hunting. . . .

I find myself with mixed emotions as always, believing the cause is worth fighting for, but not believing anyone's life is worth it either. But lives will be lost, even more, and I guess this is the reality of Viet-Nam. In order to save lives, we lost lives, but somewhere it just doesn't all quite fit together. Americans are in a real dilemma about Viet-Nam, and I can't say that I blame them. . . . I do know that I hope your life isn't too hard right now, but I'll bet you look more worried than I've ever seen you.

The green lacquer box took pride of place on our living room coffee table, but I did not look inside it more than a couple of times. I sensed that the letters and photographs belonged to my parents, especially my mother. If she were to see me reading them, as moody as she now was, how would she react? I wondered if her dark eyes would flash angrily and she would accuse me of doing something I should have known not to do. Worse, she might cry, and then what would I do?

Two Vietnamese who wrote to my parents came to the United States within a few months. Tran Ngoc Bau was the young leader of National Voluntary Services, an organization Pete and other ivsers had worked with closely. Bau asked:

> How can we express our sorrow and regrets when we heard of Pete Hunting's death in a mine accident while he was doing his assignment in the Mekong River Region. . . .
>
> Pete Hunting's life as well as his heartful sacrifice will remain forever. Pete had done something most valuable in serving mankind.
>
> We sincerely send our sympathy to you and wish that Pete Hunting has a peaceful sleep forever.

Bau visited our home in Oklahoma City. Afterward he toured the San Francisco Bay Area and marveled at the Bay Bridge, fresh shellfish, and California wine. At Muir Woods he saw the ancient redwoods. Americans lived in an earthly paradise, he observed, while Vietnamese lived in the hell of war, misery, and illness. He looked to our family for empathy:

> We never forget the Huntings who bear in their soul and their body the very living suffering of our people, who share in their heart our anxiety, our fear for the present and the future, our physical and moral insecurity, our perplexity before such an unimaginable inhumanity of this world. . . .
> I spent the most excellent hours in U.S. with you, just to be near you, to hear from you, to feel at home with the Huntings, to be sheltered under the same roof Pete had been. . . . You might consider me as your second Pete in Vietnam.

A Miss Nguyen also came to the house. My mother was suspicious of her because Pete had not mentioned her and she was not pretty like the other young women he had wanted the family to meet. After visiting us in Oklahoma City, Miss Nguyen called on my relatives at the farm in Connecticut. They didn't like her, either. They found her homely and were afraid she was a Communist spy. She had stood at a window in my grandmother's house, looking out at the lawn that sloped down to the swimming pool, shaking her head and muttering, "Too much. Too much."

At Thanksgiving my parents sent a letter to the people who had reached out to them. The letter reflected what I think of as my parents' best qualities: my father's clarity, my mother's bigheartedness, and their sincerity.

> Thank you, each of you, from fullest hearts, for your deeply moving thoughts and deeds for Peter and for us. Please forgive this general letter to tell you all over the world how much your kindnesses have meant to us.
>
> The tribute to Pete of response from so many, even some who only read the news of a stranger's death, makes us humble, grateful, and thoughtful, in a kind of awe that in the hearts of people widely separated there is a shared but individual sense of deep personal loss, joining with ours.
>
> As a family, we were always close; and we felt there was a special bond between Pete and each of us. But something in Pete in some way touched the lives or hearts or minds of many, it seems, making his life, though brief, memorable and full of meaning—an outward-spreading ripple.
>
> We think your wonderful letters express an awareness in us, thinking of him, of a sureness in him of life's truest values, underlying his fun and dedication and interest in life; a thoughtful acceptance of things as they are, so complete it was a readiness for what would be; a naturalness that reached directly, without sham or pretense, the sincerity in others.
>
> Perhaps he seems in some way special because he was an "ordinary American 'good guy' you never hear about," representing all like him who don't know they are special. Pete died where he wanted to be, doing what he believed in and wanted to do—a reminder that belief in true values and faith in humanity, put to work by a individual, can be a valued contribution in today's complex world. Perhaps Pete personified to us and those who wrote, an affirmation of brotherhood and the efficacy of a labor of love, the greatest of God's gifts. . . .

In different ways, we will always feel a special bond with so many of you. We are glad it was Pete's privilege to know such as you; and to serve with those of you in Viet Nam, and IVS, who quietly continue your work and contribute so much in the love and service of your fellowmen.

Pete returned in the goodly company of others who had served and died in Viet Nam. We are personally glad an investigation found no evidence to verify the first reports that he was betrayed. With a quiet family service Nov. 22nd, in a gentle rain so soft it was nature's own benison, Pete was laid in eternal rest in the autumn beauty of the Connecticut countryside he lived in as a child and again during his college years. We are deeply touched that memorial services were held in the International Protestant Church in the far land he loved, and in the Methodist Church of Dexter, Missouri, our home in Pete's boyhood—in addition to the lovely service in Woodbridge. We are glad to have met many of you there. Thank you, so very much, for the keepsakes we have from these services.

Our hearts are full; but much greater, than grief, is our love and glad gratitude for the years of Pete's life and for what he was—a kind and universal good guy, very dear to us, who liked and believed in his fellowmen and whose contribution counted; a practical idealist graced by fun and good cheer; a dreamer but doer.

A deep sadness will always be in us for the loss of the son we so loved, and for his hopes and plans that cannot be realized. But we have much more to be thankful for, and feel blessed in his memory; and in the family and friends who helped make him what he was, and his life full and good and of meaning.

You will always be in our warmest thoughts; to you our door is always open! And for all you have said and written and done, our deepest thanks and appreciation go out to you who cared and shared, with us, in Pete's loss.

Until the trunk containing Pete's letters surfaced in 2004, I didn't know how many people had helped my parents to withstand the blow of their son's death. Along with Pete's correspondence, I found paper bags stuffed with more than two hundred sympathy letters. Many of them were addressed to the whole family or specifically referred to Cis, Holly, and me.

If only our parents been able to demonstrate behind closed doors the openness they showed in their Thanksgiving letter. They signed it "Allan and Mary Hunting and family," but my sisters and I didn't even know they wrote it.

Some of my father's friends from work proposed starting a memorial fund. My parents wrote to IVS Executive Director Gardiner to ask if the contributions could fill a specific need in Vietnam. Pete had talked about many kinds of projects, they said, from drought relief to science education to windmills, but "he always got around to the subject of basic hamlet education." They hoped the memorial funds would help as Pete would have wished:

> In the sad knowledge that we will not again see his warm smile, we are reacting to helplessness as Pete did, directly and simply, saying in effect, "Let's get on with small beginnings. . . ." Perhaps, with Mr. Luce, his IVS team members in Viet Nam, and the Viet Namese people he so admired, you can tell us that we may help some village to build their school.

For advice about a suitable project, they turned to Bob Friedman, the prov rep who had worked with Pete in Ninh Thuan and now was back in the States. Friedman suggested four possibilities: first, the education of a Cham or Vietnamese teacher, possibly at a university in the United States; second, a textbook for elementary students, as Pete had considered the teaching materials in hamlets woefully deficient and instruction in the scientific method crucial; third, sponsorship of formal training for hamlet teachers; and finally, the creation of a rural education department at Saigon University, because Friedman believed that rural Vietnam's unique conditions justified a separate curriculum.

My parents also relied on Gene Stoltzfus. Gene met with several people in Phan Rang, including school principals and officials responsible for education, land reform, and youth.

The education chief suggested building a school. He felt that because Pete had been concerned chiefly with education, a school would be the most fitting memorial. Gene knew, however, that other funds were currently available for hamlet schools.

A second alternative was to equip a youth center temporarily being used by the U.S. Navy Seabees for residential quarters. But the Vietnamese government had already promised to renovate the center, and Gene knew that Pete had not worked much with its youth services office.

The third and best project, Gene thought, would be to build a public library in Phan Rang. Pete had at one time drawn up a proposal for a combined library and youth center, and the project had generated considerable enthusiasm. The community felt that a library would be a fitting memorial and would serve an important function in their city. Pete had estimated the cost to be around a million piasters—about 13,700 U.S. dollars. The memorial fund was not expected to cover the entire amount, but Gene thought the provincial government might contribute some money and USOM would come up with some building materials.

The library had the most potential for success, but a few problems remained to be worked out. Who would supply the books and maintain the library? Would it be private or run by the government? Where would additional funds come from if they were needed?

In February 1966 my parents informed Don Luce that they were particularly pleased by the suggestion of a library. If he agreed that this would be the best use of the funds, they were in full accord. They sent a check combining the gifts of 158 contributors.

Luce informed my parents that Nguyen Van Hoa, a prominent architect and close friend of the IVS director, had agreed to draw the plans for the library. A few weeks later, Mr. Hoa informed them that more money was needed. My parents sent another check. Pete's motorcycle was sold and the proceeds were donated to the fund. Roofing materials, cement, and the building site, on a plot near the high school and adjacent to the Boy Scout office, were donated.

Ground was broken in the fall of 1966. Things moved slowly, but both Don and Gene assured my parents that the pace was normal for Vietnam. They said that the library's ultimate success would depend, in fact, on moving slowly and allowing time for people to reach a consensus.

The building would be typical of the architectural style in Ninh Thuan Province: a one-story concrete structure with a pitched roof and a large front porch. Shuttered wooden doors and windows would provide ventilation. The interior would be a single open room with a tile floor.

Meanwhile, two new IVSers had arrived in Phan Rang. One of them, Beryl Darrah, had been charged with overseeing the library construction. Darrah had served in the army before joining IVS. He was given the responsibility of making the library a reality—a job he later described as "monumental."[6]

Phan Rang had never had such a thing as a library, and few people knew what a library was, Darrah discovered. On top of that, he soon realized that the project was underfunded. He scrounged for tables and for wood to build shelving. No provision had been made for books, but he found that the U.S. Information Agency had hundreds of volumes and was eager to donate them. The books proved to be out of date, however, and too technical for Vietnamese with limited English skills.

After weeks of looking, Darrah located an organization that was willing to donate the kinds of volumes the library needed. At first he was elated. Then someone in the Saigon IVS office determined that the potential donor had accepted money from the CIA. Darrah later wrote:

> After that, everything I had worked so hard for went crashing to the ground. They said accepting aid for any organization who had ties from the CIA would compromise our position in Vietnam. What WAS our position in Vietnam? It was something that I never figured out. . . . Half of the Vietnamese I worked with were convinced that I worked for the CIA anyway, because I didn't live in an American compound and because I worked with Vietnamese and not Americans.[7]

Despite Darrah's frustrating experience, the library was completed, even though he missed the dedication. After contracting hepatitis, he had to be evacuated to a hospital in Saigon.

The library opened in June 1968. Another IVSer, Jay Scarborough, was responsible for orchestrating the opening ceremony. He described it to my parents:

> After many unforeseen delays, the library opened on June 6, with a small ceremony consisting entirely of province officials, school principals and IVS representatives. At the time of the opening we had 1300 books in Vietnamese, about 800 in English, 400 in French and 44 in Chinese. A substantial number of the Vietnamese books—720—were bought with a $400 fund contributed by Save the Children Foundation, the first organization to give us financial aid. I have also received a promise of monies from Catholic Relief Service [sic], and the province is requesting $2000

from Asia Foundation. I hope the latter will come through, for such an amount will go almost all the way to meeting our goal of 5000 Vietnamese books.

Scarborough noted that, even before the official dedication, students and adults were borrowing books. He envisioned the library developing rapidly into a "credible and popular institution." Although he had not known Pete, he thought from what he had heard about him that the library would be a fitting memorial. He saved the hand-painted banner from the opening ceremony and sent it to my parents with an article clipped from a newspaper:

> At 4 P.M. on 6/6/68, the lieutenant governor of Ninh Thuan Province cut the inaugural band to open a library situated on Le Van Duyet Street in Phan Rang.
>
> Also present were the lieutenant governor, the chairman of the provincial committee, the principal of Duy Tan School, and a number of high school teachers in the province. On the American side were a female representative from IVS in Vietnam, a representative from the International Voluntary Youth Agency of Ninh Thuan, and members of the CORD[s] organization in Ninh Thuan.
>
> This library is named after a young American IVSer, Petter [*sic*] Hunting, who had worked in the Ninh Thuan area during the two years [1963 and 1964] and who had died in Phong Dinh. During that time, he was assigned to the Fourth Tactical Zone as the IVS leader.
>
> This library was built next to a Ninh Thuan Boy Scout office with a length of 16 meters and a width of 6 meters [about 52 feet by 20 feet]. Total cost was VN $300,000. Part of the cost was a contribution from Peter Hunting's mother and the local CORD[s] office contributed building material.[8]

Verda Bradford represented IVS at the dedication, and afterward sent my parents color slides taken that day. In one, a potted plant is being placed in a tree "to appease the superstitions of the local people," she explained. "They believe spirits live in trees and if it [a tree] is one not bearing life it must be given life to signify a rebirth of the spirits and to bring good luck to the building on the property." Other slides showed Jay Scarborough splattered with whitewash after touching up the building at the last minute and subsequently, having changed

The author's mother with Pete and Cis (1943).
Photo by Ben Stone;
author's collection.

The author's father (circa 1959). Photo by Jim Rollins, Malden Air Force Base, Missouri; author's collection.

The author (age 3), *second from left*, with her siblings, *left to right:* Cis (age 11), Pete (age 12), and Holly (age 5). Photographer unknown; author's collection.

Pete (age 11), *right*, with unidentified friend in a toy car given to him by his maternal grandfather, Popeye. Equipped with an accelerator, horn, brakes, and forward and reverse gears, the car was manufactured by the company Popeye founded. Margo Bradley's father later became its president. Author's collection.

Pete, probably on his fifteenth birthday, in Dexter, Missouri.
Author's collection.

The author with Pete (circa 1960). Author's collection.

Pete, *left*, with unidentified fellow members of the Wesleyan University yacht club (date unknown). Photographer unknown; author's collection.

The author, with a book and a cat on her lap, around
the age when Pete left for Vietnam, in 1963.
Author's collection.

The International Voluntary Services education team (Summer 1963) at the
IVS house in Saigon, *left to right:* Don Fuller, Phyllis Colyer, Dick Carlton,
Louise Ross, Chuck Ross, Carlie Allender, Carl Stockton, Anne Hensley,
Walt Robertson, Renate McDowell, John Sommer, Willi Meyers, Pete
Hunting, Bob Biggers, and Gene Stoltzfus. On the back of this postcard,
Pete wrote a birthday greeting to his mother and asked her to send his
Chinese dictionary and telescope. Photographer unknown; author's collection.

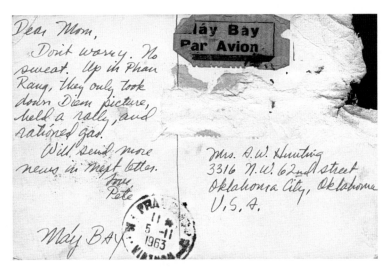

Dear Mom,

Don't worry. No sweat. Up in Phan Rang, they only took down Diem picture, held a rally, and rationed gas.

Will send more news in next letter.

Love
Pete

Máy Bay

Máy Bay
Par Avion

Mrs. A.W. Hunting
3316 N.W. 62nd street
Oklahoma City, Oklahoma
U.S.A.

After the bloody coup d'état that deposed South Vietnam's president, Ngo Dinh Diem, and his brother Nhu in November 1963, Pete sent a postcard to reassure his mother. Author's collection.

From an unwritten postcard found among Pete's papers; the caption reads, "Village notabless [*sic*] in festival dress." Author's collection.

Fishing village, Phan Rang Bay, Vietnam (circa 1963). Photo by
Pete Hunting; courtesy of Sue Patterson.

Fishing boats, Phan Rang Bay (circa 1963). Photo by Pete Hunting;
author's collection.

On the back of this photo, Pete described the scene: "Stern oarsman stands on port gunwhale and sculls the boat. . . . Took this while crossing a bay on this little ferry. Chap's leaning way out over water. [He] posed and nearly fell in the salty brine. About a minute later I discovered the bottom was made of rice straw; saw it undulating up and down beneath floorboards and was quite excited until I found it was made that way." Probably Phan Rang Bay, Vietnam (circa 1963).

Photo by Pete Hunting; author's collection.

Vietnamese women hauling manioc to market (circa 1963). On the back of the photo, Pete described the pole and baskets as the "Vietnamese equivalent of wheelbarrows, easier to haul 'in the long run.' (Last couple of days have been bad for puns.) The road to Nha Trang (Vietnamese Riviera). Ate a lobster a good 18 inches long, no kidding, I was so hungry for lobster and good seafood. Ate at François', of course." Photo by Pete Hunting; author's collection.

On the back of this photo, Pete, described the smiling woman: "Cham lady. Vietnamese women don't carry their baskets on their heads, or wear such flowing gowns." Ninh Thuan Province, Vietnam (circa 1963). Photo by Pete Hunting; author's collection.

"Montagnard stud heading to market to sell his kindling." Pete wrote on the back of this photo. "Will get about 75 cents for it all, takes all day to go back and forth to market, takes about a day to collect the wood."
Ninh Thuan Province (circa 1963). Photo by Pete Hunting; author's collection.

Pete with unidentified colleagues (date unknown).
Author's collection.

Pete and his first IVS stationmate, Chuck Fields, light a fire to smoke fish in a charcoal kiln. Ninh Thuan Province (date unknown).

Photographer unknown, U.S. Operations Mission; author's collection.

Pete with unidentified children, probably Ninh Thuan Province
(date unknown). Author's collection.

Bricklaying 101. "They didn't know you've got to soak bricks in water so's they won't soak all the water out of mortar," Pete wrote on the back of this photo. "Didn't believe me till I showed them how easy it would be for somebody to stove in the wall." Ninh Thuan Province (date unknown). Author's collection.

Well construction at Thuan Tu, a Cham hamlet, Ninh Thuan Province (date unknown). Photo by Pete Hunting; author's collection.

Residents of an unidentified Cham hamlet gather around their new well, with Pete in the background. Ninh Thuan Province (date unknown). Author's collection.

Unidentified scouts, Ninh Thuan Province (1964). Pete, a former Boy Scout, hoped to enlist the Phan Rang troop's help with service projects. The scouts had more enthusiasm for "campfire dancing" and practicing semaphore signals. They were the "salutingest bunch of young men" he had ever seen. Photo by Pete Hunting; author's collection.

his clothes, welcoming the people of Phan Rang to the library. Another volunteer, Phil Scott, looked on as several Vietnamese men wearing white shirts and black ties signed a guest book.

In her letter, Bradford said Scarborough was disappointed that the dedication had been arranged so hastily that neither officials in Saigon nor my parents had been invited. She added that the simplicity of the occasion "would probably prove to be a saving grace." She apologized that the construction had taken so long.

Don Luce visited the library eight months later, in February 1969. By this time he had resigned from IVS and was speaking and writing against the war, under the aegis of the World Council of Churches. He was impressed to see how well the library was operating. He informed my parents that young people were reading at tables and checking out books. The library was so well used that the books were fraying, but IVS was having them repaired. Only eight books had been lost. A taxidermied tiger donated by Larry Laverentz still presided over the room.

Liberation soldiers had entered the library one night during a battle with South Vietnamese troops. The wooden window frames had taken machine gun fire and a grenade had blown a hole in one wall, but repairs had been made. The fact that the library was still operating, Don said, attested to the esteem in which the people held it:

> It is a tribute to the service that the library is giving the community that the NLF soldiers were careful not to harm anything within the library. None of the books were taken, or destroyed. The tiger was left unharmed. I also think that it is an indication that whatever happens politically in this sad land . . . the library will continue. This is as Pete would want it.

He noted that in the Asian calendar it was the year of the chicken. According to Vietnamese tradition, "When the year of the monkey (1968) turns to the year of the chicken, there will be peace," he said. He hoped it was true. The people's belief in the saying was so strong, he added, that their will might make it true.

But the war would continue for six more years.

In the fall of 1968 I left home. College provided a way out of the tensions of living under my parents' roof, but the strain between my mother and me only increased after I began to take part in antiwar demonstrations in the spring of my sophomore year. Because I was in Massachusetts and my parents were in Oklahoma, it was easy at first not to tell them about the protest marches.

I was afraid to tell them that I believed the war was immoral and the United States should withdraw. I was not a pacifist, but I blamed our country's military involvement in Vietnam for Pete's death more than I did the people who had actually killed him. I thought that if American combat troops had not been sent to Vietnam in 1965, Pete would still be alive.

Only once did I find the nerve to tell my parents that I felt our leaders were wrongheaded. When I did, my mother rebuked me with the words "You are betraying your brother's memory!" I didn't believe it was true, but her accusation stung all the same.

She became an arch defender of the war, but my father did not. Interviewed by the *Oklahoma City Times* for a story about the views of "survivors of lost GIs," he stated:

I think it's a hell of a drain on the economy. I'm violently opposed to the administration's course of action. I just think we ought to end it. My personal conviction as to stepped-up bombing is that it would lead us right into what the air force has wanted for a long time—a full-scale war with China.[9]

Because my family did not discuss the war or Pete, I did not know my father's words had been published in the newspaper, but I sensed that his views were more like mine than my mother's. Once when I was home on spring break, he asked me to recommend a book that would help him understand my generation— at least those of us who were rebelling against the war, our elders, and our society and its prevailing norms. I suggested *The Uncommitted: Alienated Youth in American Society*, by the social psychologist Kenneth Keniston. Dad seemed interested, but he never mentioned it again and I doubt he ever read it. For one thing, he hated psychologists even though he had a master's degree in abnormal psychology.

I realize now that I could have talked to my father about so many things if only I had known then how to initiate a conversation of substance. When I was a student at Wheaton College, he came to Fathers' Weekend one year. I enjoyed our time together and his amusing stories about visiting my mother there three decades before. When I think of the opportunities I missed to talk with him about things that mattered to me, I feel sad that we were both so emotionally standoffish. My father could be too strict and insensitive, but he also was wise, open to reason, and, deep down, tenderhearted. I never asked him what happened to Pete. He was loyal to my mother, and we never discussed the way she took possession of Pete's memory, or her irrational behavior and depression.

A few years after I finished college, I visited my parents in Massachusetts, where they had moved during my senior year. By then we had begun to talk about Pete a little, although not about his death or how we had coped with it. Pete had been gone more than ten years and my mother could talk about him without crying. Still, I was careful around her.

I had passed the age Pete had been when he was killed. Now I wanted to understand him not just as a brother, but as a young man. I had a better grasp of the war in Vietnam and wanted to know what he had said about it. His letters were the key. If there were any chance of seeing them, I would have to ask my mother for them.

One evening I waited until my parents and I were comfortable in the living room after dinner. I said I would love to read Pete's letters. Could I?

Tears came to my mother's eyes. There had been a flood in the basement, she said. All of the letters had been destroyed.

So they were gone. Pete was out of my reach for good. I would never again see those blue airmail envelopes or my name written by my brother's hand. I would never know whether he had criticized or supported American foreign policy, or what he thought of the men who shaped it. My fifteen years of memories would have to be enough for a lifetime. It wasn't hopelessness I felt, but resignation.

It didn't occur to me to ask my mother if she was sure the letters had been destroyed, or how she had discovered they were ruined, or if I could look in the basement myself.

Around this time, my sister Carol became interested in a form of spirituality that is generally associated today with the New Age. A psychic friend of hers said she had received a message for me from Pete. Although I have always been skeptical of claims of otherworldly knowledge, I stifled tears as Cis said that Pete wanted me to know he was all right and I didn't need to worry about him. He had written the same thing to me in a letter from Vietnam.

Cis, Holly, and I began taking annual retreats in 1978. That year, we met at a state park. Cis brought four of Pete's letters that she had saved. They were the only letters of his that we had. We read them aloud and, for the first time, wept together and talked about the brother we loved so much. That weekend was a turning point for us. We grew closer and began to find our voices for talking about the loss we were all living with.

SIX

Mr. Tall American

It was a new year, 1964, and a new president occupied the White House. In his State of the Union address on January 8, Lyndon Johnson urged members of Congress to carry forward the plans and programs of John Kennedy, "not because of our sorrow or sympathy, but because they are right." In the same speech, he declared the War on Poverty.

Three days later, a fifteen-year-old figure skater named Peggy Fleming won a place on the U.S. Olympic team.

On January 8, the musical *Hello, Dolly!* opened at the St. James Theater, starring Carol Channing. Another 2,843 performances would follow, breaking the existing record for a Broadway run.

In Vietnam, Pete had spent Christmas with the IVS team at the villa in Dalat. It didn't "seem much like the season" to him, and he wished he could be home with the family. Still, he urged us not to try anything rash like telephoning. "Please don't," he stressed. "For one thing, you wouldn't be able to reach Phan Rang. For another, we might go to Nha Trang or Dalat. And thirdly, it costs about $75."

He didn't say why, but he was discouraged. His recent letters had offered clues, however. The education chief was lazy, the former province chief was in jail after the Diem coup, a schoolteacher in the next town had committed suicide, and his stationmate Chuck's mind was "just one big rusty nail," he had vented to

Cis. He told Sue, "I get so mad at the people I work with and live with sometimes that I'd like to have someone to come back to, to forget it with." On Christmas Eve, his spirits lifted a bit when the group drew names and opened presents.

The following day, fueled by eggnog laced with alcohol, Pete and several of his teammates decided to go paddleboating on a lake. He described what happened next in a letter to Margo Bradley:

> Forty-five minutes later, my drunken paddleboating partner and I had been rammed by another playful paddleboat crew. The port pontoon took on a few gallons and we sank. . . .
>
> Having had some training in drinking and having developed a modest capacity in the days of my youth at Wesleyan, I was still untouched and commenced fishing for my soggy boatmate, at which time the boat owner was fast bearing down upon us with a wrathful look in his eyes.
>
> There followed a very complicated social situation, what with all the handshaking and social amenities taking place in French.
>
> My comrades had taken to the reeds along the shore and hoisted the groggy one over the gunwale in six feet of water. Looking back on it all, one is inclined to ask himself, searchingly of course, if these things happen only to certain people. . . .
>
> Altogether, it was a very jarring holiday. No snow, one or two accidents. All the people I care about so far away.

New Year's Day found Pete nursing a hangover after a party back in Phan Rang at the American military compound. His mood had lifted and his sense of humor had returned. "Thank God for coffee," he wrote. "It has been a hot, sweaty, dusty, thirsty holiday in Phan Rang."

For Christmas, Margo had sent some books, but they had not arrived yet. He hoped her package looked as unlike a bomb as possible and thanked her in advance for the gift: "Believe it or not, the only one of Mark Twain's works I have is a well-worn *Tom Sawyer*. Having already lost a few things in the mail, there is the possibility that never the Twain shall meet."

For the twenty-eight months Pete lived in Vietnam, minus a few weeks when he came home on leave or took vacations in Bangkok and Hong Kong, he corresponded mostly with my immediate family, our closest relatives, and two women, Sue and Margo. He had dated both of them in college. While he was away in Vietnam, Sue was completing her nursing studies in Connecticut and Margo graduated from college and was working in Manhattan.

Decades later, both Sue and Margo would offer me their letters from Pete. Even after I read them, I could only guess what his true feelings had been. It was clear that he had cared deeply about each of them, although not necessarily to the same degree at the same time. I have wondered if he was the Archie to their Betty and Veronica.

Sue had saved every word Pete ever wrote to her, beginning with the notes he left at her dormitory saying he had stopped by. Some of these letters contained intimacies no brother would want his little sister to see, but Sue gave them to me uncensored.

Margo's letters, by contrast, came to me expurgated. Believing they should be shared with a wider audience but unsure how to proceed until I unexpectedly contacted her in 2004, she had typed all of the letters, discreetly omitting the most personal information. She said she had disposed of the originals.

Over time, Pete gradually began writing more to Margo and less to Sue, until in his last letter to my family he enumerated the qualities in Margo that he believed might suit them for a life together. While I could not be sure how his thinking had evolved, I could trace his shifting affections when I photocopied the letters onto different colors of paper. For Pete's letters to the family, I used white paper. I used green paper for the ones to Margo and pink for those to Sue. Then, by arranging all of the letters in chronological order, it was easy to see that the pink letters tapered off after a year and eventually ceased altogether, while the number of green pages steadily increased.

In his letters to Sue, who had become his steady girlfriend by the end of college, Pete showed a vulnerable, tender, and randy side. I'll never know if he revealed the same traits to the sophisticated Margo; what is clear, however, is that writing to her brought out the best in him. His witty, intelligent letters at first bordered on attempts to impress her but, as time went by, showed him confiding, more and more, his insights about Vietnam and what he was doing there.

Pete had been in Vietnam less than three months when, without mentioning anyone by name—Sue, Margo, or possibly someone else—he wrote in his diary about a woman he missed:

Moon is beautiful tonight. Storm has cleared. Everything in a clear pale half-light. Now and then a cloud—transparent—drives across its neighbor orb, dressing it in silver fleece threads. Wish I were home admiring it with her, or she was here admiring it with me. Wish she could've driven down from Nha Trang with me, today.

A week later, he mused about small things that gave him pleasure, things he wished he could share:

In moments of peace and relaxation, passing shadows, fragrances, and half-thoughts come to the doorstep of my mind and pass on, but do not make my acquaintance—only vaguely remembered, smiling thought-faces. Tonight the moon was a beautiful orange in a green, smoke-cloud sky, and I longed for my faraway sweetheart.

He was not without female acquaintances, however. In mid-October he received letters from two girls in Vietnam, both of whom asked why he was shunning them. "Whew!" he wrote to Sue. "Sometimes I just don't know about these people."

Bicycling home from the market one day, he found that he had acquired a small fan club:

All the students were out marching, practicing for Independence Day. I'd pass the columns of boys and they'd all say "Hey, hello" or "Ong Peck," which is how they pronounce Pete. I know lots of them. Then I had to go past the girls' ranks. They just love to tease me. All this sighing and swooning. God, I hate parades.

After six months in Vietnam and almost daily contact with Americans stationed at the air base in Phan Rang, Pete told Sue, "I really feel sorry for some of these military guys. They don't trust their wives and don't deserve the trust of their wives, either. They darn near go stir crazy, sitting around over there."

I mentioned this comment to one of Pete's IVS friends, some of whom were surprised to hear he'd had a girlfriend, or even two, back home. I said that it sounded as if he were telling Sue he was true to her. The friend didn't dispute it, but what he said next— "What time period was that?"—answered my implicit question.

At least one woman Pete knew in Vietnam was less interested in him in particular than in a potential American husband. "The cigarette girl downtown is hot for my body," he wrote. "Other day she informed me she was on the prowl for a tall, blond, handsome husband, as she slowly drew the 25 piasters out of my hand. Eeeyow." A smoker since college, he would have been a good customer of hers in this period leading up to the Federal Trade Commission's June 1964 announcement that, effective the following year, American cigarette manufacturers would be required to label packages with a warning about the harmful effects of smoking.

Half a world away from the people he cared most about, Pete was also literally up to his knees in hamlet projects. The IVS annual report for 1963–64 cited his digging of wells as an example of "how the IVS educational development volunteer operates—even outside the immediate province of education."

A high school near Sacramento had provided funds for constructing a well in coastal Thuan Tu hamlet. Pete recorded the construction project on eight-millimeter film that he sent home and we watched in the living room. The sequence begins with the image of a Cham elder wearing the traditional garb of a white tunic, his head wrapped in a white cloth and very thin legs extending from a pair of shorts.

Standing on the flat bed of his Land Rover, Pete enters the frame dressed in cutoffs and a long-sleeved shirt rolled up to the elbows. A third again as tall as any of the other adults, he tugs a heavy concrete well liner to the vehicle's edge. The muscles in his face, legs, and arms tighten with the exertion. He places one hand on the flat bed, hops down, and with five other men, all of slight build, lowers the cylinder to the ground.

Next, from several feet beneath the earth, the camera slowly pivots three hundred sixty degrees to take in dozens of children looking down from the well's rim, smiling against an intense blue, cloudless sky.

The action moves to two Cham men who are guiding a second concrete cylinder downhill in the direction of a large hole. Uphill, other arms hold taut the two ends of a rope from which the weighty ring is suspended. The lowering and rolling of the concrete well liners are repeated several times as the rings are moved into position beside the hole.

Building the well in Thuan Tu involved more than heavy lifting. It became an object lesson in the science of hydraulics and a foundation for friendship.

In a letter to the California students who had contributed to the well-digging project, Pete began by describing the hamlet's remote location along a cowpath on the far side of a settlement whose inhabitants were rumored to be Vietcong sympathizers.

He then explained what he and his Cham co-workers had learned from laboring together:

> We made twelve trips out in my little Land Rover vehicle. Each trip out we'd carry a pre-cast, reinforced concrete well ring; each returning trip we'd have a load of Cham women taking rice to market. It was a good opportunity to practice my Vietnamese, since on most trips I didn't take an interpreter, and it probably had a small "psychological" effect, as they say.
>
> The traditional method of digging a well out there was to dig a hole down to the water level, then to lay bricks or stone up to the top, starting from about half a meter or a meter under water. This had to be done during the dry season, when the water level was at its lowest. Besides being time consuming, this method never did guarantee much water during the dry season. . . .
>
> Laying bricks under [water] seems to be a bit of a problem, especially if the mason is confronted with flowing sand. With a concrete ring, a man gets inside and digs the dirt out from under the bottom ring, adding one ring on top of another, as the whole column gradually sinks. When the man reaches the water level, the work goes a lot faster, even though he must work under water.
>
> But the workers didn't take my advice and dug the well the hard way. When they reached the water level, I jumped in to show them what I was talking about. They thought this [was] quite a jolly sight, and I guess it effected a change in their attitude.
>
> They invited me to their Cham temple where I dried out over a cup of tea; they changed into their national dress so that I might take pictures, some of which now hang on the temple walls.[1]

To thank them for their contribution, Pete sent the students in Sacramento a weaving made by one of the Cham women of the hamlet. He explained that blankets of this kind were used to decorate funeral platforms and were burned along with the casket and other ceremonial objects.

Digging wells in hamlets engendered the goodwill that ivs considered fundamental to its mission in Vietnam. Successful projects also could produce unexpected outcomes. In one case, Pete found himself on the receiving end of a marriage proposal. In a letter subsequently published in an ivs annual report, he explained what had happened:

> The Cham people are one of Vietnam's cultural minorities. Actually, the word "tribe" is a bit misleading. They seem to be as advanced as the Vietnamese, using whatever standards you might wish to apply—cleanliness, agricultural methods, etc.
>
> One difference is that theirs is a matriarchal society; the mother of the bride does the proposing, for instance.
>
> I learned this when one old "Ba," whom I have occasion to meet frequently, asked me if I would be interested in marrying her daughter. I tried to be non-committal, but diplomatic, about it; but the next thing I knew, she and her daughter were standing in my yard, all dressed up, giggling and carrying on, with presents for me.[2]

He elaborated on the marriage offer in a letter to Margo:

> The Cham lady whose blankets/tablecloths I help sell offered me her daughter in marriage. She brought it up one day in a casual sort of way and the next thing I knew, she brought the girl over for an introduction and was willing to pay for palm readers and someone to read my horoscope, which is the equivalent of our blood test, I guess. Think I'll take a vacation soon.

The amity between Pete and the Cham people in hamlets where he worked was lasting. He continued to visit them even after projects were completed. The friendships were preserved on celluloid, as both Pete and his visiting teammate John Sommer filmed smiling Cham weavers at their large wooden looms.

More than forty years later, I would discover additional evidence of one such friendship when, by an extraordinary coincidence, I chanced to meet the granddaughter of the "old 'Ba.'"

Pete had thought he would be teaching English in a classroom, but what constituted "teaching" in Vietnam went well beyond the classroom. The jobs of the seven IVS education "hamleters," as they called themselves, varied considerably from province to province, depending on the problems they encountered, ideas they came up with, and the educational level of the people. While many villages were eager for education, others, such as Montagnard groups that had been relocated from the forest, did not know what a school was.

The volunteers might identify hamlets likely to support a new school, distribute classroom supplies provided by the U.S. Operations Mission, or show teachers how to make geography globes from local materials. They might suggest a teaching technique based on knowledge and skills they had acquired "from having simply undergone the fine experience that is American education," as one IVS annual report put it.[3]

Several new schools had been constructed in Pete's province under the Strategic Hamlet Program. In three months he had visited all but three, which were unreachable because of heavy rains.

He had repaired one school's water pump. He had demonstrated to the district education office staff how to use a new mimeograph machine and translated the instruction manual for them. Because there was a shortage of filmstrip projectors, he had made drawings of the filmstrips about science and health, mimeographed them, and distributed them to the schools. He had shown teachers how to make inexpensive ink from black dye and rounded up discarded medicine bottles to use as inkwells. In exchange for Vietnamese lessons, he was teaching English to the chief of hamlet education.

He reported to the IVS office that he had made seventeen trips to ten different hamlets. Sometimes he went late in the day and returned in the evening because of competing claims for the Land Rover, which he shared with Chuck.

The biggest education-related problem in Ninh Thuan was paying teachers' salaries in the poorest hamlets. Each teacher received only six hundred piasters (just over eight dollars) a month. Government support was threatened by cutbacks, which would leave the people hard pressed to support a teacher. A program was devised to pay part of their salaries with food. The food would include U.S. surplus commodities such as bulgur wheat and corn, along with rabbits.

Chuck, who had arrived in Vietnam before Pete, put his animal husbandry schooling to good use. Working with the provincial education chief and a local veterinarian, he hit upon the idea of raising rabbits as a food source. Funds to purchase the animals and build cages for them would be provided by the Office of Rural Affairs.

Pete's home movies of the rabbit project show him carrying wooden frames, followed by "after" shots of white rabbits installed in cages. Working without power tools, he built the hutches at the house in Phan Rang where Chuck had insisted they move. "I can't figure why Chuck was so taken by the place," Pete complained, describing craters filled with trash and a neighbor who threw her garbage over the fence into their yard. "I asked him why, and he said it was more like a farm than the other place. You can say *that* again."

They purchased thirty-three rabbits. Pete noted a couple of months later that the number had risen to forty-two. "Rabbits, rabbits, rabbits, rabbits," he said. "They're sort of cute, but the way I'm thinking now, they'd look even cuter in a frying pan."

A hamlet called Khanh Hoi asked Pete for financial assistance from IVS to build a tilapia fishpond. The community had been confused about the availability of self-help funds, which required the sign-off of three officials: the Rural Affairs representative, the U.S. military adviser for the province, and the Vietnamese province chief. Self-help funds had been misused under the Diem regime, but "since the coup and subsequent arrival of a fireball province chief, these misconceptions have been cleared up," Pete's monthly report stated. IVS would help with the fishpond. A portion of the proceeds from selling the farmed fish would help support the hamlet school and its teacher.

The Rural Affairs self-help guide, published in Vietnamese and English, contained detailed instructions for preparing a tilapia fish pond, in a chapter with the caffeinated title "Would You Like to Have All of the Fish You Can Eat All of Your Life at No Cost Whatever?" In the tilapia, it said, nature had provided a delicious and inexhaustible food supply. The fish would multiply "constantly," each pair reproducing as many as ten thousand young per year. Tilapia could be used in *nuoc mam* or eaten fresh, dried, pickled, or smoked. "All you have to do to receive this wonderful gift," the manual promised, "is use the natural resources you have around you and apply a little of your own time and labor."[4]

A second project, capitalizing on Ninh Thuan's existing fishing industry, was put forward by Rural Affairs man Bob Friedman. He wanted to get Chuck and Pete started on a portable fish smokehouse. They would build it in Hai Chu hamlet as a demonstration project, in the hope that other communities would adopt the idea. Smokehouses would provide fishermen with a way to preserve their catch for up to six months. Even though the people were not used to the taste of smoked fish or meat, Pete noted, "The RA man likes smoked fish, so that's how it goes."

The Rural Affairs manual gave detailed instructions for building and operating a smokehouse. The project was outlined as an easy, low-cost solution to a problem—namely, that the comparatively slow dehydration rate for fish dried in the sun invited spoilage. Smoking a fish before sun-drying it would effect rapid dehydration. The manual assumed that the superiority of the method would trump flavor preferences. "Once you become accustomed to the smokey taste," the manual stated, "you will probably like the flavor."[5]

Two weeks after the smokehouse was completed and introduced in the hamlet, Pete wrote home to ask how his movie of the demonstration had come out. On the way there, he had shot film perched on the tailgate of Friedman's jeep, "holding on for dear life [and] twisting through midair, pulling the trigger of the camera with one hand and pawing for a handhold with the other."

The movie opens on the broad plain outside of Phan Rang. Craggy mountains and a barren landscape rush by. On a footpath beside the road, a woman wearing a conical hat carries two baskets suspended from either end of a bamboo pole. A settlement enclosed by tall bamboo bounces into view.

Some eighty people, apparently the entire population of Hai Chu, have turned out, half of them children. They crowd around a table laid with several bowls of fish.

The scene shifts to a shore and fishermen bringing in their catch. From his boat, one hands a basket of fish to a woman who has waded into the water to receive it with outstretched arms.

Back in the hamlet, puffs of smoke rise amid the crowd. A Vietnamese army officer approaches, hand on hip, observing. Another man holds up a fish and explains something to the onlookers. The officer places a fish in the smoker.

A serious Pete, the only American in view, enters the scene dressed in khakis and a short-sleeved white shirt. A leather camera case hangs at his hip. When he looks in the direction of the camera and whoever has trained it on him, the scene ends.

Two years later, Friedman sent my parents a photograph of the same occasion. He explained that the fishermen of the village were very poor and had known nothing about the smoking process as a way to preserve fish. "I know you must have read much in recent months of commentary questioning the United States' purpose and goals in Vietnam," he continued. "About the worthiness of Pete's work and objectives there can never be any doubt. He was dedicated to the improvement of the Vietnamese peasant, particularly the children, and as I think I've told you before, I consider him to be one of the most outstanding persons I've ever known."

Pete was becoming known in the province and had acquired two nicknames. Although Ong My Cau, "Mr. Tall American," fit every American man, a group of elderly women marveled at Pete's towering height. Their theory, it seemed, was that a person never stopped growing. "Since I'm already a quarter to a third again as tall as they are, at the tender age of 22, they exclaim '*Ui-Cha!*' at the prospect of how tall I'll be at forty years."

The second nickname, Ong Mui Cau, was uniquely Pete's. The same group of women remarked on "the beauty, the noble incline, the strength and grandeur" of his nose. They wondered aloud how Americans, with such large noses, managed to make love.

But it was the children with whom the nickname stuck. "I'll go out to a hamlet that I've never been to before, and the kids will come out running and screaming," he said. "And then they take a second look and exclaim something to the effect, 'Hey, it's Mr. Big Nose.'"

He began taking meals in a local restaurant, where the food was better than at home, and befriended a Vietnamese neighbor who enjoyed "taking a nip or two" of kumquat nectar in friendly company.

Margo's gift of Mark Twain books arrived. Pete was grateful for a touch of humor in his off-hours, even if a sergeant at the American military compound who was "suspicious of people who think and speak in polysyllables" had found him out.

He was also reading Ian Fleming. The James Bond books were a letdown. "They're such a blow to the psyche," he told Margo, "when you read of luxury and suspense, etc. while sitting on your duff in the tropics."

Visiting dignitaries were coming through on inspection tours. In March 1964, a "storm of petty bureaucrats—otherwise called an Evaluating Committee"—

arrived with grandiose plans for economic development. One of the projects they wanted to check on was the installation of irrigation windmills that would make use of Ninh Thuan's coastal breezes. When one U.S.-engineered windmill had been put in place, its arms had promptly snapped off. Pete anticipated that the committee would recommend termination of the project, even though he was sure the windmill only needed thicker wood.

But the bureaucrats were "thinking in terms of canning factories for this province," he complained. "When you think of the planning, the staffs of technicians, the preparations that go into economic development programming in the States, and then you see these Committees come in and in two days plan a year's budget or give the province a canning factory, you can see why some people don't appreciate foreign aid." He decided to look around for a way to make inexpensive windmills from local wood.

Pete reported that U.S. Ambassador Henry Cabot Lodge, Secretary of State Dean Rusk (held over by Johnson from the Kennedy administration), and Vietnam's new head of state had all recently stopped in Ninh Thuan:

Last weekend the clouds parted and Cabot Lodge, Dean Rusk, and Premier Khanh descended, God-like. It was really quite a show. There must've been sixteen helicopters and five huge transport planes out on the airstrip. Undoubtedly unnerved the Vietcong up on the mountain considerably. Their croplands are visible from the airport.

The reason for the visit was to show Rusk one of the most peaceful provinces in the country and the potential for social and economic development which the government can exploit, thus winning back the hearts of the people (provided Vietnam gets enough foreign aid).

Describing the same visit in another letter, Pete said the trio had "dropped in for some pep talks the other day." The people accompanying them had done "quite a snow job on Rusk," he noted. "He sure must be a tired, overweight, gullible old man."

The fact-finding visits by high-level officials were precipitated by Vietnam's increasingly rocky political situation. In April 1964 Defense Secretary Robert S. McNamara advised President Johnson that twenty-two of forty-three provinces in South Vietnam were at least half-controlled by the Vietcong. Furthermore, he said, the population was apathetic and the government's position was weakening. He suggested that American dependents be sent home, that a U.S. combat unit be posted to Saigon for added security, and that U.S. officers be assigned overall command of the war.[6]

That same month, Ford Motor Company—which McNamara had joined in 1946 and led as president before joining the Kennedy cabinet—introduced one of the most popular models in its history, the Mustang.

As a civilian attached to an NGO in the midst of an escalating war, Pete, like other IVSers, had a unique vantage point compared with most Americans. He saw U.S. policy as it was developing in Vietnam, not from the lofty position of the war's architects. He was an eyewitness to the effect of shifting political currents on daily life—his own, and those of his teammates, his Vietnamese colleagues and friends, and the U.S. servicemen he knew.

In February 1964 the country observed the lunar new year holiday. The "IVS Handbook" explained its significance: "For the three days of Tet, the Vietnamese bid goodbye to the old year and welcome the new by visiting their friends, wearing new clothes, and exchanging gifts in a festival atmosphere that would rival Thanksgiving, Christmas, and Easter rolled into one."[7] But even Vietnam's biggest celebration was tempered by the simmering conflict. In Pete's case, exploding firecrackers tossed into the back of his Land Rover were less festive than unnerving.

The same date that he wrote home about Tet, the Beatles appeared live for the first time on the *Ed Sullivan Show*. I didn't watch, because my parents didn't like rock and roll. At the bus stop the next morning, though, I listened with interest to the debate about who was cuter, Paul or Ringo.

Pete heard the Beatles for the first time over Radio Australia. "Doesn't sound so bad if you're in the right frame of mind," he said.

Four little girls had recently been killed in a Ku Klux Klan bombing of a church in Birmingham, Alabama. Pete followed what he knew only as "the civil rights revolution" in articles from the *Saturday Evening Post*, *Look*, and *Life* magazines. The news of violence back home was distressing.

He worried about the emergence of the conservative Republican senator from Arizona, Barry Goldwater, as a presidential candidate. "If Goldwater is elected," he wrote, "I will not be able to say with any pride at all that I am an American. . . . It will seem to me that the American society has chosen an immoderate, inarticulate, unplanned political road which is horrifying to my ethical and moral feelings."

Meanwhile, there wasn't much new in Phan Rang besides the arrival of a new IVS stationmate. Jim Hunt was a Cornell graduate and even an Alpha Delt there. Hunt had evidently taken the military situation to heart and was stockpiling hand grenades, a cannon, boxes of ammunition, and a Thompson submachine gun. Pete admitted to feeling, by comparison, "rather country squire-ish armed only with my modest automatic rifle." Even so, he had taken the roof off of his Land Rover and folded down the windscreen to gain a free field of fire.

"I'll probably never ever see a VC," he told Margo, "but the possibility is disturbing. For that reason things get a little tense sometimes and mail means a lot." Letters from our grandmother were especially comforting: "Nana writes every so often and in her old age she only writes beautiful thoughts, sometimes little excerpts from the Book of Psalms, which I never think about until she brings them to my attention. After reading one of her letters, I always feel very much at peace inside."

If the danger of life in a war zone was real, it did not impede Pete's sense of adventure. "Really weird being over here in the middle of all this," he said in February 1964. His timing in removing the roof of the Land Rover had been unfortunate, however. That weekend, he and Gene Stoltzfus were caught in a downpour while driving to Dalat:

> It started raining at the foot of the mountains and didn't stop all the way up. It rained so hard the seats were in puddles and water streamed off the tops of our noses and trickled into our ears because of the slipstreak of wind.
>
> Well, you should have been with us on the trip back. A beautiful clear day with the wind moaning in the pine trees. On the descent, we could see over the Phan Rang plain all the way to the coast. The clouds scudded over and their shadows seemed to race us down the mountain. It was sort of a wild ride because we lost time on the curves, but it was wonderful and exhilarating, especially when we caught up with a cloud.

While the well digging and smokehouse building continued, Pete also scrounged a film projector and auxiliary power unit from Saigon. With the equipment he found, he began showing films in remote hamlet schools.

Man alive. The kids will come in, snap to attention, yank off their hats, bow to you, then proceed to knock themselves pot over teakettle vying for position. They'll stick their fingers up into the beam of light to make images on the screen while the movie is going, and the old men will swat the kids indiscriminately with long bamboo rods. . . .

[It] always turns into a sweaty brawl, half the village crammed into a room the size of our living room. This creates quite a ventilation problem; Lord knows *one* of these chaps is hard enough to take at close range. I usually wind up sitting on the floor in the back row, where it's coolest.

One of the films, produced by the U.S. Information Service, explained a method for smoking fish. Pete was showing the movie one evening when he realized he was hemmed in by rifle-bearing members of the local militia. "Looked up to find myself surrounded by bodyguards, which was somehow not as reassuring as you might think," he said. Before he left to return to Phan Rang, the police carefully examined his vehicle for bombs and hand grenades. The reason became clear two days later, when Pete learned that the Vietcong had distributed rat poison to villagers and were encouraging them to use it on Americans.

Pete's interpreter, Kim, was growing nervous about security. Since the Vietcong had "raided Kontum, bombed the Kin-do theater, and hand-grenaded the Saigon ballpark, he's taken to locking the bedroom and front door behind him," Pete wrote. "Nonetheless, he leaves the window open for fresh air."

Such incongruities were part of daily life. Amid attack scares and mounting deaths of American servicemen and Vietnamese acquaintances, Pete was feeling more and more comfortable in his new home. "I guess I'm really getting entrenched in the routine over here," he realized. "I can hardly remember what some of the luxuries are like, back in the States."

He began "infiltrating" the local Boy Scouts, trying to enlist their participation with projects such as digging wells and repairing school buildings "in the true spirit of scouting and the country's revolutionary struggle against the Viet Cong." The scouting program lacked focus, and Pete, a former scout himself, believed that service-oriented projects were more meaningful than singing, practicing skits, drilling in figure eight formations, and saluting.

In April 1964 many Americans back home watched the Academy Awards on television. That year, for the first time, an African-American man, Sidney Poitier, won the best-actor Oscar, for his performance in *Lilies of the Field*.

That same month, Pete spent a lazy Sunday afternoon napping under a coconut tree on a French rubber plantation. Nearby, the Boy Scouts practiced their semaphore signals.

"They're the salutingest bunch of young men I've ever laid eyes on," he wrote. "Makes me tired to watch all the senseless, wasted energy they put into saluting and campfire dancing. I'm on a big, frothing 'public duty' kick these days. It's a shame the way these people are so relaxed about their national situation."

SEVEN

Never "Very Good at the 'Why'"

The recurring dreams began eight or nine years after Pete was gone.

I was living in western New York State and working for the Corning Museum of Glass. After college, I had not known what to do next and I had very little ambition, so when a friend from high school asked me to marry him, I had said yes.

He took a job as an engineer with Corning Glass Works, which in those days did not employ married couples in professional-level positions. I volunteered as a docent at the museum until, a few weeks later, I was offered a menial job on the curatorial staff.

The company had built a plant to manufacture ceramic liners for catalytic converters. The "catcons" were required for new cars to comply with an Environmental Protection Agency regulation aimed at reducing toxic emissions. Because the technology was new and Corning was a glass, not a ceramics, company, equipment breakdowns occurred frequently. My husband and I lived not far from the plant, so he received most of the middle-of-the-night phone calls. Our sleep was often interrupted by someone demanding that he come out and fix the huge machines, which clogged easily with ceramic dust.

When the phone rang, he awoke cursing. He left the house and returned two or three hours later, his clothing spattered with caked white clay. When emergency trips to the plant became routine, he stopped washing his clothes and pulled on the same ones night after night, like a uniform.

Perhaps it was because we went to bed in suspense, wondering if our sleep would be disturbed. Or because on nights when he left, I was half-listening for him to return. Or because subconsciously, I was ready to start grieving for Pete. Whatever the reason, I began to dream that Pete had come home.

In one version of the dream, he returned and said he had been in Vietnam all this time and had not died. In another, he had died but returned from the dead. Either way, I felt overjoyed to see him again. Then the dream would end and I would wake up sobbing.

Thirty years later, the dream was still recurring. One morning in December 2004, nine months after Pete's letters turned up, I dreamed again that he was back in Oklahoma City. He had come home with a colleague, a matronly woman wearing what looked like a Salvation Army uniform. The two of them were employed in relief work in another country and were in the United States only briefly. I had been out to dinner with a friend and missed him. He was going on to New York to see Margo. I realized that I could still see him. I could fly to New York! I could call him on the phone!

What would I do with all of his letters and papers that I had collected? I would tell him I had organized them for him. I was glad I had done it.

On January 9, 2006, I woke for the first time from a dream of Pete coming home and didn't feel sad. That week, I had seen my daughter off to college after the holidays, gone in for my annual mammogram, and had dinner with friends. Nothing out of the ordinary.

Pete had been gone forty years.

My first marriage ended after six years and I married again, in 1982.

My new husband was involved in ecumenical church work, and we received a lot of financial appeals in the mail. One day in November 1985 a letter came from the American Friends Service Committee, the Quaker organization. I remembered hearing that Don Luce had been affiliated with AFSC after he resigned his position with IVS and left Vietnam.

When Don went to Southeast Asia in 1958 as an early volunteer with IVS, he was no radical. Raised on a small dairy farm, he had majored in agriculture at the University of Vermont and earned a master's degree at Cornell. His childhood ambition was to have a job working with people he liked, who also liked him.

He was sent to Ban Me Thuot, in the mountains. With his teammates and Vietnamese co-workers, he introduced a new variety of sweet potatoes that grew well there.

During his first year in country, he spent many hours visiting people in their homes and practicing his Vietnamese on them. One evening his hosts brought out some special rice cakes.[1] He asked what the occasion was. They told him he would know soon. Don had observed that the Vietnamese love a mystery. They had a saying that a person without a secret was a nobody. The following day, he learned that one of the guests had "gone out into the jungle" — the euphemism for joining the Vietcong. "And I was very confused," Don said many years later, "because this was a very good person and why was a good person joining the Communists."[2]

Don's early political biography was like that of many ivsers. Conservative in his outlook, he looked up to John Foster Dulles, President Eisenhower's secretary of state and a staunch anticommunist. He did not question U.S. foreign policy and accepted the legitimacy of the Saigon government.[3] It was not an ideology, however, but his personal relationships with Vietnamese that, over nine years' time, changed Don from someone whose ambition had been to like and be liked by people into a peace activist who wanted to help others even if it turned people against him.

After his first assignment with ivs, he was named associate chief-of-party. A year later, he was appointed to the organization's top post in Vietnam. He expanded what had been an agricultural program, adding education volunteers. By 1967, the year he resigned, the team was 160 strong.

When President Diem and his brother Nhu were deposed in 1963, Don hoped that the people's faith in the new government meant they could defeat the Vietcong. Before long, however, a succession of coups d'état, greater U.S. involvement in the country, and the arrival of American combat troops led Don to view things differently.

Then a friend and team member was killed. In the first Vietnam War memoir written by Americans, *Viet Nam: The Unheard Voices*, Don and his co-author, John Sommer, would write about the changes augured by the first death of an ivser, in 1965:

Late in that year, Pete Hunting, a good friend and outstanding IVS team leader for the Mekong Delta area, was riddled with bullets in a Viet Cong ambush along the road. Our earlier, almost blithe nonchalance about the war was deeply shaken by his death. Vietnamese friends were equally distressed. Since we were always much influenced by the attitudes of the Vietnamese with whom we lived and worked, we noted their shifts carefully. Some, of course, stiffened in their hatred of the Viet Cong. Others came to resent the Americans.[4]

The attitudes of the team also shifted. When USAID moved to divert the focus of IVS away from village and hamlet work toward large-scale development plans, Don resisted. The IVS board was pressured to let its young leader go, but instead stood by him.

In the summer of 1967, Don took home leave and left his associate Gene Stoltzfus in charge. Gene absorbed the growing discontent among volunteers, who complained that the war was impeding their work. Some were becoming impatient.[5]

Meanwhile, Don was in Washington explaining his team's frustrations to the IVS board: as the war drove villagers from their homes, volunteers were expected to help the refugees. In doing so, they were tacitly supporting the displacement of the rural population. Some team members asked if teaching English to Vietnamese wasn't "Americanizing" them. The board passed a resolution supporting IVS's independence and its commitment to the people of Vietnam.[6]

Don returned to Saigon in July and convened a meeting of his entire team. They voiced their concerns, but no decisive action was taken.

The following month, Gene took a vacation in Laos. As he watched American planes in the sky heading toward Vietnam, and then heard their bombs exploding in the distance, he thought, *I'm going to do something about this.*[7]

He returned to Saigon and submitted his resignation to Don, who, as Gene remembers, said "something like 'If you go, I do too.'"[8]

As word spread among the team, other volunteers wanted to follow suit. They were discouraged from leaving, however, because the plan of action was to alter U.S. policy. If it worked, IVS would be needed in Vietnam.

In the end, four resigned: Don, Gene, Willi Meyers, and Don Ronk. But on September 19, 1967, forty-five of their teammates joined them in signing a protest letter addressed to President Johnson.

The letter began with the signatories identifying themselves as IVS volunteers working in agriculture, education, and community development. They felt compelled to say what they had seen and heard in Vietnam and to speak on behalf of the too little understood, too often unheard voices of the Vietnamese. "It is to you, Mr. President, that we address ourselves," they stated.[9]

They called the war self-defeating and "an overwhelming atrocity." Further, they observed anti-Americanism growing in proportion to the escalating violence. They recommended five actions: de-escalation of the war; an end to the spraying of herbicides; the cessation of bombing in both North and South; recognition of the National Liberation Front and representation of the NLF in peace talks; and the establishment of an international peace commission, with agreement by the United States to accept its recommendations.

The letter was the first public denunciation of the war by members of the American community in Vietnam.

To avoid its being leaked to the American press corps in Saigon, Don aimed to get the letter to Washington as quickly as possible. He intended to follow correct procedure by delivering it to Ambassador Ellsworth Bunker's office for teletype transmission to the White House. He handed the letter to the U.S. mission coordinator at the embassy, who read it and asked him to return in two days.

Don explained that he wished only to transmit the letter quickly, before the news outlets found out about it and reported it without the president's foreknowledge. "A certain feeling of tenseness also contributed to our desire to send off the letter without what seemed to us unnecessary delays," he remembered.[10]

The mission coordinator left for forty-five minutes to speak privately with Ambassador Bunker. When he returned, he again said to come back in two days. He pointed out that criticizing government policy as a guest in Vietnam was unethical, and as Don later wrote:

> He added that such irresponsibility would make it impossible for us to get jobs in the Foreign Service. He said that the IVS transportation priorities would be upgraded. (We had complained two weeks earlier about our flight priority being lower than that of a colonel's mistress.) In frustration, we tried to explain that our protest was not about technicalities. . . . But he interrupted, saying he did not want to discuss U.S. policy with us, that that was not an IVS concern. We gave him the letter and left in frustration

and anger, asking that its contents be forwarded by the teletype to President Johnson. Five hours later, we made the letter public to the *New York Times*. The next morning, Ambassador Bunker agreed to see us.[11]

In addition to the letter appearing on the front page of the *New York Times*, it was published by the *Washington Post, Los Angeles Times, Christian Science Monitor, San Francisco Chronicle, New York Post, Newsweek*, and *Christian Century*.

The *New York Times* and *Washington Post* ran a series of articles about the significance of the resignations. On September 25 a *Times* editorial concluded that Don, his three top aides, and his team, all of whom knew Vietnam intimately, had effectively issued a warning that the United States was losing the "other war"—the critical civilian effort—in Vietnam.[12]

The IVS board hastily came together on September 21 to fill the positions vacated by the four who had resigned. They also authorized Executive Director Gardiner, a former USAID mission director, to leave immediately for Vietnam and mend relations with Ambassador Bunker.

When the four protesters returned to the United States, more than seventy-five members of the Senate and House of Representatives asked them for a private or small group meeting. They were asked how our country could withdraw from Vietnam responsibly and end the war and the Vietnamese people's suffering. They were urged by some to meet with President Johnson, but an interview with one of his aides made it clear that such a meeting would be a waste of time.

Some advised them to meet with Vice President Humphrey. But recently, in the presence of officials who afterward repeated his words, he had called the resignations "one of the greatest disservices to the American effort in Viet Nam."[13] No meeting with Humphrey took place.

At the suggestion of a junior State Department employee, appointments were scheduled with senior officials. When the protestors arrived, they waited two hours before being sent away because no one was available to meet with them. Secretary of State Rusk had said that their views did not reflect those of most Vietnamese. Assistant Secretary of State William Bundy claimed that the four lacked a proper perspective. More sympathetic, lower-level officials confided, however, that their perspective—because they had observed U.S. foreign policy at close range and were so close to the Vietnamese—was disturbing.

In Saigon, friends and co-workers, including some who had distanced themselves from Americans, descended on the IVS office. Some of them admitted
that they had heretofore suspected IVS of being a cover for the CIA. Others said
they now knew that some Americans genuinely cared about the Vietnamese.

After a brief return to Cornell, where he lectured and wrote from a base in the
Southeast Asia program, Don made headlines again in 1970 when he helped
expose prisoner abuse in a South Vietnamese jail.

That year, President Richard Nixon sent a delegation of ten congressmen
to Vietnam. They would visit detainees of the Saigon government in return for
permission to see where the North Vietnamese were holding American prisoners of war.

Don was working for the World Council of Churches. He accompanied the
delegation as an interpreter and one who knew about jails. Many of his Vietnamese friends had been arrested.

Tom Harkin, later to become a U.S. senator, was an aide to Congressman
Neal Smith. According to Don, Harkin convinced two members of the delegation to look into accusations of torture in the Tiger Cages, built in 1939
by the French, where suspected enemies of South Vietnam were held. A
prison adviser in the United States had likened it to a Boy Scout recreational
camp.[14] Don had heard otherwise and obtained drawings showing the location
of a secret cellblock. As he recounted years later, what they found there was
shocking:

> Using maps drawn by a former Tiger Cage prisoner, we diverted from the
> planned tour and hurried down an alleyway between two prison build-
> ings. We found the tiny door that led to the cages between the prison
> walls. A guard inside heard the commotion outside and opened the door.
> We walked in.
>
> The faces of the prisoners in the cages below are still etched indelibly
> in my mind: the man with three fingers cut off; the man (soon to die) . . .
> whose skull was split open; and the Buddhist monk from Hue . . . I re-
> member clearly the terrible stench from diarrhea and the open sores
> where shackles cut into the prisoners' ankles. "Donnez-moi de l'eau"
> (Give me water), they begged.[15]

Harkin photographed the Tiger Cages and published them in *Life* magazine. Almost four hundred detainees, men and women, were removed from the prison after a public outcry resulted.

Don kept up with many of the former inmates. One of them read about the liberation of Auschwitz and Dachau, and identified with the prisoners who remembered someone's kindness to them in a time of dire need. I was traveling with Don in Vietnam in 1991 when he was asked to come to the desk of our hotel in Saigon. A man waiting there handed him a bottle of expensive American whiskey. He had heard Don was back in town, and he felt he owed him something.

I stared at the masthead of the year-end appeal from the American Friends Service Committee. I remembered my parents mentioning Don's affiliation with AFSC. He had kept in touch with them, even visiting them in Oklahoma City while I was away at college.

Although they liked Don, my mother disapproved of his opposition to the war. Since Pete's death, she had become a staunch backer of our country's policy in Vietnam. She also defended President Nixon and Vice President Agnew (even when they left office in disgrace), and the National Guard troops who shot and killed students during an antiwar demonstration at Kent State University (when I too was in college and protesting the war).

Seeing the AFSC letter, I hoped I might locate Don if I wrote to the organization. I sent a note requesting his address, signing it with my married name. I mentioned that Don and my brother had worked together in Vietnam. Instead of replying to me, the recipient at AFSC forwarded the note to Don.

He wrote back a couple of weeks later. He said he tried to keep up with people he had known in Vietnam, but he didn't recognize my surname.

This time, I wrote a letter. I said my mother had taken Pete's death very hard and I didn't know much about what had happened to him. I wondered what his political views had been. I mentioned my opposition to the war in my college years.

It was the first time I had spoken so openly to anyone but my sisters about Pete or my family's reaction to his death. The subject had been all but taboo. To this day I can't explain why I chose that time and that person to break the silence.

A week later Don wrote to me again:

Getting your letter brings Pete very close to my mind . . . his smoking fish in Phan Rang, working on a windmill to bring salt water to dry in the salt flats, practicing Vietnamese with me. We were very close and spent many hours just in relaxed talk.

None of us are ever very good at the "why." But we all did foolish things back then. Pete was driving in an area where he wasn't known, where he had never worked, and was caught in an ambush. We were always safer in the communities where we lived and worked—people understood what we were doing. I think, tragically, Pete was misunderstood for a soldier. He became one of the innocent people—more than a million non-combatants who were killed.

I suspect that Pete would have been a part of our letter to Pres. Johnson protesting the war. Those of us who drafted that letter were his closest friends—John Sommer, Gene Stoltzfus, Willi Meyers, Don Ronk. We were all very close and would not have sent the letter until we all agreed.

We have all continued in work for Peace in our various ways—John Sommer is a dean at the Exp[eriment] for International Living (and on [the] IVS board); Gene is a Mennonite minister working on urban issues in Chicago (also on [the] IVS board) and is about to go to the Philippines for 6 months to study issues of Peace there for the Quakers; Willi teaches agricultural economics at Iowa State; and Don Ronk is in Hong Kong (I think) editing a magazine on Asia.

I'm still working on peace issues. I mentioned the Vietnam curriculum. I've done quite a bit on Korea too—edited a poetry book, went to the north as a soundperson for ABC-TV. I've been back to Vietnam since the war—saw some of the windmills Pete built still standing and still pumping salt water into the salt flats to dry. . . .

I have been much involved in the religious peace movement. . . . I was employed in Vietnam by World Council of Churches in 1968–71 until I got kicked out. . . .

My love to you, your family, and all of Pete's family. If ever I can be of any help, let me know. And please feel free to write—it means a lot to me to keep this contact.

Peace and love,
Don

In my early thirties at this time, I was a wife with a one-year-old child, living halfway across the country from my parents and sisters. The experience of being a mother was a revelation to me. I had discovered, in the bond with my little girl, a depth of feeling and a capacity for love that were new to me. My days often consisted of taking long walks, pushing my daughter in her stroller along the bike path and sidewalks of my new home, Sonoma, California.

I studied conversational French with a group of women friends. I read books by and about the psychologist Carl Jung. I tried to improve my cooking.

I had not learned my way around the kitchen from my parents. My practical father, a minister's son and one of six children, was by far the better cook, but he flew solo. He said that anyone who could read could cook, a veiled criticism of my mother. She was an avid reader, but not of recipes. After Pete was gone and I was the only child left at home, the three of us took our meals catch-as-catch-can. Often we ate dinner barely speaking, while we watched television. We went through a lot of frozen chicken potpies, canned beef slices in gravy, and cheap cheeseburgers from a place called Quick's, to which my mother would dispatch me with a few dollars. When I got to college, I was the only person who loved the cafeteria food. Eventually I taught myself to cook. If I was going to eat well, I had to fend for myself.

And then, in 1985, a year without marked highs or lows, and with no deliberation on my part, I had opened the door to something remarkable. I had found my way to Don Luce, the first of many individuals with whose help I would retrieve my lost connection with Pete.

On a whim I had reached out to Don, and he had met my curiosity with kindness. In doing so, he had dispelled a feeling that my questions were illegitimate and offensive. I didn't know it, but I had embarked on what was to be a redemptive, even miraculous journey.

Still, something he had said troubled me. If Pete had acted foolishly and gone somewhere he shouldn't have, had he invited his fate? If his youthful overconfidence had led him to take an unnecessary risk and drive where it wasn't safe, his death seemed even more of a waste.

Something else Don had written hardened me toward my mother. She said I had betrayed my brother's memory, and although I didn't believe her, I hadn't known how to refute her. By guessing that Pete would have had a hand in writing the letter to President Johnson, Don "proved" to me that my mother was wrong and I was right. Her archconservatism seemed to be a way of insisting that Pete had died both for his country and for the U.S. mission in Vietnam. I didn't think Pete was motivated by patriotism of that kind, and Don's letter confirmed it. I was years away from empathizing with my mother, even though I now understood the limitless love of a parent for a child. She had lost her first-born. Yes, she could be rigid, but I couldn't see then how like her I was.

Don said that my letter had brought Pete close to mind. I thought that Don was as close to Pete as I would ever come. I wondered if Pete's life would have taken a course like his.

I didn't guess what Don would do next. Unbeknownst to me, he shared my letter with two more of Pete's friends. Without my realizing it, these three men would launch me on a quest. Before I reached the end, I would find more of Pete's friends than I could count.

John Sommer was raised in a politically moderate household in Montclair, New Jersey. Although tolerant and open minded, his parents shared with other Americans of that era a fear of communism. His mother organized the basement in case there was a nuclear attack.

For his first three years with ivs, John felt that U.S. policy overall, if not its implementation, was right for Vietnam. In February 1965, John's parents came to visit. His father opposed U.S. policy, and John remembers, "I thought one of my objectives would be to show him we were doing the right thing. By the time he left, the measure of progress I had made was that he was ambivalent. It was when the U.S. military started coming in such big numbers, and later on in 1965 when Pete was killed and we saw the negative repercussions of the U.S. troop involvement, that my thinking really began to change."[16]

In 1967, his first tour with ivs behind him, John returned to Vietnam for four months to lead a usaid-sponsored internship program. It was intended "to convince college students of the righteousness of U.S. policy." He anticipated that the program would produce the opposite effect, and it did.

During that time, he had many conversations with ivsers about their role and what action they might take. He would have willingly signed the letter to President Johnson, had he not already returned to the United States by the time it was published.

He accompanied Senator Edward Kennedy to Vietnam as a consultant to the

Senate Judiciary Subcommittee on Refugees and subsequently graduated with a master's degree from the Johns Hopkins School of Advanced International Studies. He passed the foreign service exams and was offered an assignment in Vietnam, which he declined. He held positions with the Peace Corps, Ford Foundation, and USAID before becoming dean of the Experiment in International Living's School for International Training, in Vermont. That's where he was on New Year's Eve of 1985, when he sat down at his typewriter and wrote to me.

> Don Luce has sent me a copy of your letter to him, which I was very moved to read. He sent it because your brother Pete and I were good friends in Viet-Nam, and indeed before that when we were both students at Wesleyan, class of '63. It is hard for me, too, to believe that it's now 20 years since his death. I remember so vividly being called to the post office in Hue, where I was then living, to pick up a cable, the cable with the news, and the staggering disbelief, overwhelming sadness, and I think anger.
>
> Pete, Gene Stoltzfus, and I had in a way a special relationship, being in the same "strategic hamlet school program" in adjoining provinces. During our first two years in country, Pete was in Phan Rang, with Gene in the province to the north and me in the one to the west; we'd get together occasionally at one or the other place, enjoying the cool mountain air in my Dalat or the beach in Phan Rang or Nha Trang. We'd share our experiences in similar work, and, for sure, our frustrations. I remember one visit in particular—in part because it's recorded on film (movie) which I'd love to show you some time—when Pete took me to some Cham villages; the magnificently colored Cham blanket that I bought there hangs behind me at this very moment as I write this letter, as it has somewhere in my home or office almost ever since.
>
> I did not know of your mother's especially hard reaction to Pete's death; I always wanted to meet your parents, but geography intervened. On the other hand, I don't know that his letters would offer much insight into how he "felt about the war." As you'll recall from Don's and my *Unheard Voices*, we were not in those days politically active or perhaps even very conscious. That only came later, really in 1966. Pete's tragic death made us in some ways more emotionally involved, and dubious about our

policies, as well. For many of the frustrations to which I referred above had to do with the sorry state of the Saigon government which seemed a sorry ally indeed, and one unlikely to be very effective in achieving a non-communist solution for Viet-Nam. Speculating on what Pete's position might have been a year later is like speculating on what would have been different had John F. Kennedy lived longer. On the one hand, I think Pete was a bit more conservative than some of us, but on the other hand I find it hard to believe he could have felt differently than the rest of us, as one saw increasingly, beginning around 1966, what was happening to that poor country and its people. Indeed, I suspect he would have been proud of your position protesting the war in those later years.

As for the circumstances of Pete's death, Don has probably told you what any of us knows—the impression that he simply was at the wrong place at the wrong time, apparently in front of a military convoy for which the ambushers were waiting. I do know that when I flew down to Saigon for his memorial service, it was a very moving time for all of us—the first time most of us had lost a peer and a friend in the course of a cause in which we believed, that of a better life for the Vietnamese people. After his death, I was asked to take over his job as team leader for the southern part of the country, in addition to the Hue region, and with it the vehicle which he had been driving that last time through the verdant rice paddies of the Mekong delta.

I could go on, but perhaps this is enough for now. . . . I thank you for provoking by your letter the memories which are flooding through me as I write. I hope we will have a chance to meet one day. Meanwhile, please share my good wishes with your sisters and parents.

Sincerely,
John

The other person who replied to my letter to Don was Gene Stoltzfus. He and Pete were the best of buddies. They bought Hondas and planned to drive them across Europe after their ivs contracts expired. They also talked about staying on in Vietnam as employees of the U.S. Operations Mission and going skiing in Japan— "despite the fact that he's from the flatlands and doesn't know the least about skiing," Pete wrote. "Not that I'd be any help to him in that matter."

Gene grew up in a Mennonite community in Ohio. His father was a minister and bishop in the church. He attended Mennonite schools, including high school and Goshen College.

He arrived in Saigon a pacifist. With Pete, John, and the other 1963 recruits, his introduction to Vietnam included a month of language training in My Tho. His first Sunday there, Gene was walking to the city's athletic fields when he saw helicopters transporting wounded Vietnamese soldiers.[17]

Both Gene and Pete took home leave in the summer of 1965 and returned to Vietnam as team leaders. Gene's base was Nha Trang. Pete moved south to the Mekong Delta.

As the war intensified, ivsers struggled to maintain their organization's autonomy and distance themselves from the U.S. mission. But ultimately, Gene concluded, "To be genuine, we had to speak out more forcefully about the war and about the American presence."[18]

In the fall of 1967, the midnight oil burned at the ivs house in Saigon as Gene and others drafted the letter to President Johnson. "Some people in the office were unhappy [about what we were doing], and there was always so much to do during the day, so we worked at night," he recalls. "Everyone pitched in. Some people were writing drafts of the letter. Some people were running the mimeograph machine. People were talking about who would take this letter around to show the others."[19]

They agreed that everyone on the team should see the letter so no one would feel left out. They caught rides around the country on Air America—which belonged to "the three dirty letters," the cia, Gene said. Some but not all supported the protest. The group was "very highly polarized at the time of the letter."

Gene took the letter downtown and spoke personally about it to Bernard Weinraub of the *New York Times*. Weinraub suggested holding it until the coming Monday, when there would be more room on the front page than on a Sunday. The *Times* was the only paper the group approached. With the letter's publication, other news organizations descended on the ivs house. Don took some of the interviews and Gene handled others, telling himself, *Just act like this is routine.*

After returning to the United States, Gene gave "about a thousand speeches." He earned a master's degree in international relations from American University and returned to seminary to finish the studies he had begun before going to Vietnam. He and his wife documented human rights abuses in the Philippines before settling in Chicago and founding a peace and justice group. In 1988, Gene became the first director of Christian Peacemaker Teams, a pacifist activist group.

A few months after I wrote to Don, Gene wrote to me.

Your letter to Don Luce caught up with me via John Sommer just before I left for the Philippines in January of this year and I have been carrying it in my case ever since. I was deeply moved by your letter and the story of your life. Peter was very important to me. In 1963 I went to Viet Nam together with him, studied language together and spent many many happy days and evenings together with him. I could recount so many stories of rides on motorcycles, youthful dreams, adventures and long long discussions about Viet Nam and our role in the emerging war. At the time of his death I considered Pete among my closest friends. Only two days before his death he took me to the airport in Saigon for a trip to Nha Trang where I was living at that time. Pete was a soul brother.

The moment when I learned of his death is as clear as yesterday. I had gone to the USAID compound in Nha Trang where a cable from Saigon was waiting for me. It was handed to me by the duty officer. I was crushed. Although, during the previous two years I had come to see the face of death, with Peter's passing it touched me at the Center. I caught the first flight to Saigon and wept the whole way. I helped to arrange the funeral and desperately tried to find meaning in all of this. In that moment I felt the tragedy of Viet Nam and went on from there to know more deeply the pain that my brothers and sisters in Viet Nam were facing daily. Peter's passing was a watershed for me because it opened a new center to my emotional life which allowed me to go from that point and make what at that time were hard decisions about the war. As you know later several of us resigned, returned to the States and turned all of our energy to working against the US death machine. In a way I always felt that I had a special responsibility to work for peace because of what happened to Peter. Until today I still tell the story of Peter when it seems appropriate and would love to talk with you about your brother.

As my work in the Peace movement grew I found myself reaching deeper for spiritual strength and depth. In 1973 I returned to seminary and completed studies, worked for some years with the church, was married to Dorothy Friesen and later spent several years in the Philippines. In the Philippines I once again saw the depth of injustice and how far our world has gone from the way of shalom. When we returned to the States we settled in Chicago and have founded a little peace and justice group with which I am now working. I'll enclose a few of our materials.

The writing of this letter has moved me over a long period of my life—most of my adult experience. I have little doubt that Peter would have been with us all the way in our peace actions. At the time of his death his thinking was moving much like our own. It had not yet jelled for any of us yet but we knew within ourselves that something very big was amiss. I hadn't known of your mother's continuing pain over Peter's death. I visited your parents briefly when I was on a speaking tour in Okla. City in 1968 and that was a very special time for me.

I hope that there will be a time when we can meet. Thank you for sharing your feelings with Don and through him with John and through John with me. You can be proud of Peter's memory and live a full life with the beautiful knowledge that he continues to inspire many of us. My prayers and good wishes are with you.

Sincerely,
Gene Stoltzfus

Don and John had asked me to give their regards to my parents and sisters. I didn't.

Why didn't I?

I had dropped my guard when I wrote to Don. Our exchange of letters, along with John's and Gene's replies, felt very personal and private. I wasn't used to talking with my sisters about feelings so unexplored and intense.

More than that, I was sure my sisters would react strongly to the letters from Pete's friends. I had been on the receiving end of my mother's powerful emotions, and I didn't want to be on the receiving end of theirs. I had a strong aversion to people who did not control their emotions. I overcontrolled mine.

Although Cis, Holly, and I had begun to talk about Pete together, we still trod carefully in our parents' presence. The subject of what had happened was still off limits. I didn't even consider telling my parents I was in touch with Pete's friends.

Most of all, I considered Don's, John's, and Gene's letters to be *mine*. My sisters would have loved to read them, but *I* had taken the initiative. I didn't have to share what belonged to *me*. So I hoarded the letters and didn't mention them to Cis and Hol. Unconsciously, I was reenacting my mother's possessiveness of Pete, for which I had not forgiven her.

There had been no avowals from Don, Gene, or John that we must meet. But within a year of hearing from John and Gene, I met them.

Gene came to the San Francisco Bay Area in the fall of 1987. On the campus of San Francisco Theological Seminary, I met a big, tall, brown-eyed man. We walked and talked nonstop as twilight turned to night. I told him about Cis's psychic friend who said that Pete was helping people in Central America. Gene said he wouldn't be surprised if that's where he was. Before we parted, he said that talking to me was like talking to Pete.

A few months later, John's work brought him to California and we met at a Vietnamese restaurant in San Francisco. It was easy to recognize him, because he was as slender and black haired as in his author photo of twenty-some years past. I had brought my copy of *Viet Nam: The Unheard Voices*, which he inscribed, "For Jill, in fond memory of your brother and my friend Pete, on the happy occasion of our first meeting." As he started to write the date, he looked up and remarked that it was April 30, 1988, the thirteenth anniversary of the fall of Saigon.

I had yet to meet Don. One steamy night three years later, under a street light in Bangkok, he would shake my hand and gaze so deep into my eyes that it seemed he was looking at me but seeing someone else.

EIGHT

"At War in Another Year"

Bangkok is a dream world—telephones, television, transportation, skyscrapers, ice cream and coffee shops, banks—egad."

Pete was writing from Thailand, where he had flown in May 1964 for a week of vacation. He stayed in a guesthouse run by Christian missionaries. It was inexpensive, quiet, and peaceful. "Didn't realize how much I'd relaxed," he wrote, "until a helicopter flew over the house and I tensed up suddenly like one of Pavlov's dogs."

He liked the familial atmosphere and civility of the guesthouse. "I never was overly religious, particularly as regards the ritual, but it's so nice to have grace before the meal and to talk to dedicated and curious people," he said. "Sure beats a hotel. I feel so renewed, refreshed."

One evening, he attended church. "I could almost feel your presence there beside me," he told Sue.

Pete had not realized how stressful life was in Vietnam until he reached Thailand. No one was throwing grenades or waging war against anyone else. He could be "uncontroversial" for a change. Saigon and Bangkok were as different as night and day: "a foggy night and a sunny day."

Bangkok was so modern, it seemed like a city back home. It made Saigon look "dirty French provincial," he noted. "A fellow could really get to dislike the French after a tour in Vietnam."

It was not only the cities that were different, but also the students. The Thai youth he met went out of their way to show him Buddhist temples and other sights. Compared with the Vietnamese, they were hard working, aggressive, and unpretentious. One young man was studying law while also waiting on tables, selling fertilizer, and collecting bills. If a counterpart in South Vietnam existed, Pete didn't know about it.

Even the frogs, with their loud chorusing, were a revelation. "They must be bigger than flowerpots," he wrote. "One gave me a good start last night, perched on the tree limb somewhere outside my window."

He spent his last night of vacation in a hotel, courtesy of World Airways. His flight had been delayed when the airplane was found to have landing gear problems. He took a long soak in the bathtub and watched the movie *Tom Jones*.

Pete would not have sprung for a hotel room. He had pinched pennies the entire week, forgoing cabs and riding local buses. "It was touch and go at first, not speaking the language, not knowing my location, not too clear on my destination, nor aware of where the bus was going," he wrote. After several hours of haphazard sightseeing, he stopped for a draught in a pub and someone gave him a city map.

An attack of miserliness overtook him and he left Bangkok early. He had spent a lot of money on a set of bronze flatware for twelve. He bought it against the distant day when he would get married. "It ought to be good and black by then," he said.

Ever since his undergraduate days, Pete had worried about money. Our family was middle class, and he had attended college without a scholarship. He felt guilty about using so much of the family's resources. His letters from Wesleyan frequently mentioned expenditures such as the high cost of eating or replacing his worn-out shoes. He wanted to apply for financial aid, but Mom refused to disclose the personal information required on the application form.

His letters from Vietnam continued the financial-pinch theme. Early in 1964, he began asking my parents to withdraw part of his salary from a bank in the States and send it to him via the IVS office in Washington. In addition to receiving a modest living allowance paid in piasters, IVSers earned a salary that was deposited to an account back home. The sum was so meager that it fell below Internal Revenue Service reporting requirements. Pete referred to it as "my (guffaw) 'salary.'"

He had been with IVS about seven months when he asked for seventy dollars. "It's a contribution to my own work," he explained to my parents. "I've found the best way to get something done around here is to do it yourself with your own fund to draw from. It won't become a habit, however. I want it to build a hand-operated drilling rig with which I'm going to dig a lot of wells for the schools in the province. No sweat; just please send the money as soon as possible."

It did become a habit. He had been listening to the Beatles over Australian radio— "She Loves You" was climbing the charts—and wanted to visit Australia before heading home unless by then he was too broke. He had been digging more wells, but the USAID program was so bogged down that he was dipping into his paycheck more and more to buy parts.

He had dug a well for the school at Thuan Tu, but another hamlet was more resistant. They said digging a well would break the "dragon vein," or energy flow, but Pete suspected there were other reasons:

> It's either a case of not being able to dig because of big rocks, or the people want a well but don't want to dig it. Or, as in a Montagnard hamlet, they're afraid of disturbing the subterranean dragon. The Montagnards will probably come around and decide to dig their well, but it's amazing to go into one of those hamlets and confront some of their old people who still believe in tiger tooth medicine and dragon veins.

The Rural Affairs manual stated that wells were one of the greatest needs of Vietnamese people.[1] Providing water for some of the strategic hamlets was considered particularly vital. The manual cautioned, however, that without establishing some means to maintain and repair the pumps, and to furnish spare parts for them, the well-digging program would lose the people's approval and support.

Not only did Pete convince several hamlets of the need to dig wells, he put his shoulder to the job. Then, when the pumps stopped working, he fixed them. At Ninh Qui hamlet, scum had collected on the mechanism. The people "hadn't had whatsoever it was they should have to buy the stuff" to clean and repair it, he wrote, but "it cost only about 35 of my dear pennies to fix the problem." While showing them the scum, Pete fell into the well. "Glad there was water in it," he said. "Had darn near the whole village trying to fish me out of there. What a farce—The American Advisor."

Before long he was broke from buying books, and parts for well pumps and a windmill he was designing. He was also supporting three elementary school students, at a cost of $1.50 a month, and a Montagnard boy whose high school tuition came to $8.50 a month, including food. The boy was like a little brother. One day he brought Pete a bottle of honey. "I thought it was rice wine," he wrote. "Took a big swallow and was very confused, because it *was* fermented but it *wasn't* rice wine."

The word "penniless" entered Pete's letters in August 1964. He couldn't afford postage stamps, so he held off on sending home the films he had shot. He had accumulated such a backlog of bills that a mere three hours after receiving his living allowance and feeling the "cold cash in my sweaty palms," he was broke. Three hours was a new record.

Nana sent a Christmas package that arrived in Phan Rang several months late. The package included a check. Pete felt guilty, as he did whenever she displayed such generosity.

> I'm already very well off. . . . I'm sure there are things around the farm or some of the younger cousins for which your gifts would be well deserved. Always appreciate your letters, though. . . .
>
> One of the hamlet schools recently asked if I would help them dig a well, so if you don't mind, I'll use your check to help them out. They can use the money more than I can.

My mother's largesse drew similar comment. When she sent a check for his birthday, he wrote, "Mom is a good Joe and all that. But, Mom, you should control your generosity a little bit more. Thanks very much for your present, but it's about twice as much as I know what to do with. Maybe I'll plow it into my foreign aid program."

Adjusting to Vietnam's tempo had taken a while. Especially when time weighed heavy, a slightly wistful note came through in Pete's letters. Early in April 1964 he wrote that an army buddy was going home in August. He wished he were going home, too.

He sometimes sounded sentimental in letters to Sue. Some days, it seemed like only yesterday when the two of them had walked across the Wesleyan campus, past Foss Hill to the new tennis courts. He wondered if Wesmen were "still on a kick over esoteric folk-type music." Had she seen any of his fraternity brothers? "Here it is, coming up April," one letter said. "I remember this season used to pass so slowly at Wesleyan."

Sue worried about writing to Pete when she was low. He encouraged her not to hold back. "When you get wrought up like that, go slow, or stop and take hold of yourself over a cup of coffee," he said. "Don't waste your energy worrying about a situation you can't remedy, and just sit it out. Don't worry about me coming back; I'm coming back for sure."

She was within days of graduating from nursing school when Pete imagined her in nursing whites: "You'll be out and wearing one of those cute—gnarxryl— little uniforms. For God's sake, be careful when you go into those solitary confinement rooms." In the same letter, he reminded her he'd be heading home before they knew it. "I'll probably want to turn around and come right back over here, though," he concluded.

He was getting entrenched in the routine, managing without his interpreter, and finding pleasure in the quotidian. It was the little things, like kidding around with friends, that made life wonderful. One day a major at MAAG, the military advisers' compound, pointed out that the beer cans were unsterilized. He warned that drinkers could be exposed to cholera. Pete's hard-working hands were notoriously dirty, and he brought down the house by demonstrating how he always wiped the lip of his beer can with his thumb. "It's amazing, the depths to which humor will sink into drollery, when people are hard-pressed for comic relief," he said.

Sue must have asked how close he was to the front. There was no front line, he explained, "because 'Charlie' is all over the place. 'Charlie' is MAAG jargon for VC. You know where they got it? From the Charlie Tuna ad on TV." The nearest he had come to shooting anyone or to "plain ol' general killing and bloodletting was driving about two and a half feet up a water buffalo's ass ('scuse me, sweet) the other day when I happened upon a whole herd and applied brakes, of which there were zip, nix, naught, nary a bit. Much to my surprise. And the buffalo's."

Sampling exotic foods was another form of adventure. He visited a *nuoc mam* plant with a neighbor and his brother. Afterward, they returned to the neighbor's house to drink beer and introduce Pete to spring rolls: "They take shrimp, lettuce, mint, carambola juice, peanuts, hot sauce, beef strips, and whatever else is handy, roll all of it up in rice paper. A good trick in itself. Then one dips it all in nuoc mam, eats the package, and licks one's fingers with much concentration. At least I do. That nuoc mam smells."

In June 1964 Pete set about organizing a motorcycle trip with some of his teammates. After their IVS contracts expired, three wanted to return to the States mostly by sea. The other four hoped to persuade the Honda corporation to underwrite their overland trek across Asia and Europe. Their stops would include the Malay Peninsula, India, and Ceylon. The motorcycles would cost six hundred dollars apiece—a little less than the amount IVS allowed for a return air ticket.

The motorcycles would be delivered to Vietnam from Hong Kong. Pete calculated that because a new Honda 300 sold for a thousand dollars in the United States, he could sell it when he got home and end up in the black. He thought he might then enroll at Oklahoma University "just to warm up the think-muscles" before applying to law school or taking the foreign service exams.

In the same letter in which he laid out his motorcycling grand design, he asked if Holly and I had grown gigantic. He wanted a recent photograph of the family, this time without anyone posing. "Holly and that jaw of hers look like a shark when she poses. All my Vietnamese friends ask me, 'Who's the shark, sitting second from the left?' and want to know if that's what we call a mermaid. I tell them no, and that a mermaid is in reverse, the fish part being the lower section."

Dad had been teaching Mom to fly. She had probably wrapped up, meaning crashed, her first Cessna 150 by now, Pete teased. How about sending a picture of her resting one foot on the crumpled cowling?

And incidentally, how should he go about voting in the presidential election "from way out here"?

By the following month, Pete had discovered that Hondas sold for about the same price in the United States as in Vietnam. He decided to buy a less expensive brand whose resale value was supposedly just as good. Having found a bike for about half the cost of the Honda 300, he asked my parents to transfer $356 to his checking account.

Better transportation would enable Pete to get around more easily. If Mom and Dad ever harbored parental concerns about a motorcycle accident, the next paragraph of his July 19, 1964, letter would have raised a far worse fear:

This week the Vietnamese, especially the VC, commemorate the Geneva Accords—called the Week of National Shame. I was almost material for a VC celebration the other day. Two men came to the house asking me to take a windmill out to their hamlet the following day. I'd heard there were VC in the province, so I checked with MAC-V [the military advisory command] that evening and was warned to stay clear of that particular area. The next morning a reconnaissance plane spotted VC in the rocks along the road I would've taken. Phew.

With no transition, he asked if Holly and I were back from canoeing camp and if the reports of topless bathing suits—introduced by designer Rudi Gernreich—being the fashion were true. "What's happening to the country, for crying out loud?" he asked. "Are people wearing the things? Girls, I mean?"

Seven thousand miles separated Vietnam and the United States, and the cultural upheavals that were taking place back home accentuated the distance.

Work on the windmill continued. After a year of waiting for the education program in his province to get rolling, Pete concluded that his most significant contributions as an IVSer would be the things he did on the side, like digging wells and engineering a windmill with two pumps so it could be adapted to different locations.

The windmill design was evolving. Pete had altered the trapezoidal wooden arms, or fans, twice. He had tested three different kinds of pumps. He was almost there, but the experimentation was costly and he was seeing "bleak days financially." Mom and Dad were ignoring pleas to send his checkbook. He supposed it was good they were.

A blotchy eight-millimeter movie taken around this time shows Pete doing the carpentry work. He enters the scene dressed in baggy khaki pants, a T-shirt, and white sneakers. He sits down in the shade opposite a small Vietnamese man. They grasp the handles of a two-man saw. Sawdust flies, and a bright green gecko on a tree watches as they push and pull. Pete turns to the camera and beams his "fish face"—a grotesque smile that is a kind of joke on the Hunting side of the family, whose men have the angular jaw and long face it requires.

Things were just moseying along, he told Margo. One day he fixed a pipe for a school well. Another, he visited a new hamlet school. The next, he wrote letters, studied Vietnamese, or worked out a new project on paper. After that, he visited yet another school and talked about planting gardens or raising rabbits and pigs. He bought a new radio, but it didn't work. It was typical of his frustrations.

But what really got on his nerves were the supercilious people he worked with.

> They know I'm only 22. That isn't a problem with the Vietnamese, who are generally very easy to get along with, but it is with the overseas American bureaucrats. They sit behind their desks and say, "No, it'll never work." I wish someone would pay me $8,000 a year for that.
>
> Sent some pictures to my mom the other day. Dad reported she wept for relief to see me actually alive in Vietnam. What are you all reading in the newspapers over there, anyway?

Although the violence was growing worse, Pete steered clear of it. Ninh Thuan Province was considered more secure than the Mekong Delta. One teammate there was stationed in "some very bad territory." He had told of leaving a school only five minutes before the Vietcong entered and removed the flag. The same friend had driven across a bridge just as a battle commenced on the river below him. "He's very casual about it," Pete said.

Vietcong propaganda sprang up regularly in one area where Pete had dug a well. "The first few times I went out there, they were a bit on the formal side, shall we say. By the end of the project they'd invited me for tea at their local temple and given me a lesson in the Cham language," he said. "During my stay I'd given 60 or so people a lift into town in the back of the Land Rover, including one hysterical woman who'd just learned her son had been wounded and killed in a VC encounter north of town."

One night, Pete was awakened by a sergeant who said he would have to come over to the MAAG compound. He was issued a revolver and assigned a battle station. The chief of police had informed the Americans that a suicide squad was infiltrating Phan Rang. The chief had agents in the Vietcong; Pete allowed that both sides probably had agents. The following day, the scare was over and he was back at his house. "Takes all the glamour out of being a civilian," he said. "Makes you feel left out."

Kidding aside, he acknowledged the trouble farther south:

Down there the communists are less discriminating and have tried plant-ing plastique [explosives] in IVS handlebars, etc., considerably shaking the faith of some pacifists on the team who think of themselves as "friends of the people" and who naturally assumed the feelings of tolerance and goodwill were reciprocal.

Less than a week later, however, danger had come close. An American sta-tioned at MAAG was shot down in his observation aircraft. The younger brother of a Vietnamese neighbor also was killed. "I knew him, too," Pete said simply.

In a lighter moment, he asked his Vietnamese friends where the local stills were hidden and how they mixed their drinks. They mixed them with women, they joked. "Well, we mixed up a few . . . but I can only remember how he threw the first one together. A little gin, carambola juice, crushed ice, vermouth, sugar. . . . It's very hard to use chopsticks under such adverse conditions."

He played a running game with the neighborhood youth. At night they tossed small rocks through the door at Pete and his housemates, now Jim Hunt, a Cornell Alpha Delt, and former teammate Larry Laverentz, who had taken a job with USAID. The boys considered everything that wasn't tied down fair game, including Pete's Land Rover, which they pushed out of sight. Pete retaliated by throwing water balloons at them until he realized they loved it. "Next thing," he said, "they'll want us to throw soap at them, too."

Security rose and fell. In June, things quieted down in Phan Rang, although less than ten miles off a battle was under way on a mountain.

Americans seemed more optimistic since the latest change of government in Saigon. At the same time, some intellectuals in South Vietnam had seesawed to feeling more anxious. Pete guessed that they were worried about what might happen to the country, and more so themselves, after it was pacified. Was the real problem not getting their fingers into the pie?

He observed a growing restlessness with President Johnson's inaction in neighboring Laos. Referring to the liberation forces in Laos and Vietnam by their old names, he wrote:

[Johnson] continues to dabble in political clichés without doing anything positive about Laos. When the Pathet Lao and Viet Minh pushed through that last offensive, what they were doing was securing the Ho Chi Minh trail. Right now, the Viet Minh quite blatantly use the Vietnam–Laos and Cambodia–Vietnam borders as refuge. A lot of people are really burned about it. Laotians and Vietnamese are getting quite impatient with Johnson, too.

With almost a year in Vietnam under his belt, Pete turned twenty-three in June 1964. On the same day, General Maxwell Taylor was appointed U.S. ambassador to Vietnam, replacing Henry Cabot Lodge.

Also that June, General William Westmoreland replaced General Paul Harkins as commander of U.S. forces in Vietnam. Harkins was said to have "fed Washington rosy reports" and not only emphatically maintained an optimistic outlook but also demanded the same of his staff.[2] According to journalist Stanley Karnow, Westmoreland was the corporate executive type, a manager. With Taylor, he would Americanize the war. Lodge had not been a team player.[3]

On July 27, President Johnson sent five thousand more American military advisers to Vietnam.

Pete continued to regale us with stories of his escapades and his insights into Vietnamese culture, but increasingly he also discussed the military and political situation. The education aspect of his job—the English teaching he had hired on for—had not yet coalesced. His work was more about meeting needs as basic as food and fresh water.

His frustration with bureaucracy and American policy was mounting. As a government major, he probably took a special interest in the development of programs. College courses were nothing, however, compared with the experience of observing strategy and policy in the making—and observing it from the unique vantage point of a civilian volunteer in a war zone.

In July 1964 he compared ambassadors Lodge and Taylor, and generals Westmoreland and Harkins:

> Of course, there's a lot of talk about Gen. Taylor and Westmoreland. It is said that Cabot-Lodge resigned as much because of his frustrations in trying to expand rational economic development programs as because of political call of duty. . . . It's not all that bad, but we've got more than enough Goldwater types in the ranks and officers than is healthy for our country or Vietnam.
>
> Taylor never believed in the A- or H-bombs as providing wholesome

security, bucked a lot of Air Force Brass Command and senators with stakes in Atomic Energy Commission contracts, and didn't begin to gain ground with his way of thinking (i.e., preparedness for nibbling wars of conventional or guerilla nature) until Kennedy put McNamara in. Moreover, Taylor is a staff man, which Lodge has not been.

Westmoreland is a "field and troops" general rather than a staff general, such as Harkins was. . . . Harkins did more to confuse Washington on military and civilian matters in Vietnam than all of USOM and the rest of the military put together, and is particularly responsible for the confused and ineffective American effort in the last years of Diem and first few months of the [South Vietnamese military regime that ousted him].

What [the new South Vietnamese premier] Khanh did was to snub growing French attempts to have Viet policy their way, and in turn to pick his own American advisers—colonels and majors whom he knew and respected from the field—putting Harkins out in the cold where he belongs. As a result, the Viets are now winning this war. The provincial aid program for this province is an amazingly good development program, thanks to Khanh's delegation of authority, and flexibility of our province chief.

Also just recently north of Saigon, 800-odd VC attacked a Vietnamese artillery company . . . which numbered about 100 men including several American military advisers. The Viets and Americans had few rifles and bullets, but lots of artillery, and were firing howitzers at 30 yards, propping them on jeeps and walls to get the angles, their backs to wall, stripped to their jockey shorts. Amazing story of pluck, as heard on the MAC-V grapevine.

He had gotten wind, through Sue, of bad news from home. My father had been in a helicopter accident but fortunately had suffered only broken bones. Trouble always came in threes; there was Dad's crash and two recent flights of Pete's:

Going down [to Saigon], the hydraulics system of a cargo plane failed and we landed like a fast freight car running off the end of the runway, mulching up beaucoup meters of cornfield before stopping. I thought, Well, that was exciting.

Then on the return trip, landing on a short runway the pilot reversed [propellers] and only the port-side prop reversed, sending us skewering up on a wingtip straight for an 8 by 8 concrete pillbox, which we were about to enter the hard way when the pilot—with much effort—winged the bird over to transverse the runway in the opposite direction. From there on down the rest of the strip we merely fishtailed back and forth on each of the wheels in succession.

As if that weren't enough, he returned to Phan Rang to learn that six Vietcong had been killed the night before in a hamlet where he was working. Two more Vietcong had been killed and another captured the week before. Unheard-of numbers of villagers were informing on the insurgents. Opinion and morale among American military officers had risen.

Fighting in the mountains and hamlets, American aircraft getting shot down, Vietcong insurgents killing and being killed—in retrospect, it is hard not to see Vietnam in 1964 as a country at war. But Pete perceived the situation differently. On July 11, 1964, he wrote, "We'll probably be at war over here in another year." He didn't object, as long as someone smart was giving the orders.

The struggle still held the possibility of victory for the South and defeat for the Communists. American combat units had not yet been sent to Southeast Asia. The word "quagmire" had not yet become affixed to the conflict. "Vietnam" was not yet synonymous with a foreign policy debacle. All that lay ahead.

If Pete was sometimes sentimental in his letters to Sue, he was witty, insightful, and generally at his best as a correspondent when writing to Margo. His letters to Sue began to taper off in the summer of 1964, while his letters to Margo became more frequent and richer in content. He and Margo seemed to exchange ideas and questions, as when Pete replied to her apparently lighthearted inquiry about libations: "No, there is no *blanc de blancs* here, but . . . I've found a place where it is possible to get Black and White scotch, cognac, gin, and soda. A little dark, black room out behind the granary sort-of-situation. Also, can get some good home-brewed sake and kumquat nectar, which is reportedly quite powerful. Maybe they put gin in it, which relegates the potion to the ranks of ordinary drinking and rubbing alcohol."

In August, he apologized to Sue for having been so long in writing. He made excuses: he was busy, and in a bad mood after a long meeting in Saigon that had been a waste of time. He'd also had a close call with "some people I'd rather not have close calls with *at all*."

He elaborated on the close call in a letter to Margo a few days later. He had recently gone out to a hamlet to repair a windmill. People came running toward him and said to go home. There were "unfriendlies" nearby, and they were well armed. It was the first time he had been told about trouble. He supposed he had probably come closer to danger, but without knowing it.

Pete was put out with Sue. She said she had withheld her feelings about dating other people because she felt guilty, as if she were deserting Pete. He thought he had made it clear when he left for Vietnam that he didn't object to her dating other guys. It wasn't his right to object, especially since he was too "gun shy" to make a commitment to her. "People change," he said. He didn't want her to martyr herself for his sake. Moreover, he appreciated her frankness and in fact agreed with her about not being exclusive. He summed up, "To be sure, I don't have much confidence in the 'us' part of our relationship, and I feel troubled and sad a bit, but again what can I say?"

Two weeks later he returned to the subject. Perhaps his last letter had been blunt, and he hoped it hadn't offended her. "Sometimes I think I can't understand you at times, which was probably just as true at Wesleyan, though unrealized," he admitted. "It seems we've both changed a good deal."

He seemed to want his freedom but not to be the one to break things off. In a letter home around this time, he said that Sue had more or less thrown in the towel. The reason he gave was that she was unhappy he might stay longer than two years in Vietnam. She may have been unhappy, but Pete and conceivably both of them may have been outgrowing the relationship. He had so many options—employment with the U.S. Operations Mission, graduate school, a motorcycling adventure with friends. "Everything is in a mess," he wrote, "but it's a wonderful mess to be in, to have so many wonderful alternative ways of doing so many wonderful things."

Along with two of his buddies, Pete was now considering staying eight more months in Vietnam when their IVS contracts were up. He explained their rationale to my parents: "It would seem a waste to have spent all this time, to have learned the language, to have built good reputations without bringing it all to fruition by drawing a sizeable paycheck for a few months and without sticking our foot in the *real* U.S. government's door." Coincidentally, if he postponed his motorcycle trip, the weather would be better.

The work was taking a new direction and Pete liked it. USOM had sent two new men to his province, who would do the kinds of things he had been doing. Finally he would be working primarily with teachers and youth. The newly formed Vietnamese Voluntary Youth, in Pete's words "yet another Peace Corps inspired by IVS," would organize university students to take up the kinds of projects IVS had pioneered in hamlets. "When we go, VNVY will replace us," he said. "After the war. It sure will have been an interesting and variety-filled tour when I'll have finished."

In the meantime, he would teach English a few days a week. He already taught classes every night, besides tutoring the deputy province chief—a man with the approximate rank of a U.S. lieutenant governor. Pete admired his energy:

[He] makes everybody else look sick, including the Americans. If everybody in the Vietnamese government were like him, the war would be won in two years. I wouldn't be surprised if it was won in two years, providing President Johnson or whoever would act according to his principles. Foreign confidence in the U.S.'s willingness to back its principles fell to such a low that people were surprised we just didn't sit back and let North Vietnam shoot torpedoes at us. I think many Vietnamese had lost faith in us; even now, they seem skeptical.

The reference to torpedoes followed, by two weeks, Congress's granting the president authority to retaliate against North Vietnam, which was alleged to have attacked two U.S. destroyers in the Gulf of Tonkin. The resolution also gave the president authority to expand the war in Vietnam. All but two senators voted in favor of it.

In the summer of 1964 President Johnson signed the Civil Rights Act, which guaranteed African Americans equal voting rights, education, and access to public facilities. The bodies of three missing civil rights workers had been found in Philadelphia, Mississippi. Race riots broke out in several U.S. cities. When his plane was shot down over North Vietnam, Lieutenant Everett Alvarez was captured, becoming the first American prisoner of war there.

I spent four weeks at canoeing and sailing camp. We bought a new puppy and named him Dash, after our first Dalmatian male. Pete alluded to these things on August 25 in reply to a letter in which I had asked about his safety. Over the course of his two-plus years in Vietnam, Pete occasionally tossed off a remark about getting shot, but in this one he addressed directly, if briefly, my concern:

Thanks very much for your letter—it sounds as though the family has had a pleasant summer, especially you and Hol.

My summer has been pretty interesting, although (as you know) it's always summertime over here.

You don't need to worry about my security over here. It sounds much worse in American newspapers than it is in my province. Our province here is quite peaceful, and the people are very friendly, even though we can see guerilla croplands on the mountainsides at the end of our airstrip.

This past month I (1) went to Saigon for a team meeting of IVS Education advisers and (2) after the meeting I worked with a youth camp with 14 Vietnamese youth. We painted a hamlet school and the hamlet "town hall" which was actually a house, and we repaired the hamlet's road.

I took some movies of the windmill I built and gave to one hamlet, so I'll send those along soon.

Can you please ask Mom or Dad to send me a checkbook or cashiers' check from my credit account for 600 dollars? I want to buy a Honda motorcycle and insurance. . . . (IF there is no emergency necessitating that the family use that money.) . . .

Well, thanks again for your letters. I always enjoy hearing about "the new Dash" from you. How about taking some close-up snapshots of the family the next time everybody is together? Thanks loads.

Much love,
Pete

A few weeks later, Pete wrote that security was about the same, and people seemed to be on tenterhooks until after the presidential election. It would be his first time to vote. He wasn't pro-Johnson, but he was anti-Goldwater. "If he wins I'm just liable to haul off and expatriate myself out of sheer disgust," one letter said. Writing to Margo, he worked up a lather about the candidate who, in accepting the Republican nomination, had declared that "extremism in the defense of liberty is no vice."

On September 20, there was yet another coup d'état in Saigon. The mood of the people had shifted, Pete noted, reflecting the increasing instability of the country.

Last year, people still had a lot of hope. This year, people's opinions are black or white, black in the majority. The experts are at a loss to forecast what will happen in the next three months. The Delta situation remains the same, leading us to believe the vc have done as much as they could and are now on a new strategy, which is aimed at toppling the country from the Central Lowlands.[4] Nha Trang, to the north, has been sinking fast, mostly due to the incompetence of that province's chief—lack of political and military savvy.

I drove right by a vc flank the other day unawares. Funny war. Wish I had time to go into it at length.

ivs headquarters in Washington attempted to allay the concerns of families back home. John Hughes wrote on September 11, 1964:

You are all aware of the disturbing headlines which have crowded the pages of the newspapers in recent weeks.

On previous occasions we have passed along to you any current, special information we receive concerning the situation in Vietnam. At this time, we have no "inside reports" on what is happening that would point the way to the future course of events. We do want you to know, however, that Don Luce, our Chief-of-Party, keeps us closely apprised of the welfare of the team. He is in touch with us by cable and telephone whenever he feels there is cause for anxiety over any incident or development.

In the past, ivs team members have avoided involvement in hostilities by being careful and prudent, by keeping up on intelligence reports about insecure areas, and simply not traveling where there might be trouble. The military is always informed as to their whereabouts and our Vietnamese friends keep them alerted to what is going on. The absence of incidents attests to the wise course our leadership staff and individual team members have followed. Carl Stockton, who was recently appointed Education Team Leader, says, "I doubt that the increased danger we are facing is much more than say, driving down the freeways or being in Jackson, Mississippi, Kansas City, Missouri, or New York City."

We are proud of every member of the Vietnam team for the courage and steadfastness they have continued to display in the face of repeated periods of tension, insecurity, and instability. Perhaps this is a time when IVS can render its greatest service to the people and government of Vietnam — by providing an element of stability and direction, especially to the restless youth of the country.

As it was recently expressed by the Deputy Education Chief of USOM, speaking of the contribution of the American presence in Vietnam: "No matter what happens politically in the country, the things we have worked for cannot be taken away: the schools, the books, the teachers — and most important, the challenged and cultivated minds of the people we have reached. These cannot be erased overnight by political changes."

The role as trusted friends and advisers that IVSers have made for themselves among the Vietnamese people has not gone unnoticed. The recently resigned Ambassador, Henry Cabot Lodge, has spoken with admiration of the strong impression IVSers have made in going about their tasks with quiet competence and understanding.

We hope you find some satisfaction and reassurance in reflecting on the importance of the task your sons and daughters are carrying out in the struggle for human welfare and stability in Vietnam.

Pete finally bought his motorcycle. The Honda's previous owner was "not exactly an old school-marm" but had treated it well. It had a bit of a kick to it.

During my demonstration ride, I was flipped off the tail end, right in the middle of a busy traffic circle, as the owner was demonstrating its excellent decelerating and accelerating performance characteristics, dashing into a solid phalanx of automobiles, which magically opened up. I felt like Moses at the Red Sea, or something, when suddenly I found myself dumped on my stern. I've bought insurance, and a helmet is on its way.

He was still grappling with his future. He might apply for a six-month job as a USOM provincial representative or assistant prov rep, make some money, and build up his résumé for a future position in government. He might take a three-month vacation back home, maybe even get married. Or he might stick it out in Vietnam for another six months and then come home, get married, and go to grad school. He and Sue had all but quit communicating, while Margo was writing more and more. "I'm getting sweeter and sweeter toward the latter," he admitted, "although not as yet foaming around the mouth."

Work was going well enough, but lately he had soured on the character of the Vietnamese. Someone had broken into the house and stolen fifty dollars that had been entrusted to him. Larry had also been robbed. Even so, Pete believed he was starting to get somewhere with the local youth.

It was the rainy season again. Phan Rang had not seen sunshine in two weeks. The rainfall was slow and steady, unlike up north, where everything was under water. People just sat on their roofs until their houses washed away and they drowned. It was terrible.

Could things in Vietnam get any worse?

NINE

Trip to Vietnam

Although by now many years have passed since the day I was held for questioning in Vietnam, I can still picture the policemen in the small room where eight of us sat crowded around a desk.

One of them was round faced and wide eyed, like a Cambodian friend of mine back home in California. Another, the highest ranking of the three, had a thin face and narrow eyes. I thought I would never forget any of them, but time has erased the third man's visage from my memory.

The policeman with viper's eyes meticulously copied the information from my passport and visa onto a sheet of paper, pressing through several thicknesses of paper and carbon paper. Likewise, he copied the information about three of my four American companions.

My fourth companion, Don Luce, would eventually minimize the seriousness of our predicament, but his ashen face could not disguise that we were in trouble. We had trespassed by stopping in a hamlet and asking questions about people who were there thirty years ago. We had left Mr. Phuong, our government-assigned guide, behind in Nha Trang. Don had left his passport and visa in his hotel room there. No one in the group we had left behind knew where we were.

Curious children reached their arms toward us through the bars on the window. Of the five of us Americans, I was the only one who understood no Vietnamese. Later, someone said a few of the women had asked the officials why they were arresting us. Why not just let us go?

Unbeknownst to us, the village of Ho Diem had been a Catholic and anti-Communist stronghold during the "American War." Some of the women guessed I was a nun. Before leaving for Vietnam, I had cut my hair short.

The height of our ill treatment, Don would say in retrospect, was the top man's refusal to allow Mike Fairley to use the bathroom. I thought being detained and interrogated for hours and paying a hundred-dollar "fine" the next day in exchange for my freedom and documents was worse. Chuck Cable, another former IVSer, smoldered when officials said we could not visit the Peter Hunting Memorial Library, which he had helped build, and in fact could not stop in Phan Rang at all.

Our trouble had begun that morning when Mr. Phuong assured the five of us that we could deviate from the group itinerary. While we visited Phan Rang and Ba Ngoi—places we had special reasons for wanting to see—the others would remain in Nha Trang, along with Mr. Phuong. He had developed a crush on a woman in our group and wanted to spend the day with her at the beach. He had said it would be all right to go without him.

Don was a known friend of the Vietnamese people. He spoke the language fluently. Our Vietnamese driver would be with us. What could go wrong?

It wasn't illegal for Americans to travel to Vietnam in 1991, but it wasn't easy. A Treasury Department ruling of 1988 permitted U.S. citizens to visit Vietnam with some restrictions. Financial transactions were limited to paying for things related to travel, such as meals, hotel rooms, and transportation between cities. Personal items could be purchased for use and consumption in Vietnam, but only goods whose value was one hundred dollars or less could be brought home, and only if they were for personal use and not resale. The ruling forbade charging purchases to a credit card. It was a moot point. Most merchants accepted cash only.

The United States and Vietnam were four years away from restoring diplomatic relations. There was no American ambassador in Hanoi yet and no consulate in Saigon, whose name had been changed to Ho Chi Minh City.

Under the Trading with the Enemy Act, placing a telephone call from the United States to Vietnam was not permitted. To get a visa for Vietnam, American citizens had to go to another country, such as Thailand or Malaysia.

The Sonoma County Health Department recommended a formidable list of immunizations, including those for cholera, typhoid, hepatitis, and plague. A measles, mumps, and rubella vaccine and a tetanus booster, along with a regimen of antimalaria pills, were strongly advised.

Nevertheless, when Don wrote to me early in 1990 that he was organizing an educational trip to Vietnam, primarily for former IVSers, I said I would go. Vietnam was tugging on me.

"Look at the bomb craters," someone in our group of eighteen exclaimed as the Thai Airways plane descended over Hanoi. The pits looked large enough to warrant identification on a city map. Tears ran down my cheeks as I stared out the window. A thousand miles of crying lay ahead.

Early in 1990 I began considering in what way, come November, I might observe my fortieth birthday and, two days later, the twenty-fifth anniversary of Pete's death. The question occurred to me during Epiphany, the time of year associated with enlightenment. More than remembering Pete's death, I wanted to acknowledge his influence on my life.

Don's letter said the tour would leave in August. We would visit schools and attend briefings on development and U.S.–Vietnam relations. Don would meet us there. He was going in advance as an interpreter for an American public health association.

One night, with the trip a month away, I dreamed I was in Vietnam with Don and Pete. The following day, I received a letter from Don saying he had postponed the trip until January 1991. Things were more tense in Vietnam than usual, he explained, owing to political changes in Eastern Europe and sensitive negotiations over Cambodia. No problem, I replied. I'd go in January.

For my birthday that year, I received a travel alarm clock and two drain covers meant to prevent roaches from crawling up the pipes and into my hotel room. The next day, Veterans' Day, I sowed wildflowers in a community peace garden. On November 12, the anniversary of Pete's death, I ate a chocolate éclair, one of his favorite desserts.

Getting the immunizations for my trip proved harder than I expected. A war with Iraq was looming, and American soldiers being deployed to the Persian Gulf had top priority for medicines. The shot hardest to come by was for the plague. Eventually I skipped it. My doctor preferred not to treat a case of the plague but said ordinary antibiotics would suffice if he had to.

The more significant preparation for my trip was emotional. I didn't do it well.

Sometime that summer, I told my sisters that I was planning to go to Vietnam. Holly and I spoke by phone about it, and afterward she wrote to me. She had been going over our conversation in her mind ever since.

She explained that she had been feeling frustrated and anxious about our parents, who were declining mentally and physically. She and Cis, who both lived much closer to them than I did, were intervening in one crisis after another. Holly had just watched a television program about Vietnam before our phone call. Thoughts of Pete had been on the surface, she said.

Her feelings about him were complicated. She had repressed a good deal of the period following his death. She found herself drawn to male friends who invariably turned out to have been born the same year as Pete. "It is as though I am still trying at times to fill the hole he left," she said. "I think sometimes that time hasn't filled the hole, but merely reshaped it."

She missed the brother who would have been a marvelous uncle to her three children, and who would have answered her questions about growing up and rebelling against her parents. She felt deprived of tangible evidence of his life. "Mom's hoarding, or privacy, grief, or whatever cut us off from not only a healthy family grief—that sounds strange, doesn't it—but also from a 'normal' cycle of individual grief," she said. "The suppression of even the utterance of his name for so many years enshrined him rather than loosening the unhealthy hold his death had on all of us." Lamentably, Pete had left "so few 'documents' in his legacy to his little sisters."

And now I was going to Vietnam. I had kept to myself what I was learning about Pete, and about meeting his former teammates and corresponding with them. Holly felt excluded: "It was like being on the outside again, unable to get close, to get comfort, to understand better the facts and feelings of an experience that altered all our lives." If she had been in my position, she said, she would have told me, and Cis, and maybe our parents. She reassured me that I had always been one of the most significant people in her life and that she loved me. She was happy I was going to Vietnam. She hoped I would share with her my impressions when I returned. She hoped I would write about them someday.

I'm ashamed to admit that I balked at Holly's letter. It was honest, gentle, and reasonable, but I felt the old discomfort of being confronted with someone's intense emotion. I emphatically did not want that emotion foisted upon me. Still reenacting my fifteen-year-old self's apprehension of my mother, I could not empathize even with the sister I was so close to. I could not let down my guard. I wanted distance.

I did not handle all of my trip preparations as badly.

My daughter, May, had heard me talk about Vietnam and the uncle she had never known. She had also heard me wake in the night from a dream about him. Before I left for Vietnam, I dreamed that Pete's body was being taken to a mortuary. I was holding a slip of paper with the time and cause of his death. I begged the mortician not to take him away. My crying woke my husband and then my daughter before it woke me. She came into our bedroom and asked, "What's wrong, Mommy?"

With my somewhat arch feminist leanings, I had held off buying May a Barbie doll. Playing at the houses of her friends, whose mothers were more accepting of Barbies than I, she loved to dress the dolls. When I sensed that she was uneasy about my going away, I thought I should buy a present that she could look forward to opening when I left. There was nothing she wanted more than a Barbie doll, so I promised her one.

I asked her first-grade teacher if I could bring a map of Vietnam to her classroom and talk about my trip. I thought it might help May if Mrs. Olrich and her students occasionally looked at the map and talked about where May's mom was that day. She agreed to do everything I asked.

On the first page of a notebook I bought to take along, I wrote down May's measurements. Don had said that his partner, Mark, knew of a good shop for kimonos, and I planned to buy one, or an *ao dai*, and matching shoes for my daughter. In my notebook, I outlined her bare foot—seven inches long from heel to big toe—as she stood on one leg, balancing with her hand on my shoulder.

"How much longer will it be dark?" May called out from the back seat. She had opened her present and was straining to see the shoes and other accessories that came with her Barbie doll. We had left home early. In another fifteen minutes it would be light and we would be in San Francisco.

It was New Year's Day, 1991. I was flying to Seattle, where I would meet up with the others in Don's group. Everything went fine until I landed at Sea-Tac

Airport but my suitcase didn't. This was the first sign that my trip to Vietnam would be about emotional baggage.

Calls to the airline produced no results. Because of the national holiday they were short-staffed. Stores in Seattle were closed, but that evening, I got a ride to a Safeway and bought aspirin, Pepto Bismol, soap, band-aids, and a razor. If worse came to worst, I could pick up new clothing in Thailand. I was more worried than I knew. I didn't sleep on the long flight to Tokyo.

In Bangkok, I watched my traveling companions pull their suitcases off the carousel. When mine didn't arrive, an airline employee led me to a lost-luggage room the size of a high school gymnasium. Suitcases covered the floor and I surveyed them hopelessly. Just as I was catching up with my group on their way out of the terminal, there was my suitcase off to the side on the floor.

I walked outside into the humid night. Under a streetlight a few yards away, a middle-aged, brown-haired, gray-eyed Don and his dark-haired, slender Mark were greeting everyone. Don and I shook hands and exchanged a look that said we had a lot to talk about.

Only three members of the group had been IVS volunteers. Some were with universities or humanitarian groups. One couple was looking for soldiers who had gone missing in action. Chuck Whalen was a retired U.S. congressman from Ohio who sponsored a bill that had cut funding of the war. Darlene Cook Fairley, who would later be elected a Washington state senator, had worked as a medic with Catholic Relief Services in Vietnam. Her husband, Mike, was an IVS alumnus.

We arrived at our hotel in Bangkok to find scaffolding covering the entrance. A couple of prostitutes slouched near the lobby. The air conditioning was off. It was good preparation for Vietnam, Don told us.

I shared a room with one of the other single women. In the morning, the high-frequency hum of a mosquito awoke me, or was it the hammering? Carol and I opened the curtains to behold a small jungle, complete with calling birds and scampering monkeys. It was early and the palm trees were black. When the sun rose, their bark turned to dusty green.

We went sightseeing in groups of four and five. Through a fence, we peered at the U.S. Embassy's private tennis courts, saw the vast produce market on the river by boat, ogled enviously the luxurious Oriental Hotel, and toured the Temple of the Golden Buddha. Don and Mark, meanwhile, spent the day filling out forms to obtain our visas for Vietnam. That evening, they invited us to visit the red-light district with a friend from Empower, an organization whose volunteers rehabilitate sex workers. The Vietnam War had created an enormous sex trade in Thailand, Don told us. Some in our group went with him, while jet-lagged others like me crashed after dinner.

Tomorrow, Hanoi.

We flew out of Bangkok in two shifts. The first group's reception was less than hospitable. Airport officials in Hanoi informed Linda James that she did not have the right travel documents. She was sent to wait on a bench and was ruing her decision to come to Vietnam when Mr. Phuong elbowed his way past the authorities, took her in hand, and herded the group into a van. [1]

Things went easier for the rest of us. The grosgrain ribbons I had tied on my bag for identification were gone and the airport personnel were on edge, but I breezed through customs.

We registered at an old French colonial hotel whose walls badly needed a coat of paint. I settled into my room. A half-used bar of soap and an orange comb with a few strands of black hair lay on the sink. I covered the drain on the bathroom floor. An empty light fixture dangled from the ceiling. I lowered the mosquito net over the bed.

Outside, a motorcycle backfired. I thought back to the summer when Pete was home for the last time, in 1965. The same sound had sent him diving to the street. Afterward, my mother laughed when she told the story. It seemed odd that a dramatic illustration of the danger he lived with in Vietnam struck her as funny.

Car horns honked, but bicycles far outnumbered automobiles. I met up with a few of our group and we ambled down a shady street. January was the wedding season, and we took pictures of car windshields covered with brightly colored crepe paper streamers. Driving seemed unsafe but the cars looked festive.

I saw my first water buffalo on a city street. I was surprised that its hide was not tough looking, like that of a rhinoceros, but soft and mink brown, and that it moved gracefully.

Back in my hotel room, I climbed into the nest I had made. I pulled close a flashlight, book, alarm clock, and heaps of Kleenex for the head cold I had picked up. For some reason, I felt afraid.

I wasn't as well informed as others in the group. Some had learned Vietnamese as IVSers. Some had picked up key words and phrases before our trip. I found that I had no ear at all for the language. Without cognates, which were common in the Romance languages I had studied, I could find no way in.

After a couple of days, I started feeling homesick. A good friend who was a nurse and hospice director had warned me before I left home that I might feel more emotional than usual. A wound that wasn't completely cleaned out would heal only superficially, she had told me. Over time it would fester. She said I was going to the source of a deep wound, and it would hurt to open it. "Don't be surprised if you feel a little crazy at times," she had said.

I suspected the cold medicines I was taking were the cause, but I began feeling weepy. My fellow travelers seemed to accept my condition better than I did. It must have been obvious to them that journeying to a land where one's sibling had been killed would be difficult. But in my family we had been expected to bear up, so I felt self-conscious and embarrassed to be letting loose — which actually amounted only to tears occasionally rolling down my cheeks.

One day we traveled to a Hmong village far from Hanoi by way of the winding road to Dien Bien Phu, where in 1954 the Vietminh dealt the decisive blow to French colonial control of Vietnam. The road into the mountains took us past an old French tank and a monument to the Vietnamese soldier who had disabled it with a grenade. When we got to the village, children crowded around us. Tom, a professor from New York, had brought a box of crayons and doled them out one per child. Chuck Whalen tried threshing rice by hand with a low-tech bucket-and-rope system.

That night, we slept in thatched-roof houses built on stilts. The rooms smelled strongly of lacquer, as if our lodging had been readied hastily. Beyond the houses, the peridot rice fields and distant blue-gray mountains beneath a paler gray sky composed a picture of utmost serenity.

We returned to Hanoi for a briefing with the deputy foreign minister. The meeting room was furnished but the decor was jarring. The floor was covered with a large red and gold carpet. The chairs were upholstered in orange velvet and topped with white antimacassars. Blue curtains puddled twelve inches deep or more onto the floor. A cabinet at one end of the room was missing half its drawer pulls. Two immense, exquisite floral arrangements almost harmonized the scene.

We were seated in a U around a table. Chuck Whalen, the ranking member of our group, sat at the closed end beside the deputy minister, who had strikingly long ears. He told us that Vietnam was eager to improve its relationship with our country. After the meeting, he shook everyone's hand.

The following day we saw the modest home where Ho Chi Minh had lived. Security police watched us carefully. As the group moved along, I lagged behind to find a better camera angle on the house. A young man in uniform gestured to me, apparently urging me to catch up with the others. Then his unfriendly expression broke and he asked, "Are you American?" Usually, Vietnamese people thought we were *Lien Xo*—Russian. I nodded. He said earnestly, "I love Americans."

Security was stricter when we arrived at Ho Chi Minh's tomb. We were instructed to leave our purses and all other belongings, except for our camera equipment, in the van. Mr. Phuong then collected our cameras, which we were not allowed to use. We were forbidden from talking. We queued up in pairs and marched in silence up the steps of the tomb, around corners, and into the room where Ho's body lies. He was lit in an unearthly yellowish white, neither smiling nor frowning.

A guard pointed abruptly to a man with us, ordering him to remove his hat. With a swat, a woman was instructed to take her hands out of her pockets. They wanted more than reverence from us; they meant to exact obeisance. I couldn't help thinking how different is the experience of visiting the Lincoln Memorial, a tribute to freedom in an atmosphere of freedom.

We were also watched closely when we visited a museum. A man in a black jacket followed us into every room, studying our reactions to the anti-American propaganda.

That evening, I lay down on my bed and watched a gecko on the wall. If this were a hotel in the United States, I thought, you would ask yourself how you had arrived at such a sorry state as to be staying in a place so shabby. Here, you just said, "This is Vietnam." Mark had told us in Bangkok that we wouldn't be staying in anything less than a Holiday Inn. What holiday? Where?

Linda had seen a dog butchered the day before. Darlene, who had worked in Vietnam in the 1960s, had once been fed a rat. Grotesquely large snails had been brought to our lunch table. The meat was ingeniously wrapped with a strip of green onion, so that with one little pull it slipped out easily. Still, it was so foreign. It was all so foreign.

Negativity had, I knew, stolen into my attitude. I had a bad cold, didn't like being stared at, and was homesick. The high point of my trip, visiting Phan Rang, where my brother had lived, was several days away. We had not received official permission yet to go there.

What was bothering me was not really the run-down hotel or the food or the strangeness of Vietnam, but the fact that I was in a country that for years I had associated with death. My brother had believed in the future of Vietnam. The country I saw was in tatters. I wanted to find something to love about this place, something to make it all right that Pete's life had ended here. The countryside and parts of Hanoi were lovely. For the rest, I sympathized with the Vietnamese, working so hard to advance, but the place didn't speak to me.

On our last morning in Hanoi, we took strong coffee with sweetened condensed milk and ate anise-seeded baguettes. Mr. Phuong showed us the monument to the defenders of Hanoi who shot down then-Lieutenant John McCain's airplane. Tom, the professor in our group, said that when the North Vietnamese found out they had captured the son of the admiral in command of the U.S. Pacific Fleet, they considered their prisoner a real prize. We were in central Hanoi beside a lake.

I asked Mr. Phuong to tell us more about Senator McCain's capture. He seemed reluctant, so I pressed him. McCain had parachuted into the lake, he said. The people all around were excited and got into their boats "to go out for him." Looking at where it had happened, I tried to imagine how terrifying that sight must have been for McCain. Seeing the look on my face, Mr. Phuong assured me, "He was a good swimmer." But hadn't he been injured? I asked. "Oh, no," he said, smiling. I persisted: "How deep is the lake?" "Only one and a half meters deep, and very muddy," he said dismissively.

In fact, McCain suffered two broken arms and a broken leg when he ejected from his aircraft. Then, as a prisoner of war in the Hanoi "Hilton," which we would visit next, he was held in solitary confinement, beaten, and tortured.

We learned that McCain had recently been in Hanoi to discuss normalizing U.S.–Vietnam relations. When he visited the prison and asked to see his old cell, he is said to have told the Vietnamese with him, "Just don't close the door."

Apart from my own emotions, the impending Persian Gulf War added a sustained bass note while we traveled in Vietnam.

The preceding August, Saddam Hussein had sent Iraqi troops into Kuwait. The United Nations responded by issuing an ultimatum to withdraw the occupying forces. UN Secretary General Perez de Cuellar traveled to Baghdad to meet personally with Saddam, and U.S. Secretary of State James Baker went to Geneva for talks with the Iraqi foreign minister. When the talks broke down, Baker went to Saudi Arabia to discuss U.S. plans for war in the event that negotiations failed altogether.

The UN Security Council passed a resolution authorizing the use of force. Iraq was given a deadline of January 15 to leave Kuwait. After that date, UN member states could use all necessary means to force compliance with the resolution.

When our group left for Asia, many Americans still hoped that Saddam Hussein would back down. War was possible but not inevitable, it was believed.

One member of our group had brought along a shortwave radio. He followed the news and kept us informed of developments.

As efforts to avert war seemed less promising with each day, our mealtime conversations turned to speculation about what might happen next. We sought Chuck Whalen's opinion as Congress debated authorizing President George H. W. Bush to use force. So far from home, it was hard to gauge the situation based on the scant news we had.

With the rest of the waiting world, we counted down the days as the January 15 deadline approached. In the meantime, we asked questions: Was this a conflict over oil? Did the president have constitutional authority to send U.S. combat forces to Iraq without Congress's having declared war? Before our very eyes we could see the effects of isolating a country economically from most of the world; would it not be wiser to try economic sanctions before going to war? We wondered whether, if war broke out, we could be stranded in Vietnam for a while.

On January 12, Congress passed a resolution giving President Bush the authority to use force. Under General Norman Schwarzkopf, who had served in Vietnam, American forces were readied for Operation Desert Storm.

We boarded an old train for the eighteen-hour trip south to Hue. The window of the compartment I shared with two other women had a bullet hole and a large crack like a spider web.

The old train clattered noisily on the tracks. To pass the hours, we sang pop tunes and stood in the corridor dangling our arms out the windows to catch the breeze. In the middle of the night, the train screeched to a stop. We were deep in the countryside and there was no train depot. From out of the darkness, men, women, and children ran toward our car, hawking handicrafts and warm sodas.

In the morning, we pulled into Hue after a mostly sleepless night. In the hotel, I went straight upstairs to the room Linda and I would share. I lay down, trying to resist sleep because Linda would be coming up soon and I didn't know if she had a key. A knock on the door awoke me. I opened it to find a prostitute, looking as surprised as I was. Someone—a man in our group, if what one of the women with us later said was true—had mistakenly told her to come to the wrong floor. He was evidently unaware that the stories were numbered differently here than in the United States.

I lay down again, but I couldn't relax because of a disturbing noise outside. Someone was crying, and in the cry I heard fear. The drapes had been closed when I let myself in, and I had kept them closed in anticipation of a nap. The heavy fabric, backlit by the midday sunshine, was the color of blood. As I listened to the god-awful sound beneath the window, I began to cry.

There was a second knock on the door. I opened it to find my cheerful roommate standing in the hall. Linda swept into the room and flung her suitcase onto the other bed. Moving toward the crying sound, she asked, "What's that?" Then, with a single sweeping motion, she parted the drapes to reveal the source of the crying. Just beneath our window was a goat confined to a small pen. In her trap outside the hotel kitchen, she would soon be slaughtered for someone's meal. Mine?

Pity and sadness welled up in me as I realized that the goat's death was inevitable. In that moment, I felt as trapped as she. I had come to the place where I must confront my brother's death just as surely as she must face the knife. I couldn't save her and I couldn't save Pete.

After lunch, we took a cruise down the Perfume River. Stepping out of the boat at the Thien Mu Pagoda, we were greeted by the fragrance of frangipane flowers. An old Austin sedan—the car that the Buddhist monk drove to Saigon in June 1963 before immolating himself—was parked in a bay. A monk strolled on the grounds with us. Tom asked him if he communicated with Buddhists in other countries—meaning, did the government permit it. "Yes," he said, "but only with the sounds in our minds."

We left Hue in a private van and headed south on Highway 1. Not far from Quang Ngai City we turned onto increasingly narrow unpaved roads. It was hot when we arrived at My Lai. The place where hundreds of men, women, and children were massacred was lush and still. In contrast to the near hush of the clearing where once a mass grave had been dug, photographs in a museum shouted the horror of that day in March 1968 when American soldiers opened fire on Vietnamese civilians. It was also an American, a helicopter pilot named Hugh Thompson, who heroically set his chopper down in the midst of the melee, forcing his fellow soldiers to stop their killing spree.

An angular, Soviet-looking monument dominated the site. A guide urged us to place sticks of incense on a memorial. Right or wrong, her instruction did not go over well with some in our group. The remorse and shame among us were palpable, but feeling manipulated, not everyone wanted to participate in the ritual. Others lit their incense, hoping that the watchful eyes following us would see that Americans were penitent.

The long-awaited day arrived. Mr. Phuong cleared five of us—Don, Chuck Cable, Darlene, Mike, and me—to visit Phan Rang and Ba Ngoi. We would miss sightseeing in Nha Trang and sunbathing on its white-sand crescent beach, but we were eager to go to Ninh Thuan Province.

We set out on Highway 1 in the morning sunshine. We were about to encounter trouble, but in our elevated mood we did not guess what lay in store for five freewheeling Americans breaking away from their official itinerary.

In northern Vietnam, the weather had been cold and damp. Here the air was warm and dry, softened by a gentle wind from the South China Sea. My cold was gone and I felt healthy and happy. Now the same breeze that used to brush Pete's cheek was brushing mine.

I knew he would have traveled this road. Separated from him by so many years, I now felt close to him and his life here. I could almost imagine him pulling up alongside our van in his jeep.

We stopped in the town of Ba Ngoi, near Cam Ranh Bay, where during the war there had been airfields and a large U.S. navy base. Mike and Darlene had been married at a villa here. They had brought their wedding photo and wanted to have a new picture taken at the house. We climbed out of the van and immediately were surrounded by children.

Slowly we made our way up the sandy street. Darlene and Mike spotted the villa. We were admiring the architecture when a man came out of the building and walked over to us. He and Don exchanged a few words. Then Don said we should follow him. "We are invited to a meeting," he said.

In Vietnam, I would soon learn, you don't decline such an "invitation." It means that you are being asked to explain yourself.

How could we have known that the Communist Party was having a regional meeting that day in that villa? The officials around the table where we all drank tea wondered. We wondered at the absurdity of our timing.

In Vietnamese, Don explained what we were doing there. His tone and facial expression clearly communicated, "You see, it's all very innocent." Behind the courteous facade of our hosts was suspicion, equally clearly communicated.

Thirty minutes later, Darlene and Mike were showing the officials photographs of themselves on the terrace in wedding attire. After polite good-byes and much smiling, we returned to our vehicle and were on the road again. We congratulated ourselves for having wriggled free of a ticklish situation. Don explained to me that the smiling faces of the party officials had masked nervousness and that Vietnamese people often smile when they are uncomfortable.

Back on Highway 1, we could see a hamlet out our left window. Chuck, who had brought along a lot of photographs from his ivs years and was shuffling through them, thought the hamlet was where his former cook had lived. He wanted to stop and look her up.

I was impatient to get to Phan Rang and mindful that our last stop had not gone as expected. On the other hand, Chuck had lived in Vietnam and I had not. This was his first trip back since he had left in 1968. When would he have this chance again?

We all agreed to stop. We pulled into Ho Diem. An enormous pig waddled alongside a wall.

As we climbed out of the van, we again magnetized curious children. American tourists were rare in Vietnam in 1991, especially in the countryside. Americans who spoke Vietnamese were even more rare.

Chuck asked some adults about his cook while Don looked for someone who remembered an American who built a windmill. This was the man's sister, he said, indicating me. A young mother came over and patted my arm, smiling and looking into my eyes. She told Don that two Americans had worked in the hamlet when she was a little girl—a black-skinned man and a tall man with a long face. We knew she was describing Chuck Fields and Pete. A lump rose in my throat.

We had been in Ho Diem only a few minutes when a middle-aged man invited us to tea. It would have been rude to refuse his hospitality. I knew this meant we would not be leaving any time soon. We entered a small house with a dirt floor. Someone brought us tea and Don explained who we were. Children and adults at the door and window jockeyed for position to see us.

Time passed slowly, but finally Don said we would leave. We thanked our host and made our way back to the van. Chuck, the driver, and I took our seats. Darlene and Mike were getting in when a man ran toward us waving his arms. The gesture was not friendly.

Someone was suspicious of the five Americans who had stopped unannounced, asking questions about the days before the Communist victory. Security had been alerted. We were invited to a meeting.

We were led into a small room with a desk and one chair. After some scrambling, chairs were brought in for all of us. For the second time that day, Don explained that it was all very innocent. This time, he was less convincing.

I was afraid when I saw the color drain from his face. *They got Pete and they're going to get me*, I thought irrationally. Le Ly Hayslip's account of her girlhood in South Vietnam came to mind. Her captors had painted her legs with honey to attract stinging ants.

At least two hours passed while Don answered questions and the man in charge hand-copied the information from our passports and visas. Finally we were told that we could return to our group. We could not take our travel documents, however. For those, we would have to come back in the morning. Authorities at a higher level would decide what to do next. We would return to Nha Trang under escort. We would not go to Phan Rang.

As we headed north, I was worried but also relieved. Mostly, I was disappointed. This was the day for which I had come to Vietnam. But now would I not see the city where Pete had lived? Had I come on this trip for nothing?

I seized the opportunity to learn something about my brother. Turning to

Don, I said I had a hard question for him: What happened the day Pete was killed?

Don had been walking home to the IVS house in Saigon when someone came running toward him. He knew immediately by the look on the man's face that something terrible had happened. After the initial shock, he went into his room and closed the door. To this day he could not remember anything about the next hours. He had completely blocked it out. All he knew was that he wanted to be alone. He didn't want to have anything to do with anyone.

I asked if he had identified Pete's body.

No, he said, but Pete was carrying a lot of identification. I took this to mean that Pete could not be recognized from the multiple gunshot wounds to his head.

His body was flown to Saigon, Don continued. At that time, there were already frequent flights bringing in casualties. Bodies were put into refrigeration until they were flown home.

He said that because Pete had been so dedicated, after his death the team leaders, including himself, were hard on volunteers if they treated their service "as some kind of lark in an exotic place."

When we arrived back at our hotel, a happy, suntanned bunch were there to greet us and hear about our great day. When they learned how things had turned out, they shared our disappointment. Chuck and I took a long walk on the beach and grumbled. By dinnertime, I was angry. Sitting beside me, Tom said how sorry he was that I didn't get to see the library. I spouted off, "Why did he come here, anyway? To these people?"

In the morning, a military escort came to the hotel for us. Our entire group followed them to a meeting with uniformed officers. While we offenders sat through Mr. Phuong's explanation and Don's apology, the rest of the group waited in the van. An hour later we were informed that we would have to go to Phan Thiet, where others would decide what to do about us. Soon we were on the road again, still under escort and with no passports or visas.

The officials had reiterated that we could not stop in Phan Rang. As we came to the edge of the town, someone in the back of the van called out, "I have to go to the bathroom!" Someone else chimed in, "So do I!" Our driver had no choice but to stop. He pulled over at a café.

A woman came forward from the back of the bus. As she passed me, she leaned down and said quietly, "Jill, *go*." The bathroom request had been a ploy to force our driver to stop so I could set foot in the town Pete had called home. I stepped into the street. Seeing the faces, I wondered if any of these people had known my brother. Chuck Cable pointed in the direction of the library, but we couldn't see it. Five minutes later, we were on the road again.

When we reached Phan Thiet, the capital city of Binh Thuan Province, Mr. Phuong left Don, Mike, Darlene, Chuck, and me in one room while he spoke with authorities in another room. Eventually he came out with the verdict. "They are going to let you go," he said, "but it will be expensive." They wanted one hundred dollars U.S. from each of us. My four companions, who were not only Vietnam hands but had lived there on subsistence wages, were indignant at the outrageous fine. I didn't see that we had a choice. For a hundred dollars, I was only too happy to get my travel documents and freedom back. Each of us also had to sign a confession. Don felt so bad that I had missed seeing both Pete's windmills and the library that he insisted on reimbursing me.

Back on the bus, I asked him what I had just signed. He told me that the top line said "From the Office of Spies." He must have been joking, because I have since had the document translated by someone who interpreted the same words as "From the Office of the Police Chief." It stated that we had broken the law by venturing where we did not have permission to go.

We were in Ho Chi Minh City (which many Vietnamese still call Saigon when Americans are not nearby) on the night of January 16. A group of Australians we met in our hotel, the Majestic, told us that President Bush's threats had worked and Saddam Hussein had backed down. There would be no war. We went to bed relieved.

Unfortunately, the Australians were wrong. In the early-morning hours of January 17, Operation Desert Storm began, with massive air strikes and missile attacks on Iraq and Kuwait. It was ironic to hear the news over breakfast in this country where so many had once fought and died. Hearing that our nation was again at war, we just shook our heads.

My trip had been emotionally demanding and disappointing in some ways, but it also had been cathartic. Vietnam was no longer a legend. It was real to me. It would never again be just a place of death. As time passed, I grew more curious about Pete's life there, not just how he had died.

Two years after my fortieth birthday and the twenty-fifth anniversary of Pete's death, both of which had inspired my trip to Vietnam, I wrote about the journey in a newspaper column.

I had been able to leave my brother in Vietnam, I said. I had a new perspective, a newfound authority over my own life. When I celebrated my birthday, I didn't feel the twinge of sadness I used to. I thought of Pete, but on reflection I felt that, if he had to die, at least it had happened in the birthday season.[2]

TEN

"A Promise Is a Promise"

I n early November 1964, a deadly typhoon struck three northern provinces in South Vietnam. Pete was transferred temporarily to one of them, Quang Ngai, to assist with flood relief. His assignment was to coordinate the volunteer efforts of Vietnamese youth.

He rode his motorcycle as far as Nha Trang to catch a flight to the disaster area. As he boarded the Air Force C-123, he learned that Vietcong had surrounded the city. He hadn't noticed as he drove through town.

Hoping his letters didn't sound too melodramatic, he admitted to Margo that at times he got carried away with the life he was leading, "being such a young man and so impressionable, as we all are in our early years. Last Saturday, for instance, I was actually shot at."

Pete was a passenger in a cargo plane flying at an altitude of seven hundred feet when it was fired upon from the ground. "There we were, buzzing along the coast of Quang Ngai when there were two 'thwack' noises which roused me out of a peaceful slumber," he wrote. "Sounded like a hammer dropping on a piece of glass, but without the tinkle of flying glass, that was quickly followed by ricocheting noises right out of a cowboy thriller." Pete reported that, except for a Vietnamese colonel, who turned gray, he and all the other passengers grinned at each other and looked out the window. The insurgents in Quang Ngai were much more audacious and desperate than those in Phan Rang. "Don't tell Mom, maybe," he told Cis. "Tell her I'm very careful."

A group of students from Hue University had shown up at Quang Ngai to help, wearing neckties, silk shirts, and pointed Italian shoes. They had brought no other clothing. Despite the disastrous conditions, they expected someone to offer them meals and lodging. After four days, when province administrators had not instituted a program they could carry out immediately, they complained bitterly. Instead of taking the initiative and organizing themselves to a task, they waited for the government to direct them.

Pete, along with one of his teammates and a student from Saigon, investigated the situation, discussed it among themselves, and in two days wrote up their recommendations for a student-run relief operation. The students would rebuild houses, teach preventive health practices, clean out wells, and perform other manual labor. It was not the work the students had in mind—they had hoped to hand out rice but were too late to assist with emergency food rationing; still, it was what the flood victims needed.

The other IVSer and the student flew to Saigon to muster support. Pete stayed in Quang Ngai to get things ready for the volunteers who would come up from Saigon University.

Meanwhile, the place was a mess. Mud covered everything. When you stepped into the muck, you could sink up to your knees. "Like as not, there's a dead cow at the bottom of the hole," Pete wrote. "People living in schools, eating dead animals, rats, dogs."

By December, the Saigon student corps had still not arrived. It had been the least rewarding month yet with IVS.

Before Pete left for Quang Ngai, another project involving Vietnamese youth had gone better. He wrote to Margo that he was in soaring spirits, despite all the natural disasters, political intrigues, and impending government crises.

CARE, the private international relief organization, had donated five bags of used clothing to a poor hamlet. Pete's job was to organize distribution of the garments, working alongside the people and ostensibly playing a subordinate role.

The assistant province chief marshaled the Boy Scouts and Girl Scouts to Ba Thap hamlet, where they sorted the clothes into family-size bundles. They went house to house and distributed 850 garments. It was cold and windy, and the people appreciated the clothing. The assistant chief listened to families who needed special help. He inquired about the overall needs of the hamlet. The people were impressed. They showed their appreciation by singing and dancing.

Some of the donated garments baffled the recipients:

We found an old castaway girdle that must have come from some mastodon of a D.A.R. [Daughters of the American Revolution] Old Guardian Society whip. Had a lot of fun with the hamlet chief joking about possible uses for the contraption. Finally decided he could sew up the bottom and use it as a bag when he goes to market.

Another wonderful old soul found some children's long underwear in her bundle—the type with the cloth socks built in, i.e., no holes for the feet, but a large hole midway up the garment. She was mystified as to what the garment was used for. Ah, a good day. We're beginning to make headway with a province youth program.

Pete observed his second Thanksgiving Day in Vietnam at Nha Trang with his teammates. Although there was no turkey, it was a wonderful holiday and a much needed rest from the "limp, do-nothing state of inactivity" in Quang Ngai. The team took an all-day cruise around an island and sunbathed, swam, and snorkeled. As he explored the coral reefs, he was enjoying himself immensely, until he realized he was not alone.

I met *the ugliest fish*, the most monstrous thing not having legs that I've ever seen. I can distinctly remember thinking to myself that this reversal of roles and elements was half-pleasing, half-terrifying, what with me being down in the soup, and no glass walls, and what-all; when suddenly this camouflaged fish moved—I don't know which creature was more startled. . . . [I] made a quick 90-degree vertical retreat, probably not unlike a Polaris launching, snorkel askew and flappers flipping. Was much relieved to regain the protection of the motor launch.

In a letter home, he wrote that he hoped his sisters had been happy and beautiful on their birthdays. He would be glad to get home and see how much the two younger ones had grown. Could it be true that Holly was learning to drive? And would we please have some family photos taken? "Only, please for Heaven's sake take them reasonably close up, and maybe give Mom"—who never drank alcohol—"a shot of vodka or something so everyone won't look so posed. Such medicine should not be necessary in Jill's case, I don't think."

My parents acceded to Pete's request, apart from my mother taking a drink. We went to a studio for the sitting. For Christmas, Mom sent Pete a photo of herself and Dad, and Holly and me.

She also sent a portrait of herself alone, even though she was superstitious about it. Her father, to whom she had been very close, had sent her a portrait of himself shortly before he died. I think my mother may have believed that her own death was imminent—not that sending a photograph to Pete would be the cause, but an omen. Not only did she tend toward hypochondria, worrying about the latest illness she read in the news, but my parents' marriage was under a strain. My father was teaching an attractive younger woman to fly. To this day, my sisters and I doubt that Dad had an affair. Mom was possessive, however. She lost a lot of weight and they argued bitterly. Unfortunately, their bedroom shared a thin wall with Holly's, and she couldn't avoid overhearing their angry exchanges.

Pete spent Christmas in Dalat with the IVS team. He returned to Phan Rang to find a box of presents from home. What he liked most was the family photograph. He was amazed to see how "chic and big" Holly and I were. "Really makes me homesick," he wrote to my mother. "I'll live, but I mean I'm anxious to get back. And you and Dad look so *young!* Everybody over here looks so old; it's a funny thing."

To Cis, he confided that Mom "must have a tapeworm or something to be so sickly and thin."

He added that "Holly seems to be built on a grand scale—don't tell anybody I said that. Jill looks to be a definite asset to a smart girls college and modeling." He hardly recognized us. "I'd hate to get shot over here without having a reunion first," he wrote, "to get to know you guys all over again. Pardon, I mean 'young ladies.'"

For almost six months, beginning in the autumn of 1964, Pete vacillated between staying in Vietnam and returning to the United States when his IVS contract ended the next summer. The instability of Vietnam, the likelihood of being drafted (his 2A deferment "in support of the national interest" was good until June 1965), and what he called his "woman quandary" added up to a difficult decision.

In January 1965 he wrote to Nana and Uncle Jim that he was considering extending his time with IVS as a team leader for two more years. He would be able to save a sizable portion of his salary. Could they recommend a stockbroker?

Vietnam might fall before those two years were up, however. In that case he would have no job with IVS. On the other hand, if the war went well and "we see the light and make progress" it would be worthwhile to stay and assist with the post-war recovery. It was better than getting drafted. In fact, he said he would enlist before he was drafted. Perhaps it would be good to get some military experience under his belt.

"The war over here is in a pretty bad way," he wrote on January 7. "Morale is pretty low, what with a virtual political vacuum of the last year." There was cause for hope, however, given that things hadn't gone down the drain altogether and the insurgents had not captured the Mekong Delta or grown beyond a certain level. He understood that some people, particularly in the States, seemed to have given up hope. "Perhaps that's because they never got to know the Vietnamese at first hand and therefore do not know their potential strength," he said.

A job with the U.S. Operations Mission would pay ten times his IVS salary, but he hadn't even considered USOM lately. "Even though the pay is good, the work's frustrating, too far from the grass roots, and USOM is in chaos," he wrote. "They don't have enough flexibility or freedom in their jobs, except the province reps. . . . IVS is the real answer in this country."

The better option if he stayed in Vietnam seemed to be extending his service with IVS. Then, sometime in 1965, he could take two months of home leave. Maybe he would get married then. He had been thinking about it a lot, he said. His wife could return to Vietnam with him and teach English or work in the hospital. The IVS job, which would mean a promotion, would pay upwards of three thousand dollars a year, with an additional three hundred dollars of living and clothing allowances, vacation pay, medical benefits, and insurance. He could help with Holly's college expenses, just two years away. "Enough pay to finance school and perhaps marriage," he thought aloud in a letter to Cis, "although on the latter point I run hot and cold, being in agreement with the principle to some extent, but undecided on the person."

His letters to Margo seemed to fish for her thoughts about his future options. He weighed returning to Vietnam as a team leader for eighteen months in the Delta. He thought about going to law school, if he could get into a good one. "That would make one of my old professors blink like a horned toad in a hailstorm," he said. Alternatively, "I just might retire if I jolly well feel like it. Get married. Have twenty kids. Sit in my long johns in front of the television set, drink beer, watch the ballgame, burp great resounding burps—if I'd not die of boredom inside of two days."

He said that Sue had called it quits when she learned he was considering staying in Vietnam. Margo did not. But neither did she give herself away. "One thing that would clear up a lot of questions would be to know how that girl Margo thinks," Pete wrote to us. "I suppose, just out of ignorance, that I could haul off and ask her, but some sixth sense tells me that this isn't the thing to do."

In January 1965 he wrote that he wanted to marry "a girl who isn't hell-bent on producing families, family planning, diet control, and all that other stuff." Margo had spirit and character. They could talk on the same level and about subjects of interest to both of them. "I wish I understood women!" he exclaimed. "What do my sister advisers have to say about all this, hey?"

His letters to Margo deepened. He shared with her the exhilaration of life in Vietnam, as when he described a motorcycle ride:

Everyone has his moments of glory over here. The other day as I was cycling to Nha Trang, the weather quite beautiful, I came upon a covey of doves eating rice upon the road. . . . They were flying and flapping all about me. A few of them were going in my direction, at my speed, and it was so beautiful to see them in flight, so close, against the evening sky. Ah well, so much for the moving prose style of exiles.

On another occasion, he suggested what they might do for fun if she were with him:

If you were over here we could go hunt up some pigeons eating rice grain on the road. You come up on them so fast that you're in among them just as they get off the ground and you can see them flying right there in front of you, a foot or two above or below, left or right, and sometimes it's very beautiful. As a rule, I'd say very few people ever get to see birds flying up close like that. But then, we Honda owners are an elite, blessed, and charmed bunch. Some pigeon watchers have gotten carried away, overcome by the beauty of it all. You're right in there with the flock of pigeons and it all looks so graceful and effortless.

Increasingly, he confided his disappointments as well as his joys. "I'm pretty glum," he told Margo one day. "Every time I meet a Vietnamese Special Forces military truck, the driver scares me to death with his games—chicken, sideswipe, race-you-to-the-one-way-bridge, etc."

There was only one problem: The young woman to whom he was growing closer was not just anyone. She was, as he said to a relative without naming her, "a very controversial person."

In a letter home in February 1965, he wrote, "The girl I've come to appreciate is a Catholic, and I know how the family feels about Catholics in general."

Pete would not have been the first in our family to marry someone who was not of the Protestant faith. One of my uncles had married a Catholic and my mother's cousin had a Jewish husband. The more significant issue was that "this Catholic happens to be none other than Margo B." Her last name, Pete continued, "puts Nana in a violent temper, and I also love Nana very much, too."

Margo's father and my grandfather had been business associates. But the reason my grandmother reacted so strongly to her last name became clear to me only years later, when I located the woman who might have become my sister-in-law.

President Johnson narrowed Pete's options for him. On February 7, 1965, he ordered the first air strike against North Vietnam, in retaliation for attacks on a helicopter base and army barracks at Pleiku. The following day, he directed that all dependents of American personnel, civilian and military, be withdrawn from Vietnam. The American Community School in Saigon was closed indefinitely. Pan Am Flight 842 left at noon on February 9 with the first group of returning families.

The USOM newsletter, "The Cyclo," bid them good-bye: "Write us your news so we can keep up with one another. We wish you all the best in your travels!"[1] The same issue reported the disappearance of a high-ranking employee, Gustav Hertz, who had not been seen since he went for a ride on his son's motor scooter on February 2. He was the second USOM man to go missing.

The first, Joseph Grainger, had been captured by Vietcong more than five months earlier. Later, U.S. officials learned that after he staged a hunger strike and a daring escape, his captors had shot and killed him. Only one other American civilian, a female secretary who died in the bombing of the U.S. Embassy in Saigon, had been killed in Vietnam.[2]

Beginning a new marriage in Vietnam was now "conveniently out of the question" for Pete. Besides, he had not seen Margo for almost two years. He appreciated her and wanted to get to know her better. But if after seeing her he were to return to Vietnam, he would have to return alone.

His three choices, as he saw it, were IVS and Vietnam, military service and Vietnam, or graduate school, married or not, but no Vietnam.

Pete didn't know how tense he felt until, in February 1965, he took a five-day vacation in what he called "the cradle and source of fawning self-indulgence."

He flew to Hong Kong alone. It was not unusual for IVSers to take vacations by themselves, because their stations were far apart and it was difficult even for good friends to coordinate their schedules. "At first," Pete wrote, "I had to persuade myself that I would have a good time despite being alone. Then I ran across an ex-Yale naval type also going solo."

They each bought a new suit and sport coat. Pete also bought shoes, a cashmere sweater, and binoculars. Then they set off to explore the island.

> The first day we set out for a methodical reconnoiter of Hong Kong and discovered most of the shops closed for Chinese New Year; we ate at a number-one spot known as Jimmy's Kitchen and were reduced to quivering, jellylike bundles of raw nerves by firecrackers. The first one must have been a magnificent five-incher; it put Bill in a doorway and would have had me in the gutter if someone had jabbed or elbowed me at that exact instant. As it was, I had to "cool it" with a fish face as I unbent after what must have looked like a curiously intent examination of the curb. The rest of the day we just flinched and bravely marched ever onward through clouds of shattered firecracker shrapnel.
>
> After the firecrackers, we dusted off and pulled ourselves together, resolved to descend upon—perhaps ascend is more appropriate—the Hong Kong Hilton—to take it by storm, albeit a very meek storm. It is a glittering, magnificent showcase of wealth and Continental, curly haired,

tight-silk-slacked manhood, which appears to be oriented toward male or female roles in the field of ballerinying, indiscriminately. So rich; they probably aren't even aware of the war in Vietnam except as it provides conversation fodder and sick jokes.

Pete was awestruck. Practically every floor of the hotel had a bar, and he checked out each one, from top to bottom. "Let it be known the Hilton has some very good bars," he said, even though he preferred the faded grandeur of the very British, less gaudy Peninsula Hotel. The luxuries of hot baths and good food were wonderful, but Hong Kong was another world. When he returned to Phan Rang he told Cis, "Everything about my life in Vietnam is natural, and everything not included is strange."

On his next trip to the IVS house in Saigon, he regaled his teammates with an account of his holiday. Phyllis Colyer, who with her husband, David, was posted to Nha Trang, recounted his description of Chinese New Year in a letter to my parents the following year:

> Tonight is Chinese New Year's Eve in Hong Kong, and, like Tet in Vietnam, it's the loudest, wildest night of the year. But the din and spectacle in Hong Kong is like that of no other city. Although this is our first Lunar New Year here, I have the feeling that I know what is going to happen, so vivid was the account Pete gave us in the Saigon IVS office last March of his vacation in Hong Kong at this same time.
>
> If it's possible for one person to enact the explosiveness of a whole city, I think Pete did it. Not since hearing my grandfather expound on the antics of his early horse trading days have I heard one person so enjoy the telling of a good story — one filled with wit and pure joy of living. That was the way Pete did everything. I think he must have built his windmills and dug his wells with the same vitality that he would burst into our house in Nha Trang with, after an hour and a half's drive from Phan Rang, bringing news, Cham blankets to sell, and filling the room with his continual energy — the same energy which burst from him atop an office chair as he dramatized the explosion of an enormous string of firecrackers hung from atop the President Hotel.

With her letter, Phyllis enclosed a check made out to the Peter M. Hunting Memorial Fund. "But tonight that doesn't seem like enough," she said. "Tonight

I feel like going out and setting off a rocket for Pete. Tonight we'll certainly stop at the President Hotel and remember Pete's unusual capacity for both work and fun."

Pete was more of a letter writer than a diarist, so it is not surprising that he wrote his last journal entry, on March 5, 1965, eight months before he was killed. What is surprising is how far his ideas about Vietnam's future had evolved.

A USOM administrator, Doc McCreery, had come to Phan Rang for a meeting with Pete and Mr. Si, the interim chief of primary education for Ninh Thuan Province. Mr. Si had requested only nineteen new classrooms and thirty new teachers for the following year. Using a formula worked out by USOM, McCreery calculated that 40 percent of the children in the province were not in school. Pete was surprised that his estimate was correct. Mr. Si explained that parents wanted their children to stay home and help out instead of attending school.

In Pete's view, McCreery was insensitive, while Mr. Si lacked the vision to grasp the long-range benefits of educating children. But what motivation did students have? They could receive a technical education, but there were no jobs for technicians. The only positions for educated Vietnamese were with the government, and the government stifled self-motivation and encouraged corruption.

USOM brought in "a technician here and a power saw there" but missed the big picture. The country needed factories and foreign workers who could train Vietnamese to take over their jobs. "So far, USOM has the belly buttons and assholes," Pete said, "but hasn't got the backbone of an aid program."

Vietnam's great challenge was to modernize itself. But to oppose the Vietcong was to eliminate an efficient and profitable path to modernization, he wrote.

They'd revolutionize, build up industry, all right, after a breathing spell. While, if we win, we've got to buck Vietnam's Tammany Hall, the rich vested interests, etc. . . . If we take this war seriously, we have a moral right to prosecute an equally vigorous and well-planned economic development program in this country after the war.

Not one to dwell on abstractions, Pete changed subjects and recorded the latest antic involving neighborhood children. After a period of their yelling "Ong My," Mr. American, at him through the windows of the Tuong Nguyen eating club, he went outside and plotted his attack on the ringleader:

I laid in wait for a good fifteen minutes, finally caught the rascal, carried him in to the kitchen, saying "Uhm, *biftec* [beefsteak] of young child should taste pretty good," in Vietnamese of course; asked the cook what he thought; he agreed, brought up a perfectly horrid butcher knife to do the meat cutting with. Well, that kid was in a definite panic. I let go of him with one hand to direct the waiter to hold a pan to catch the blood, and the child fairly shot through the doorway, which was full of interested children waiting for the knife to fall. God, they're a sanguine lot.

Three days later, the Ninth Marine Expeditionary Brigade landed at Danang—the first U.S. combat troops to arrive in Vietnam. They joined the 23,000 American military advisers already in country.

Earlier that week, a bombing campaign named Operation Rolling Thunder began in North Vietnam. Nearly 70 percent of all American prisoners of war eventually released by the North were pilots downed on Rolling Thunder missions, which continued through October 1968. That same month, American B-57 bombers struck South Vietnam for the first time.

Back home *The Sound of Music*, a movie about a family who resists and eventually flees an invading army, opened in theaters across the country. Film critic Pauline Kael called it "a sugar-coated lie people seem to want to eat."[3]

On the same day that the first marines arrived in Danang, Pete wrote home that he had decided to extend his service with IVS. Instead of staying two more years, however, he would sign an eighteen-month contract. "Personally, when Johnson brings in American combat troops for the big battles, I don't think we'll be here very long," he said.[4]

Otherwise, not much was new. Phan Rang was "very peaceful and serene," but farther north things were much worse. One hundred fifty miles—the distance to Phu Yen Province, where the fighting was—didn't sound like much, but in Vietnam it was like another world.

In less than a month, the peace and serenity evaporated. As part of their strategy to take Pleiku, Qui Nhon, and Danang, the Vietcong tried to seize Phan Rang. Pete was unaware of the attack scare until he went out to see a hamlet schoolteacher, whose reaction was, "My God! What are you doing out here?" Pete hurried back to town. Then he joked about going out to see a second teacher:

But I never made it because the VC threw an ambush and I got shot full of holes and they killed me. Nope, just kidding. I missed falling into it by about five minutes. They captured a guardsman and I met the guard company as it was retreating. I shudder to think what might have happened if I'd gone to the second hamlet first, instead of vice versa.

Now with a definite plan to accept a promotion with IVS, Pete's thoughts turned to his two months of home leave. He considered traveling by ship so he could take his motorcycle. He thought it would be fun to surprise Mom by just riding up to the house one day.

He considered flying by way of Europe with Gene Stoltzfus. Then they learned it was cheaper to buy a round-the-world ticket, traveling west to east. He could sightsee in Europe on his return to Vietnam.

He discouraged my mother from making elaborate plans, such as agreeing to Nana's suggestion that the family rent cottages on Cape Cod. He didn't want any uncomfortable, tear-filled reunions, he told Cis. He was going to need gradual reorientation. "I don't know how I'll react to getting back to the Land of the Big PX, as they call it. Maybe I'll write an ode to the Family Thing With Outdoor Grill in Backyard; maybe I'll explode; maybe I'll cower hunched down in a corner and giggle at the plate glass window. Maybe I'll die of an overdose of McDonald's hamburgers."

After spending time with the family in Oklahoma City, he would go to Washington to see John F. Kennedy's grave at Arlington National Cemetery. He also wanted to visit our great-aunt in Chevy Chase, Maryland, and look in on Bob Friedman and Colonel Kosta, two friends he had made in Vietnam. The IVS orientation was scheduled for the same time, and he wanted to check out the new team. He wondered if he should look into a job with the State Department.

From Washington he would go up to Connecticut. He would visit relatives there and see what possibilities existed at Yale for doing graduate work in law, political science, or economics. Then he would head to Wesleyan to see some friends graduate. He might also do some recruiting for IVS on campus, although the news coming from the States made him doubt he would be successful. He may have heard that a group called Students for a Democratic Society had staged its first antiwar protest on April 17 in Washington.

On the way home from Vietnam, he would lay over in Honolulu for four days. While there, he would look into the master's program at the East-West Center.

He would reach Oklahoma City on May 22. He was glad his home leave would start there. It would be too much of a shock—for himself and, he may have thought, for Margo—to start on the East Coast. "I didn't realize how immersed I'd become in my work and in the almost entirely masculine environment of MAC-V compounds, military airports, and work associates around the province headquarters and hamlets," he admitted to her. "Coming back to Saigon I feel very rough and countryish. Meeting some of the IVS girls in Saigon, or USOM secretaries, or visiting Peace Corps girls, all of them my own age or perhaps younger, I feel sort of awkward." He would see Margo in New York City at the end of his trip.

Although he had nailed down his next eighteen months, he still had the problem of choosing what to do when his contract was up. It was a decisive time not only for him, but for IVS. The organization was not up to full strength because of the trouble recruiting volunteers for Vietnam. USOM was threatening to terminate contracts with IVS and to bring in Peace Corps volunteers. It wasn't such a bad idea, Pete thought.

Vietnam was also at a critical juncture. "The VC are going to have to reassert themselves and make a comeback soon, or they've had it," he said. "They were blocked at Danang by the Marines, have been blocked at Vung Tao just recently by the Airborne, and must do something quick.[5] Rumor has it they'll try to take and hold Kontum or Ban Me Thuot, which are mountainous areas. Supposedly, they'll be aided by the rainy season now beginning."

Pete would return from home leave a regional team leader, which would mean moving to the Mekong Delta. "Thank goodness," he wrote to Nana. "It's safer down there."

Meanwhile, wrapping things up in Phan Rang brought a "final flurry of activity." Pete was working on another windmill. "I'd promised the people of one hamlet; as an IVS–Vietnamese project it didn't measure up to all the standards of a good program, because there won't be any follow up, but a promise is a promise and the people should be able to handle the rest of the work," he said. "Cost a lot of money, too, which I paid out of my own pocket. Next year I don't think I'll be so philanthropic."

He had hoped to bring home *ao dais* from Saigon for Holly and me, but when he went downtown to look into it, he "found that a prohibitive set of esoteric statistics" was needed, including detailed measurements. When he was home, we could make shadow drawings and life-size paper cutouts, he suggested. On second thought, however, "Flexing muscles, jumping over chairs, racing dogs, tripping over rugs, driving compact cars, and playing golf" — of these, only driving applied to Holly— "are all activities for which an ao-dai is poorly suited. Ao-dais enforce inactivity, come to think of it, so I suppose I should wait and see how receptive the sisters are to such a useless thing. Boy! I was trying to imagine what everybody looks like, the other day."

I saw Pete for what would be the last time in the summer of 1965.

I remember his homecoming clearly. It was a warm afternoon and I was returning from school. As I walked across the lawn, I saw him step outside onto the front porch. He had been watching for me. I cast my armload of books onto the grass and ran to hug him with both arms.

My father recorded the moment with an eight-millimeter camera. Time has since eaten away at the film, and blotchy blues, yellows, and pinks spread from one frame to another. Some of the images, crackled and pale, resemble a hydrangea blossom, or a brain.

Still, I can make out Pete in a long-sleeved white shirt. He embraces me, at six feet almost a foot taller than I, and my head rests on his chest. A few frames later, we are standing side by side. With one arm around me, he draws me close and, head cocked downward, looks into my eyes, smiling. I smile back at him.

Another film, of the day Pete soloed for his pilot's license, held up better. My father was rushing him through flight training in a single-engine airplane. While Pete was still in Vietnam, Dad had sent him the FAA "Student Pilot Guide" and a prep booklet for the private pilot test so he could begin studying there. When he got home, he started building cockpit time right away.

As a former schoolteacher, my father believed in the primacy of knowledge. He taught his students to understand the weather, one's aircraft, and its instruments. (Two years later, the FAA would publish the "Instrument Flying Handbook" that he wrote.) What to do in an emergency was equally important.

Pete's flight training would have included a lot of practice in touch-and-gos. For a touch-and-go, the pilot briefly sets his wheels down on the runway and immediately takes off again. My father stressed taking off and landing because they were, of course, essential and prime occasions for pilot error. By comparison, a thunderstorm was less hazardous. I was once about to board a small plane during a storm when my father told me not to worry. If lightning struck, he said, it wasn't dangerous unless it hit the gas tank.

Scott Robinson, whose parents and mine were very good friends, described a day he practiced touch-and-gos when my father was his flight instructor:

> We were following behind a pilot who happened to be doing touch-and-gos, too. It was working out fine, for as we touched down and then took off again, this fellow was above and opposite us. When we were in the downwind part of the pattern we could look down and see him doing his touch-and-go on the strip.
>
> Suddenly our "shadow" pilot was nowhere to be found. I remember your dad quickly looking around, and suddenly he grabbed the mike and called to the officials at our base, the larger airport a half-hour away, Wiley Post Airport, blurting out, "I have an emergency, a pilot is down at El Reno." He tilted the wing, pointing downward for me to see in the plowed farm field below the small twisted clump of metal and fabric at the end of the runway. Tragically, this pilot had pulled up too steeply after his last touch-and-go and had stalled, nose-diving into the earth.

After five hours of instruction, Pete soloed. "That would normally be considered quite fast," he told Margo, "but in my case not so amazing because of family tradition and vast experience in the model airplane production field." Dad had all the ratings a pilot could earn, he explained, including a hot-air-balloon license. In his off time, he took on an occasional student "in order to refamiliarize himself with the fear of God so necessary in bolstering the hard-nosed vigilance over flight standards and procedures" for his line of work.

In the home movie of Pete's first solo flight, he first performs a walk-around, a visual inspection of the Cessna 150. He takes off, and several frames later the camera is fixed on what looks like an empty sky. Then the little plane comes into view. Pete lands and taxis toward the camera, then turns away, shuts down the engine, and climbs out. Next, although this ritual was not captured on film, Dad would have torn a large section from the back of Pete's shirt and signed and dated it. The day a pilot solos is a day never forgotten.

Pete was glad to be home. He kidded Margo, "No bicycles in the road. Everybody speaks English. Flying lessons. Short shorts. Big healthy robust, bosomy girls."

Driving in the States took some getting used to. At high speeds, he clutched the steering wheel nervously. He zoomed off highways and onto exit ramps without realizing it, careening at full speed through gas stations alongside the road. He slammed on the brakes at intersections when a car approached, certain the driver would shoot forward, as in Vietnam, regardless of who had the right-of-way.

My parents were proud of Pete. Mom was prone to launch into a "this is my son newly returned from Vietnam spiel," as on the day the two of them met up with one of her friends and her child. "A Little League type opened fire on me the day after I arrived, with an imitation carbine that shoots paper explosives all too realistically," Pete told Margo. For a split second he was all nerves. He retreated to a quiet place, "whereupon junior attacked from an unexpected quarter."

Otherwise, Pete's only concerns were a cat that pounced and a pair of Dalmatians. "The male thinks it's a lap dog and likes to perch atop my knees and lick my face with bovine eye. As a member of the Great Society, I suppose I must submit to this sort of thing and consider the cat and dog as half-human, as everybody else seems to do."

One evening my family went to a steak house for dinner. Pete told story after story about Vietnam. When my mother remarked that he was eating slowly, he said he'd gotten used to unhurried meals. When my father paid the bill, Pete commented that for the same amount of money, he could have built a classroom in Vietnam. He wasn't bitter. It was just an observation.

We went to the Robinsons' one evening. Scott Robinson, who was nine years old at the time, later recalled the visit:

When Pete shook my hand, he winced a little in pain. He showed me the wound on his palm. He then showed me the round scab . . . perfectly round. The rough, oozing, blackened scab took up most of the skin in the center of his palm. He explained to me how the blade of a windmill to bring fresh water was being hoisted up to him in a rural village. A gust of wind came before the bolt could be screwed on, and his palm had to hold the blade on the shaft or it might have been blown off and destroyed, falling to the ground far below, also possibly hurting not only himself, but those Vietnamese workers helping him.

The news of his death not long after gripped me, and it has done so all this time, as firmly as did his handshake.

Pete turned twenty-four that summer. I gave him a birthday card and wrote inside, "You really are a cool brother. It's been great having you home. I wish you weren't going back."

Just before leaving for Washington and New York, Pete passed his pilot's check ride. The FAA examiner had been kind, or at least had looked the other way at some things that were questionable. Pete claimed to have heard the man's brain grinding when he examined logbook entries that showed how quickly this student had learned to fly.

Pete performed some sloppy takeoffs, recoveries from engine stalls, and turns around a fixed point. On a short-field landing, he was rattled by the sight of gullies, trees, and cows close to the runway. "To hell with cows!" the examiner had shouted. The check ride was just about over when, taxiing back to the hangar, Pete nearly collided with a parked Commander jet.

When he related these details to my father, he may have exaggerated. He was probably a good student with a good aptitude for flying. But Dad must have wanted very much to give his son the one thing he had asked for that summer—namely, help in getting his pilot's license—or he would never have hurried a student through flight training.

A few years after Pete was gone, Scott Robinson told my father that he wished he could go beyond merely flying, to understand the principles of aerodynamics. After pondering this awhile, Dad said, "Understanding the principles behind things is what life is all about, and that's what my son, Pete, comprehended."

ELEVEN

"An Open Question"

I don't know if you remember me," the voice on the phone began, "but I knew your brother, Pete." It was August 2000. The woman had just asked if she was speaking with Jill.

Her name had been Sue Patterson, she said. I hadn't seen Sue since I was twelve years old, but of course I remembered the pretty nursing student my brother dated during his Wesleyan years. She visited my family one summer at Round Hill Farm. The next year, she came to Pete's graduation wearing a blue suit that matched her big, clear eyes.

I liked Sue. She made an effort to get to know Holly and me, and even corresponded with us. "I don't know how you manage to stay in one piece with all the laughing you do," one of her letters said. When she graduated from nursing school, she sent us a picture of herself in her stiff white cap and starched uniform.

Now Sue was living in Massachusetts. Recently, after interviewing for a job in Middletown, Connecticut, she had stopped at Pete's alma mater. A librarian led her to a newspaper clipping about Pete that included the names John Sommer and Gene Stoltzfus. She had located Gene on the Internet. He gave her my address, from which she found my phone number.

Our conversation moved over the years like stones skipping across a pond. We told each other about our marriages and divorces and children. She asked about my parents, and my sisters by name. My mother and my sisters and their families all lived in Arkansas, I told her. Dad had passed away in 1997.

I mentioned the difficulty we'd had coping with the trauma of Pete's death. My sisters and I talked about Pete now, I said, but we had only four letters he had written to Cis.

Sue told me she had saved every word Pete ever wrote to her, including notes he left at her dorm to say he had stopped by. She offered to lend me the scrapbooks she kept them in. "There may be some references to a hot-and-heavy make-out session," she said, but it was so long ago that she had no reason to be embarrassed now.

I thought I detected a note of uncertainty. Not wanting her to regret the offer she had made, I asked if she would like to think about it.

Three years elapsed before we spoke again. I assumed incorrectly that she had reconsidered.

I was getting used to these letters and phone calls from out of the blue. They came infrequently, but when I received one, it meant a lot to me. The circle of Pete's friends I was meeting was expanding.

Two years before, in 1998, IVS alumni had gathered in Portland, Oregon, for a reunion. During a session devoted to memories of teammates no longer living, Larry Laverentz had talked about Pete. Mike Fairley told him that he and Darlene had traveled in Vietnam with Pete's sister—and in fact had been through an ordeal together there. Soon afterward, Mike sent Larry my address.

Larry had joined USAID as the prov rep for Ninh Thuan after his IVS service. It was during that time that he and Pete shared a house in Phan Rang, he said in a letter. They both had busy schedules, so they did not spend a lot of time together, but he knew Pete to be dedicated and highly esteemed by province officials. He remembered him most for his "giving spirit" and sense of humor. They respected each other. They never argued.

One of Pete's projects had made a special impression on Larry:

> I recall how hard he worked on building a windmill, an extra project for him. He was so excited as it neared completion and finally worked successfully. Pete also worked with the youth service on projects. Needless to say, as the province representative, I considered his presence to be a great asset.

I am glad to have the opportunity to pass on my thoughts about Pete to you. I have always felt remiss in not being able to discuss my impressions of his commitment and success with a member of his family. At the time of his death, I was on my way out of country for thirty days. Apologetically, I must say that I didn't do any follow-up after I returned.

Vietnam developed some kind of "hold" on many of us, particularly us IVS types. It was easy to get caught up in the adventure and romanticism of the war and all of the peripheral activities. We were generally treated with friendliness, dignity, and respect by the Vietnamese. They seemingly had an ability to block out the war and continue to laugh and go on with life, despite the potential for tragedy in their lives. To some degree, I at least fell into a similar pattern. Vietnam did have a significant effect on my life.

He offered to tell me more if I wanted to talk sometime. "Thanks for listening," he closed. "I have felt the need to acknowledge, in my eyes, Pete's true spirit and greatness."

A week later we spoke by telephone. After that, we continued the conversation in letters and e-mails.

I learned that Larry had majored in agriculture and economics at Kansas State University. In a senior seminar he heard that a group called IVS was seeking volunteers. He signed up to leave for Laos in August 1960, but when a civil war broke out there, the plan fell through. "I got tired of staying home and helping my dad feed cattle, so I went to graduate school," he said. IVS called the following May and asked if he could leave for Vietnam in June. He agreed and, after a two-day orientation in San Francisco, left with four other new recruits.

He quickly discovered that the good intentions of IVS were inadequate to the situation in Binh Dinh Province, where he was assigned:

My initial assignment was misdirected, poorly thought out, and not practical. The idea was to improve the grass for cattle. I came from a large farm in Kansas. The Vietnamese did not need my technical expertise and were much more attuned to what was going on than I was.

I would ask farmers, "How can I help you?" Almost universally they said they wanted rat poison. They were overrun by rats. The rats lived in the rice fields and came into the houses in the rainy season. The government agricultural affairs office organized rat hunts, where farmers were digging rats out of the dikes between the rice paddies and killing them with hoes. We went to a village office where they had piled hundreds of dead rats on the front steps. We could hardly walk up the steps. In America, you'd have put them off to the side, not on the front steps, but they were proud of their accomplishment.

A few months later the agricultural affairs office organized cadres from every hamlet to distribute rat poison. The U.S. government was into quantitative analysis. They had told the Vietnamese they needed to measure the results of the rat poison. Cadres were directed to cut off the tails of the dead rats, and according to the province chief they collected over 900,000 rat tails in a couple or three weeks. There were more rats than people—and Binh Dinh province had the first- or second-highest population in the country.

Later, through ivs, demonstration plots were established to grow plants for the production of warfarin, the anticoagulant in rat poison.

Larry and Pete shared a house across the street from a Chinese hotel with a restaurant. Sometimes they went there for a bowl of *pho*, the noodle soup described by veteran journalist R. W. Apple as Vietnam's national passion.

The two bachelors had a cook and a maid who understood no English. ivsers learned Vietnamese in language classes taught by northerners, but Pete and Larry picked up the southern dialect spoken by their household staff.[1]

For language practice and female companionship, they went to bars. Relationships with women required discretion, as Larry explained:

Dating in Vietnam was a difficult thing. Girls worked as barmaids and many times as prostitutes also. If you wanted company, you'd go to the bars.

Vietnamese girls were very vulnerable, and if you wanted to have a relationship with a girl from a nice family, you could, very easily. I visited families who knew me by my reputation, but a girl couldn't be seen with me in public or she would be labeled as a prostitute.

Pete was young and good looking, so there would have been some Vietnamese who would have said, "Let me fix you up." But it would have been in the company of a sister or parents, and hands-off. Pete and I tried to be very careful.

After working for USAID, Larry returned to the United States and worked in the Foreign Service Institute's Vietnam Training Center, in Arlington, Virginia. He was talking with another employee one day when Pete's name came up.

"As I recall," Larry said, "this person had some ties to the CIA. We talked about the fact that they found Pete's vehicle with thirty-eight bullet holes. A squad of Vietnamese had killed him. Through intelligence, they tracked them down and assassinated them. In most cases the Vietcong would not deliberately set up an ambush for a civilian. Pete may have run into a squad by happenstance."

Why would intelligence track them down and kill them? I asked. I wondered if going to such lengths was customary.

"To send a message: 'You don't do that to an American,'" he said. The killing had been brutal, and, moreover, the victim was someone who was there to help the Vietnamese and do good.

Larry recalled that about three months before Pete left Phan Rang, he began carrying a gun.[2] If he'd had a weapon with him, Larry ventured, he might have tried to defend himself. "He was in good condition. He obviously had a very benevolent side, and he also had a very strong determination and will. When I think of Pete, I think of someone who was strong and active, with a very strong spirit."

Don Luce had said only that Pete was driving in an area where he wasn't known, was probably mistaken for a soldier, and was caught in an ambush. The rumor about retribution was news to me. I had not considered that Pete's death could have had repercussions beyond IVS.

"I tell a story," Larry said as that first phone call came to a close. "Every IVSer has similar stories. If you hear a story from me or from another IVSer, there's some commonality in terms of experience, motivations, and unselfishness."

He said he would try to find an address for the man who said Pete's killers had been eliminated, in case he remembered more.

Later, I related our conversation to a friend. She asked how I felt when I heard that the squad that killed Pete had been tracked down and killed. Well, I said, it was wartime. Pete's colleagues had told me they expected a certain amount of danger. Don even implied that Pete had taken too much of a risk. But the thought of people avenging his death had not crossed my mind. To be honest, I told my friend, it was a little unsettling that the story gave me some comfort. If the rumor was true, there had been others who, like my family, were dead serious about what happened to Pete.

Chuck Cable, one of the group I dubbed the Phan Rang Five, had been sorely disappointed when authorities refused to let us stop in Phan Rang. He had lived there for two years and worked on the library, overseeing some of the construction and rounding up electrical wiring, switches, and circuit breakers.

In 1968, he had escaped the violence of the Tet Offensive because he was on vacation. He returned to Saigon on the second flight after Tan Son Nhut Airport was reopened. He then spent several nights in bomb shelters after one plane bound for Phan Rang was destroyed and another was delayed by rocket attacks.

A few months after our 1991 trip, Chuck learned that our trouble with the local authorities had caused him to miss a party in his honor. Thirty former students and fellow teachers had assembled at the home of an old friend in Phan Rang to welcome him back.

He thought the same friend could tell us about the condition of the library. He offered to write to him. It was months before he received a reply, and it was inconclusive.

Chuck wanted to help me learn more about Pete, and he did. He suggested former volunteers I should call, who had either worked on the library or known my brother. During a phone call, he gave me a list of names and offered to look up their phone numbers in the IVS directory.

"There's an IVS directory?" I asked. There was not only a directory but also an alumni association. I joined as a Friend of IVS. I received a roster of former volunteers, with listings of the country to which each person had been assigned, from Algeria to Zimbabwe, and their years of service.[3]

Chuck also suggested I call a man named Bert Fraleigh, who had worked in the Office of Rural Affairs. He might have known Pete.

I sent a note to Fraleigh, asking if he'd be willing to talk with me.

Yes, he had met Pete, the phone conversation with Fraleigh began. "I was taking care of various field operations for USAID, and there were IVS guys in the provinces," he explained. "They were not working directly for us. I met Pete because there weren't many Americans in Phan Rang." He recalled that Pete was a good singer.

At the time Pete was killed, Fraleigh had been working primarily in Saigon. Other USAID people would have known more, he said, but the road Pete was driving on was a main highway. It was highly traveled and not considered dangerous.

I said that the *New York Times, Washington Post*, Walter Cronkite, and others had carried the story that Pete was led into an ambush.

"Impossible," he said emphatically. The prov rep would more likely be singled out. "Pete would have been the last person the Vietcong would target."

I asked him about the rumor that Pete's killers had been identified and eliminated.

"We did mount a program called Operation Phoenix, to infiltrate the VC and identify who among villagers was a Vietcong spy," he said. "Those spies—we got to them and encouraged them to defect or they were assassinated. The CIA mounted that program. As to imagining to delegate two CIA guys to go out and shoot the guys who got him, in Vinh Long Province, where Pete lived, we didn't have any CIA people that I know of. If there were visiting firemen, they would be from Saigon."

Visiting firemen? Who am I talking to? I wondered. "What are visiting firemen?" I asked.

"CIA people in Saigon who would go through the province," he answered. "A fireman was someone who was just passing through."

And doing what? I was afraid to ask.

But since we were on the subject, I asked if any IVSers were CIA.

I had posed this question confidentially to a few former volunteers. Some had not hesitated to name a teammate they suspected. Interestingly, no two names were the same. No one mentioned Pete.

Over the years, when I had mentioned a brother who was a civilian volunteer in Vietnam, some people asked if he was a spy. My parents had been so silent about him that I hadn't entirely dismissed the question. But the same people who jumped to the spy conclusion had never heard of IVS. Moreover, they were, like me at the time, ignorant of the tremendous civilian effort in Vietnam and of the hundreds of Americans living and working there before U.S. combat troops arrived.[4]

At last I was making my way to people who really knew something.

"There was an IVSer who was CIA," Fraleigh told me. He worked with Montagnards in the highlands. "They were primitive. Dressed in G-strings. [He] was so effective that they almost considered him to be their king," he said. "The CIA hired him to help the Montagnards with self-defense. He armed them and organized them against the Vietcong. The Montagnards were never really conquered, and he is one of the very few people responsible for this."

He asked if I knew what Pete's IVS assignment had been in the Mekong Delta. The more questions he asked, the more I realized how little I knew. He recommended a book of essays about Vietnam in the early 1960s, to which he had contributed a chapter about the Rural Affairs program he had helped Rufus Phillips establish. "We were hand-picked by John Kennedy," he said. "Basically, its purpose was to counter the Vietcong and to help the Vietnamese develop their backbone to fight for themselves. It required great patience, and Americans don't have patience."

IVS must have investigated Pete's death, he insisted. As chief-of-party, Don Luce or his deputy, Mike Chilton, would have gone to the area where the ambush occurred. There would have been an official report, and someone must have sent my parents a copy. There would have been no reason to prevent them from knowing exactly what happened.

My father had passed away six years earlier, and my mother's memory was by now greatly diminished, but I didn't want to say so. Nor did I want to tell someone who seemed fairly emphatic and who scarcely knew Pete that my family didn't talk openly about him.

Fraleigh urged me to keep looking. Someone would have made a report.

Paul Worthington was one of the first IVS volunteers in Vietnam. He went over in 1957, returned to the United States after his service, and returned to work for Rural Affairs.

In 1963, between his two tours, he married Linda, a widow with three children. They went immediately to Berkeley, California, for a semester of training with other U.S. Operations Mission employees headed for Southeast Asia. Having served with IVS, Paul already spoke Vietnamese. Linda took classes at the Monterey Language Institute.

"There certainly were people in Rural Affairs who later were CIA, or who came out of the CIA," Linda explained when I called her. "In those days, you never said if you were CIA, but Rural Affairs was not a CIA program. It was a community development program." She named someone who after his IVS service went to work for what is sometimes called "the company."

Paul and Linda lived first in Saigon, then in the Mekong Delta. It was so safe, they felt, that they enrolled their red-haired, blue-eyed seven-year-old in the local kindergarten. They lived in Vietnam until February 1965, when all USOM dependents were evacuated by order of President Johnson.

IVSers stayed.

People were confused about IVS, she said. "The U.S. military couldn't understand how these young, mostly men were out riding their motorcycles, talking to the people, and all that. Because they weren't military, they were considered loose cannons. They weren't following anyone's orders."

In the 1990s Linda served as co-director of IVS. The other co-director was Don Luce. When the organization closed in 2002, the office files were given to Goshen College in Indiana. Many of the old papers were discarded then, Linda said, and it was possible that any reports or communications related to Pete were now gone.

I asked who else might know what had happened to him. I mentioned the original report of a land mine explosion and the subsequent story that two Vietnamese friends had led Pete to his death.

I told her Don had written to me in a letter, "We all did foolish things back then." She cautioned me not to unquestioningly accept his version of events. She doubted he would be inclined to believe that a Vietnamese betrayed an American.

"Personally, I believe that is exactly what could have happened," she said. She did not wish to challenge, however, whatever "myth" had formed around Pete's death. She had heard that he had been killed by a land mine. In any case, she assured me, "Nobody ever accused Pete of wrongdoing in any way."

She urged me to talk to more IVSers who were volunteers around the same time as Pete. "See what they know," she suggested.

In the fall of 2003 a friend invited me to go to Italy for a writing retreat she was organizing. At the time, we were editors of a food, wine, and travel magazine.

A few years earlier, I had become interested in truffles, the mushroom relative that grows underground. I had hunted the delicacy in Oregon and Europe, met truffle "royalty" in Italy, published recipes and articles about truffles, and started a newsletter for devotees. I hoped that in Italy, away from the distractions of the office, I could bring into focus a book I wanted to write about this most mysterious of all foods.

One afternoon the other writers and I were talking about our goals. I told them about my passion for truffles. Then, for some reason, I took a detour. I said that my interest in the subterranean food might be related to something that had happened in my family, something we had buried. I talked about my brother and the family that treated his death as a secret. That afternoon, in the golden beauty of the Umbrian countryside, I realized that the story I wanted to tell was about Pete.

I returned home and told my sisters what I was going to do. They were glad. We talked about the four letters from Pete that we had. Holly remembered seeing a green lacquer box containing sympathy letters from Vietnam in our parents' storage locker. She offered to find it and send it to me.

She asked if it would be useful to have Pete's journal. Pete kept a journal? So seldom had we talked about our brother, I hadn't even known a journal existed. Holly kept it on her bedside table. The following week, she sent it to me.

The brown leather book contained thirty-nine pages of entries. They began on June 20, 1963, after Pete had kissed Holly and me, "the sisses," good-bye at the Hartford airport and left for his IVS orientation in Washington. Tucked inside the journal was a note from October 1964 with the price, 540 dollars, of a motorcycle and the address in Hong Kong for ordering it. There were five wallet-size photos of young women, two with a name on the back and another whom I recognized as Pete's high school sweetheart, Judy. There were two snapshots of friends lounging on the porch of the Alpha Delta Phi house at Wesleyan. There was a draft of a letter to friends and family, written in mid-July when he returned to Vietnam after his two months of home leave.

Bert Fraleigh had mentioned the name of Don Luce's deputy, Mike Chilton. I found Mike's name in Pete's journal. He was one of "a good crew" who had visited Pete at Phan Rang.

When I called Mike, he seemed surprised that Pete had written about him. I reminded him of the day that the assistant province chief's servant had opened a champagne bottle so violently that half the wine was lost. Hearing this, Mike laughed heartily. Pete had described that laugh.

I asked about a Major Cook who had upbraided Pete when he arrived at Phan Rang without the proper letters of introduction.

"Ah . . . Major . . . Cook." Mike said. Cook was the senior American officer in Ninh Thuan Province. Someone asked him how many Vietcong were within his sphere of influence. Two hundred eighty-nine, he had declared emphatically. "It was typical of American thinking," Mike said. "Everything was right in Major Cook's world."

I mentioned Pete's complaints about his first stationmate, including his indignation that Chuck Fields corrected his Vietnamese when he himself had studied five languages. Mike chortled. "Chuck worried about everything," he said.

I brought up the differing accounts of what happened to Pete that day on the road from Can Tho. I asked if he thought Pete had been targeted by Vietcong or had driven into an ambush set for the convoy that found him soon afterward.

"What happened to Pete is an open question," he said.

Another question I asked Chuck Cable concerned the man who called my family with the news of Pete's death. Chuck didn't know who it was, but he gave me the address of a former ivs administrator, John Hughes, who might know. I wrote to Mr. Hughes and asked if it would be all right for me to call him. Certainly, he replied. He suggested a time for us to talk. His note also mentioned that he had attended the memorial service for Pete in Connecticut.

Our conversation began with my saying I remembered almost nothing about the service. Did he?

I knew from Sue Patterson that some ivs representatives had been there. She remembered them as cold and unfeeling. Hughes could recall very little. He named the men Sue would have met: himself, Executive Director Gardiner, a former volunteer named Tom Luche, and Pete's teammate and friend Willi Meyers.

Hughes did remember, however, Pete's last visit to ivs headquarters in Washington, when he was home between assignments.

"He brought me some herbs he had picked up from a Chinese merchant," he told me. "He said they were reputed to be a great asset to one's sex life." Hughes stashed the herbs in the back of his desk drawer.

He visited my parents once in Oklahoma City. I asked what his impression had been. To most people, and maybe to everyone but my sisters and me, my parents seemed to cope well with the loss of their son. Hughes confirmed this. They seemed to accept things matter-of-factly, he recalled, "with no morbidity and no rehashing of the sadness."

"Do you have any idea who made the phone call to my family that day?" I asked.

"It fell to me," he said.

I couldn't believe I was talking to the man whose voice I had heard just before summoning Dad to the phone that sad, long-ago day.

I was jolted out of myself to realize that the question must have stung. "I'm so sorry," I said. "I didn't know."

That morning, Don Luce had called from Saigon. "John, it's urgent," he said. "Before the press gets hold of this, we have to tell the parents."

"As acting director, it fell to me to tell them," Hughes said. "I did have the courage. I had to say, 'Mr. Hunting, I have sad'—or maybe I said—'I have bad news from Vietnam.' I don't think we talked very long. I felt so terribly for your parents. It was one of the hardest things I've ever done."

I asked if he had been concerned about the safety of the other team members. Did other parents want their sons and daughters to come home?

"Yes," he said. "Being alerted to the potential hazard in Southeast Asia, Arthur Gardiner prepared a letter addressed to later recruits, saying, to be casual about it, 'Let's face it—there are hazards there. We think there's a useful role for IVS.' We tried to be frank and realistic."

"Have you seen the movie *The Quiet American?*" I asked.

"I couldn't stand the thought of seeing it," he said.

"Why do you think Pete brought you the Chinese herbs?"

"I don't know what my reputation might have been, but I think it was probably just a waggish thing to tweak a bureaucrat, a desk man. Something for a laugh. 'Here's something authentic from Southeast Asia.'"

I laughed.

"I'm glad I gave you a laugh," he said.

TWELVE

"Too Much Talk about Danger"

Saigon is awash with green uniforms," Pete wrote to Margo when he returned to Vietnam in July 1965. After an absence of just two months, he was surprised to see the Pearl of the Orient so changed. American military vehicles now strangled the flow of traffic. Jets and helicopters churned up the gray skies. It was a little depressing.

He had come back by way of Europe. He and Cis had arranged to meet in Paris, but the plan fell apart. She was traveling with a friend whose morning ritual included considerable time in front of a mirror; to cover her thinning hair, she wore a wiglet that required an hour just to be fastened to the top of her head with hairpins, and then teased and combed. Their trip had started in Spain. By the time they reached Paris, Cis was at wit's end. Trying to hurry her primping friend had been futile. When they finally arrived at Orly Airport on the appointed day, Pete's plane had already landed.

"I bashed myself to American Express" hoping to find a message there from Cis, he wrote to my mother afterward. After two hours of looking for her, he checked into a hotel and deposited his suitcases. He returned to American Express, where he ran into a friend from Wesleyan. They climbed the Eiffel Tower together, worked up an appetite, and went to a restaurant where Pete consumed an octopus. Finally, jet lag overcame him. "Was *dead* tired," he told Mom. "Never been so tired!"

Late in the evening, Pete and Cis crossed wires one last time before he gave up and went to bed. The next morning, he flew out. "Cis can really be a meathead when she works at it," he complained. They would not see each other again.

In Venice, as in Paris, Pete ran into someone he had met at Wesleyan—a young woman traveling with her twin sister and aristocratic grandmother. He sunbathed on the Lido until he "parboiled" himself. He loved La Serenissima's architecture and cuisine, the orchestra playing Strauss waltzes on St. Mark's Square, and the gondolas and accordion players outside his hotel room. At night, on the canals, he could almost sense the ghosts of Marco Polo, Lucrezia Borgia, and "assorted poisoned troubadours."

He laid over in Rome, but the Eternal City was a letdown. He found the Coliseum surprisingly small—not much larger, in fact, than the Dexter, Missouri, high school gym. "Can you imagine feeding Christians to the lions in the Dexter High School gym?" he asked Mom in a letter written from Karachi, Pakistan. "I was expecting a bit more in the way of running space. Tomorrow, Singapore."

If Rome had disappointed Pete and missing Cis had exasperated him, Margo had left another impression. Had he not been returning to Vietnam, he told my mother, he'd have flipped over her:

> She was so easy to talk to, joke with, relax with. Physically attractive (Yaow!) but poised and mature. . . . We're both the type of person that can keep control until I finish what I'm doing in Vietnam and some questions in our separate minds are settled. I guess what this means is, we both found each other attractive, thinking in a serious way, but it's "wait and see."

In the same letter, he compared Margo favorably with another young woman whom he had gone out with a few times in Oklahoma City. "More domestic, less world- and travel-oriented" than Margo, she also seemed to have a devious side and a potential to dominate a man. What he liked about her was that she was "natural" and "fresh."

Margo, by contrast, had been "a long time unlimbering." She was a lady, he told Mom, "like you are a lady." Her interests were broad and complemented his. "If someone said to me, 'You must marry tomorrow,'" he summed up, "it would be Margo. I'd have more confidence in what I was getting into."

Saying good-bye hadn't been easy. In New York, he nearly missed his plane because they didn't hear the boarding call.

Back in Vietnam, Pete didn't broadcast his feelings about Margo. But the friend he considered his best buddy remembers Pete's response when he asked how things had gone with Margo. Pete shook his head slowly from side to side and said, simply, "Ohhhhh, Gene."

In Connecticut, Pete had met Margo's sister and brother-in-law and talked with her mother about the exotic flowers in Vietnam, some of whose English names he didn't know. Now back in country, he asked Margo to tell her mother that although American soldiers were buying everything in sight, they had left some gladioli on Saigon's Street of Flowers. "As soon as I get some more film," he promised, "I'm going to go down there and eh-eh-eh-eh-eh the whole street to solve the problem once and for all as to what kinds of flowers are there."

At a New York restaurant, he and Margo met a man who suggested Pete write a novel based on his experiences in Vietnam. The conversation may have planted the seed of an idea, because on July 16 Pete sent my parents a short letter asking them to take an article he enclosed to the office of a newspaper in Oklahoma City. He hoped they would publish it and let him contribute four or five stories a month. If an Oklahoma paper didn't want the article, he asked my parents to send it to the *New York Times* or *Christian Science Monitor.*

With his cover letter to the editor, he enclosed a photograph of himself with a windmill he built. "Don't mean to push it on you," he explained, "but it's the only one I have coming close to the topic of IVS or NVS hamlet cadre work." Both IVS and the organization it inspired, National Voluntary Services, were to be featured in an upcoming ABC documentary scheduled to air in August. Pete was one of two IVS spokesmen who had been interviewed, and if the newspaper cared to scoop ABC, it could, he suggested. His new job as a regional supervisor would provide frequent opportunities to travel in the Mekong Delta. He could report on conditions there in his free time.

The article began with Pete stating how different he had found Saigon after being in the States only two months. During that time, President Johnson had committed another 50,000 American troops to Vietnam, bringing the total to

125,000. The recent buildup threatened to overwhelm what had been a massive civilian aid effort.

> It is depressing in the sense that our efforts along social, economic, and (indirectly) political lines will be all the more eclipsed. For civilians connected with the foreign aid program, there is a mental tension created by an unmeasureable dilemma: These new soldiers and military adjustments are needed, but at what number of troops do we lose sight of the social, economic, and political aspects of the war? Will we reach a point where we cannot maintain our position of the past, a propos the Vietnamese trust in our non-colonial interest, our good faith? As our troops pour into the country, will the Vietnamese forget why *they* must keep fighting the Viet Cong?[1]

His concerns for Vietnam were dispelled somewhat on July 15, he continued, when he heard Prime Minister Nguyen Cao Ky address students at a leadership training camp. Pete and other IVSers had been present to offer encouragement and technical and logistical support. The thirty-four-year-old Ky, who had assumed office just one month earlier, identified with the Vietnamese youth who were eager to help their country develop. He exhorted them to rise above setbacks and criticism, admitting that his job required the same resiliency he was asking of them.

Even more than Ky's remarks, the students' enthusiasm and receptivity to their new leader boosted Pete's hopes for the country:

> During certain moments of the ceremony, a fraternal, trustful atmosphere seemed to envelop audience and speaker alike. The trainees felt a great pride in what they were going to do, in the fact that their youthful Premier was coming to meet and talk with them. . . . At least two students also took the opportunity to apologize for the Premier's tardiness, noting that "Young men are always late," a quote having various ribald connotations which are perhaps appropriate, considering the Premier's reputation as a playboy.

The emergence of a unified student volunteer movement in Vietnam was a recent development. In the last days of the Diem presidency, dissident students had been a force for change. Successive governments, backed by the United

States, mistrusted the young activists. Then, in November 1964, eight hundred students volunteered in disaster areas after central South Vietnam was ravaged by floods. More than five thousand people had died, and many more had lost their homes.

Over several weeks, the young volunteers collected clothing, distributed relief commodities provided by the government, staged theater performances to raise money, and canvassed for donations. Some students came face to face with corruption, as they saw officials take for themselves what was meant to help flood victims. Others proved, as Pete had seen in Quang Ngai, more demanding than resourceful. In the end, however, the students accomplished much good.[2]

The gains of their disaster relief efforts energized student leaders to request permission from the government to organize a program the following year. After three months, the government granted tacit support. The American aid mission also backed the program, in part, allegedly, to keep the students off the streets.[3] More than eight thousand students devoted a portion of their summer break to the 1965 Summer Youth Program, building bridges, repairing roads, teaching in classrooms, providing child care, distributing medicines, painting hospital furniture, and, in general, mixing with the rural population. It was the first exposure for some of them to non-urban Vietnamese and to hamlet and village life—which one ivs annual report held to be "the purest repository of what is traditionally Vietnamese."[4]

Of the thousands of volunteers who participated in the 1965 Summer Youth Program, three hundred were chosen for the monthlong leadership training camp that July in Saigon. ivsers such as Pete assumed a supporting role as the trainees carved out three goals: to unify and strengthen the country's youth movement, to serve the people of rural Vietnam, and to develop an aware citizenry and leaders for the country's future.[5] From these three hundred student leaders, sixty-six were chosen for the nascent permanent social service organization National Voluntary Services, established on the ivs model.

For the last four months of Pete's life, working with Vietnam's promising youth would be a top priority. The newspaper article that he asked my parents to submit reflected his immersion in Vietnamese affairs, and specifically in a national youth movement that had no American equivalent. A busy newspaper editor, let alone his or her readers, may have found the substance of the article difficult to comprehend. The situation in Vietnam was complex, but as my father would say, Pete grasped an underlying principle—namely, that the country's youth were playing an important role, and in fact were the most promising counterforce to the claims of the Communists:

> Having contact with IVS volunteers through workcamps, English classes, and cultural programs, a fairly large number of Vietnamese university students set up their own organization, NVS, which sends five-man cadre teams out into the provinces.
>
> . . . They leave the security, joys, and pleasures of Saigon to live and work in the country for one year, or in the case of rotating teams, a half year.
>
> . . . NVSers are idealistic and highly motivated; what they lack in experience they make up in enthusiasm and perspective. The Vietnamese peasant has long felt that Saigon, the Government, and the Vietnamese educated classes were progressing without concern for the agricultural countryside. NVSers know that they must "bridge the gap"; in effect, they are doing what the communists have promised to do if once they control the country.

He went on to distinguish between the youth corps, which he called "cadres," and government "cadre teams." The government units lived in province or district capitals, making daily visits out to hamlets. Their objective was to show the government's benign face and undertake short-term improvements, such as digging wells, repairing fences, showing movies, and distributing educational materials. The NVS cadres lived in the hamlets for six months or a year, in teams of five, and adopted the local standard of living. An NVS agriculture volunteer could work with farmers for an entire crop cycle. A health volunteer could "follow a rat poisoning campaign from beginning to grisly end."

The students were constructive and idealistic, Pete explained, yet realistic about their country's social, economic, and political conditions. They were critical of the American presence at times, he acknowledged, but they grasped the stakes of the war. NVSers would "balance, soften, cushion, augment and explain the government's activity in the countryside," he stated. "This is a very reassuring thought as new American military transports drive by one's window from dawn to dusk."

In addition to keeping tabs on the Summer Youth Program, Pete's new job entailed no end of waiting in airports, flying here and there to check on team members, answering and asking innumerable questions, and placating, assisting, and smoothing the ruffled feathers of disgruntled volunteers. It didn't have the "glamour," he wrote home, of daily contact with teachers and farmers, as his hamlet education job in Phan Rang did. He had less time to write letters, except when he was waiting for an airplane.

Not only were in-country military transports free for IVSers, but by this time flying could be a safer way to get around the Mekong Delta than driving. The procedure for volunteers was to go to the airport, put their name on a passenger list, and wait for a flight. As IVS alumnus Ray Gill, a member of Pete's new team, recalled:

> You went out and talked to the army guy who controlled the flights on
> Air America or on a military spotter plane—which was a Piper Cub-type
> plane—or got a place on a helicopter. Helicopter was the preferred way
> of going in and out. On a Piper Cub there was only canvas between you
> and bullets. Air America planes were obvious targets. Helicopters were,
> too, but they were very maneuverable and had door gunners. You got the
> fresh air, too.[6]

Pete carried his Vietnamese textbook with him for such lulls, but keeping up his language studies was a challenge. "I sure wish Vietnamese was closer to Chinese than it is," a letter home said. "Every day or two I study some Vietnamese. Every time I pick up the book I wish I could have the time to study the Chinese, too." The pressure to study Vietnamese was "very great," he told Margo. "When I study one language or the other, I feel guilty about not spending enough time on the other. And there's the French to study, too. Impossible situation."

Now that he was a certified private pilot, he also needed to keep his license current. He obtained a U.S. Army aeronautical map of his new region—which comprised all of the area designated by the military as IV Corps, in the southern-most part of the country, plus Bien Hoa and Vung Tau, which were closer to Saigon. On a Mobilgas road map, on which the oil company's Pegasus trademark indicated the locations of Mobil gas stations, he plotted a triangular cross-country flight between Dalat, Nha Trang, and Pleiku.

There was a French flying club in Saigon, and he planned to make contact with them on his next trip to the IVS house. The club's aircraft were old Piper Cubs, he had heard, single-engine airplanes with "band-aids patching up the holes" in the yellow fabric covering. "I shudder to think of the crates they're flying," he said, "or where they fly them."

He had planned to set up his regional headquarters in the city of Can Tho, but the influx of American servicemen had created a housing shortage and inflated prices. Over a six-month period, rents for many of the good houses in the most secure areas of Can Tho tripled.[7] New housing construction could not keep pace with the demand. Pete was forced temporarily to live out of his suitcase during the week and return to Saigon on weekends. Eventually he settled in Vinh Long, a city about twenty-one miles away.

Despite the minor frustrations, Pete liked the job, he told Margo on August 2. Even a vexing experience that began when his motorcycle blew a tire had turned out all right. The flat tire surprised him because

(1) Honda is the perfect motorcycle; (2) I'm the perfect motorcyclist; ergo (3) this sort of thing is just not supposed to happen. Then, at the tire repair shop, two students started a fight with a fruit vendor. I became worried when one of the students disappeared from the mêlée. A cyclo driver and I backed against a wall near a door, waiting and watching the crowd and bystanders, expecting a grenade to be tossed my way. Cyclo driver was a good man. One situation where speaking Vietnamese made all the difference. Tense moment.

The same afternoon, after taking a shower, he caught his bath towel in the ceiling fan, putting enough of a load on the voltage regulator to shut down the system. "I was trying to perfect an overhand towel snap as opposed to the common underhanded snap known in locker rooms throughout the world," he explained. "If successful in developing this new method, I may well shoot into international prominence."

Later the same month, as Pete was giving a friend a lift on his Honda, the bike slipped on a turn. "I made contact with a taxi, with mostly my nose," he told Margo. "I caught a fast glimpse of my friend sliding down the middle of a mud puddle backwards, trying to lift himself out of it all the while. We had our laughs. Picked up the machine and off we went."

Pete found his moments of levity, but conditions had grown very serious.

Three months earlier, fifteen thousand Vietnamese had left a Vietcong-held area in Kien Tuong Province and were squatting around the district capital of Cai Be. The refugees were "literally eating grass," Ray Gill recalls. The people had been forced from their homes by a program of bombing and artillery fire intended to drive out the population and thus deprive the Vietcong of sustenance. "It's not so much people trying to escape the vc," Pete wrote to Margo, "but the possibility of being bombed, though [they are] glad to be rid of both and expecting relief support from the government."

He took the head of National Voluntary Services to Cai Be to show him the situation. NVS was sending a team there to start up a self-help organization among the refugees. Pete hoped NVS would also help build houses. IVS agriculture volunteers would teach intensive gardening.

On another occasion, Pete and Ray asked some of the refugees, who were too afraid to return to their homes, what they knew how to do so they could help them do it at Cai Be. They said they knew how to make rice "wine," really a whiskey. Pete went to Saigon and scrounged around for copper tubing and other supplies to get them started. "We used to go to the compound," Ray remembers, "and they would hold a glass right under the drip and fill it. They wanted us to taste it. It burned all the way down. We tried to keep a straight face, but we always turned down second helpings."

Pete described a visit to a rice wine distillery in Ba Xuyen Province — most likely a research trip for the refugee project — in a letter to Margo:

> I'll never again enjoy rice wine unless I drink it far from Ba Xuyen. The water they use to make the mash is dipped out of a murky looking canal instead of a mountain spring. The boilers are made of galvanized tin painted over with aluminum paint! Have you ever heard of such a thing? As if that wasn't enough, there were all these diseased inebriates standing around. To my horror I was told they were the workers. It's a wonder people around here are still alive. Me, for instance.

She would have enjoyed the previous day's drive to Ba Xuyen, he told her. Some people didn't like roads with potholes and bumps, but he did. It tested his skill. He described the route:

> The road winds alongside one of the Delta's primary canals. On one side are banana trees or palm trees hanging over the bank with water buffaloes

tethered beneath them, kids climbing all over their backsides. The sun was bright and casting long shadows, and there was a slight breeze in the treetops, blowing the palms. On the other side of the road were some hamlets — thatch houses with kids and pigs running all over the place. Maybe I'll shoot a roll of film for you on the way back.

Two months and twelve days later, with fateful consequences, Pete would take the same road.

Recent news from home took Pete by surprise. It wasn't the race riots that August in southern California that startled him, but the fact that Cis had gotten married without his knowing it. She had been engaged and planned a September wedding, but when it appeared that her fiancé, Frank, might be drafted, they moved up the date.

"Didn't she like Europe?" he asked in a letter home. "Did Frank look sort of pale?" Pete sent a large Cham weaving as a wedding gift. It was blue, and he wondered if she might take the hint and "have a boy type baby, which seems a helluva thing to say about one's sister. . . . Staggering thought, one of my own sisters hauling off and doing such a thing."

He reckoned that the two "young monsters" — to our faces, he called Holly and me his "favorite youngest sisters" — were "making daily raids on the city's clothing stores in anticipation of school. What a pair of beauts."

He regretted he'd had only two months of home leave instead of three, so he could have seen more friends and relatives. One of the friends he hadn't seen was Sue Patterson. "Figured it best that way, sort of having come to a mutual prior understanding through correspondence," he said. "I was surprised to get back and see a letter from her."

Pete had learned that his Chinese professor from Wesleyan was going to pass through Oklahoma City with his wife and children, and he hoped we would see them and give them his love. The Wus stayed with us. I remember the two little children as being alarmingly energetic.

Mr. Wu was one of the only faculty members whom Pete said he missed and would like to see again. My father recorded his and his wife's greetings to Pete on a reel-to-reel tape recorder and subsequently sent the tape to him. They said they were proud of him. When they drove away in their station wagon, my mother fretted that they would never make it to their destination, somewhere farther west. Mr. Wu had learned to drive only days before taking his family on this cross-country adventure, and his uncontrolled, nervous mien at the wheel convinced them that trouble lay ahead.

Along with soldiers, American correspondents were pouring into South Vietnam. Most were men. One notable exception was Rose Wilder Lane, the only child of *Little House on the Prairie* author Laura Ingalls Wilder. Lane was seventy-eight when *Woman's Day* magazine sent her to Vietnam on assignment.

In her early life, she had been a best-selling author, a highly paid magazine writer, a personal friend of the king of Albania, and, in her thirties, a communist. After World War I, while traveling in Russia, she was arrested by the secret police and claimed later that her knowledge of Marxism had been useful. In time she repudiated communism and became an outspoken critic of the New Deal. She opposed Social Security, claiming that the hundreds of jars of put-up food, grown in her own garden and stocked in her pantry, were her social security.[8]

Woman's Day editor Ellen Tighe asked Lane to report on the conditions of women and children in war-torn South Vietnam. In June 1965, the day before she was to leave, the Defense Department tried to pull the plug on her trip. There could be trouble if anything were to happen to this intrepid septuagenarian. But Lane prevailed.

From the top of the Caravelle Hotel in Saigon, she observed mortar fire flashing in the distance. Unlike the reporters Pete complained about, who were either lazy or afraid to leave the bars, Lane traveled beyond the capital, even flying on helicopter missions.

For her long piece, "August in Vietnam," she interviewed a young man whose home, like hers, had once been the Midwest:

> Peter Hunting from Dexter, Missouri, . . . complains that there's too much talk about danger. It's keeping young men from volunteering for ıvs in Viet Nam, he says; and ıvs needs volunteers. There are only 40 ıvs men in the whole country, and opportunity for ten times as many. . . .
>
> The Viet Cong's no bother, Peter Hunting says, unless maybe they'd hit our village in the night, but how safe are you on American highways? No ıvs man has had any trouble with the Viet Cong; all you need is ordinary good sense. Any time they start moving someone tells you right

away. They wreck schools and they may kill teachers, so you help get her out of the way and hide books and so on; then you just go in the other direction. And come back when they're gone.

The peasants are fine folks, you have the time of your life. . . . The food is good; a little rice, plenty of fish and fruit and delicious vegetables of all kinds that haven't even a name in English. You feel fine. There's not much sanitation but the people are healthy because they eat right; Americans eat too much. . . .

What's important, Peter Hunting says, is the progress. It's wonderful. The people keep on going right ahead. The standards of every village in his district are higher than they were two years ago. That's something to see. Peter Hunting's only complaint is the publicity about danger; it's exaggerated, and it's keeping men from volunteering for ivs in Viet Nam.[9]

By the time the December 1965 issue, with Lane's article, entered circulation, Pete was dead.

In early September, during the same week that the casualty figure for American forces in Vietnam—650 deaths since 1961—was released, Pete wrote a long letter to Margo. It was an invitation to enter into his world and share his fascination with Vietnamese folkways, his frustration with a member of his team who was six months behind with his monthly reports, and his analysis of where American foreign aid was failing and how to correct it.

He had observed an ingenious method of making fertilizer:

The people make a huge, tall tower out of bamboo, with a palm frond roof. Instead of a floor, they hang about 50 bundles of palm fronds tied at the end, like drying tobacco. After a few days, thousands of bats will appear—big ones six inches to a foot from wing tip to wing tip—sleeping up in the tower during the day. In the evening, the people come out and broom the guano to the side. It makes excellent fertilizer. No kidding. It's amazing how these people have picked up these methods. Just goes to show you what people can do without science and industry.

He wished his job were more challenging and gave him more responsibility for administering foreign aid. Perhaps he was impatient, he granted, but the system badly needed improvement. At present, resources were allocated by American technicians working in cooperation with Vietnamese officials. They spent too much on baseball stadiums and strips of superhighway, office complexes and air conditioners, and cars and housing. Too little money went to the provinces for developing schools, hospitals, roads, and bridges and training teachers. The lack of time devoted to development was even worse. "It's amazing our foreign aid has worked as well as it has," he concluded.

He credited President Kennedy with having chosen thinkers for foreign aid advisers and for having placed American representatives in every province of South Vietnam. The problem with the prov reps was that they necessarily spent all their time with Vietnamese officials, and only the good ones made time to "follow a program down to the last brick being laid in place," he said. "They're the exception and not the rule."

The missing element was the "cadre concept"—the grassroots, team approach IVS was taking in Vietnam and Laos. The Peace Corps projects in Asia were, he believed, too individual oriented and lacked continuity unless a volunteer possessed "an enlightened personal feeling of responsibility."

What he found most frustrating was that the U.S. Operations Mission appreciated IVS but looked upon it as a "freak organization." The solution, he felt strongly, was to form cadres that would integrate the volunteers with the administration of foreign aid.

Acting on his analysis of the problem, Pete wrote a letter to friends and family, hoping to enlist their support for the solution he believed in. He explained his new assignment as an IVS regional supervisor with a team of twelve volunteers stationed in the Delta. He praised his team's efforts in assisting refugees, teaching English, and serving as liaisons between Vietnamese youth, the government, and Catholic Relief Services. "The problem," he stated, "is that we simply do not have enough recruits." IVS still needed education and agriculture technicians, but the volunteers would now also work with refugees.

He appealed to everyone reading his letter to encourage people they knew to apply to IVS. He asked them to urge their congressional representative and senators to plug IVS-Vietnam in their public appearances. The Washington IVS office could provide members of Congress with the names of volunteers they represented.

Late in October, a few days before 25,000 war supporters marched on Washington, D.C., Pete struck a wistful note in a letter home. He had spent a Sunday morning at the Saigon zoo with a group of students. He had seen a goldfish "about a half a yard long with a mouth the size of a milk pail" spring for a piece of bread held by a Vietnamese soldier, and had helped pull the man to safety by his belt and pant legs. In other countries, zoos were virtual geography lessons and parents taught their children about the world by showing them exotic animals, he noted, whereas in Vietnam three-quarters of the animals were from their own country. Seeing the families together left Pete feeling homesick.

He'd had another close call that he didn't write home about. He and Ray Gill had driven the road from Cai Be to My Tho, a distance of some twenty-five miles, through Vietcong-penetrated country. Pete was at the wheel, driving fast—his standard practice, according to Ray, to outrun danger.

> The Vietcong would take unexploded artillery, remove the fuses, rewire the duds, and bury them in a dirt or gravel road. They disguised them very well. Then they ran wires into the rice fields and waited. When a vehicle came along, they quickly connected the wires and exploded the artillery. IVS vehicles looked just like USAID vehicles. The Vietcong would blow up any American vehicle.

At one point on their route, an explosive device detonated immediately behind them. They knew they had narrowly escaped being blown up by a land mine. Ray remembers:

> We were both pretty scared when we got back to My Tho. We talked to MACV. They said road conditions had worsened on Highway 4: "You should not drive for a while. Stay off the roads. If you have to go out to Cai Be, wait 'til you get a chopper."
>
> We agreed we wouldn't drive out there again 'til we got an okay from MACV.
>
> I went to Bangkok for a week of vacation. Pete probably got tired of sitting around. Choppers weren't going that way. There hadn't been any incidents on the road.
>
> The intelligence was very tentative and you took your chances. We didn't think bad things would happen to us. The incident on the road was scary, but it was proof.
>
> I touched down in Saigon and went out to the IVS house. Don Luce told me the news. It was just unbelievable. I'd been looking forward to

getting back and getting to the work Pete and I had going. It was one of the saddest days of my life.

I have another thought: If I hadn't been in Bangkok, I'd have been dead, too.

A week before my fifteenth birthday, Pete called home and spoke with my mother, Holly, and me. Afterward, he told Nana about the call. He said he hadn't gotten a letter from any of us in a month or two. Mom wasn't feeling well. Dad was in California with a helicopter project. I had come back from summer camp "with an overwhelming crush on one of Oklahoma's young, very young, men."

He had his hands full with new IVS recruits. "Two of them are girls, which means trouble, a priori, and sure enough they are trouble," he wrote. "Always wanting attention and Western food and that sort of thing. I'll live, though." The female volunteers were a fine bunch, he was sure, but an administrative headache. "And they are so uninhibited and unruly. Man alive."

Two days later, he asked in his last letter home, "Is Jill over her enormous crush? Boy, I sure wish I could have been around to see the phenomenon."

He was thinking of quitting IVS in June, before his contract ended. Working for USOM instead, he would make more money. Or he might hire on with a construction company. He wanted to get married and go to graduate school at the same time, if he were to get married.

Returning to the subject of Margo, he enumerated more of the qualities he admired in her, addressing my mother:

The thing about Margo is that she's (1) quiet and poised, though not a mouse—very reserved and discreet, is what I'm trying to say. (2) She has a special sense of humor and I can be as droll as I want and she appreciates it. Maybe droll is not the word. (3) She's got a roundabout way of expressing her feelings, sort of like Chinese or Japanese paintings—delicate and reserved, but says what she feels at the right moments. I mean, she's not precipitous. (4) She's not a sports or athletic type, but appreciates taking walks and playing golf, and sunning or digging in the sand pile. . . . (5) She's got a broad outlook even though she votes Goldwater—likes French *chansons*, etc. (6) In summary, she's most like you, and Jackie Kennedy, except she isn't brittle, as I thought Jackie Kennedy was just a bit.

Margo was not raised to be a housewife, as I was not raised to be a garage mechanic, though she'd do all right and isn't ambitious as I'm ambitious to some extent. On the other hand, she's less idealistic and excitable than I am, but still she's not money-conscious. Mostly, she's a hard girl to figure. She's the only girl I know that has some special qualities you have, a lot of breeding, that doesn't consider Oklahomans or Missourians as "quaint" or "novel" though she appreciates my background, enjoys my company when I cast puns or corny anecdotes.

Well, I don't know if the attraction we had for each other will last. I think it will. This summer was the first time in six years we ever told each other how we felt about the other, and the attraction was based on that six years of acquaintance.

Many years later, after I found Pete's letters, I remembered something my friend Patty told me when her husband died. She said that, in the grieving process, it helps to write a letter to the person who is gone.

I wrote to Pete and said I was sorry I hadn't written to him more often. I asked him how he had come up with a way to build a windmill. I said I was proud of him and would love him forever.

I had told my brother while he was alive that I loved him, and I'm sure he knew it, but I wish I had told him more often.

THIRTEEN

Pete's Long-Lost Letters Surface

Three years after Sue Patterson called and offered me her scrapbooks with Pete's letters, I stood inside a highway gift shop in southern Massachusetts, waiting for her. It was All Souls' Day, November 2, 2003.

I had spent the previous two days in Vermont, visiting my daughter at college. Sue and I hadn't spoken since August 2000, but knowing I would be coming east for Parents' Weekend, I had written to ask if we could meet.

A woman about sixty years old with penetrating blue eyes stepped out of a car. I recognized her at once as Sue. Indoors, where we talked and drank coffee, she asked again if I would like the letters. We realized that we had misread each other, both of us thinking the other was reluctant when Sue first said she would share Pete's letters. Now our only consideration was how to get them safely from Massachusetts to California. She suggested bringing them out and the two of us spending a day making photocopies.

Sue was now a hospice administrator. When I told her that my mother had transformed our living room into a shrine to Pete when I was in high school, she nodded. The "shrine period" could last two to three years, she told me, and the grieving period usually lasted about a year.

She thought Pete must have been lonely in Vietnam and must have sought female companionship there. I didn't know. I asked, though, if she recognized a name my parents had mentioned: Margo Bradley. "Yes," she said evenly. "I think I heard that name."

Over the next few months, Sue and I tried to find a few days when she could visit me in California, but meshing our schedules proved difficult. In the meantime, she sent me a spool of audiotape. Inside the three-inch-square box was a note from Pete, saying he had bought a tape recorder for fifteen dollars and was going to send it. It was to be a graduation gift from her father after she finished nursing school. "Love you, Sue, think about you all the time," the note ended.

Since reel-to-reel tape recorders are hard to find, I took the tape to KQED Radio in San Francisco, where I had begun contributing commentaries on the subject of war and peace. As a favor to me, one of the engineers transferred the audio onto a compact disc. I drove home with it, wondering what it would be like to hear Pete's voice again for the first time in forty years.

I popped the CD into my player.

"The first of our little recordings are beginning," he said on July 6 or 7, 1964. "I can't think of anything to say. Sort of strange, talking to the box here. It's a terrible substitute, especially at twelve o'clock at night." Slurping noises followed.

The voice wasn't what I was expecting. I was surprised that I could have forgotten how my brother sounded.

It was the spring of 2004, a season that ushered in a series of amazing discoveries.

"We have a big surprise for you," Cis told me, unlocking the door of Mom's house in Hot Springs, Arkansas.

I had flown there to help my sisters decide what to do with our mother's possessions. Dad had passed away seven years before. For a few years afterward, Mom lived in her own house next door to Cis. Then she suffered a stroke and needed more help than her caregiver could provide, so we moved her to a nursing home in the neighborhood. Physical therapy restored some of her mobility, but my sisters and I eventually realized that she would not be able to return to her home.

By now, dementia had robbed her of many of her memories, but it also had softened her personality. She didn't worry as much. She was more relaxed with us and laughed easily. From her small room, she admired the beauty of the cardinals and trees outside her window, often exclaiming how tall were the loblolly pines, as if seeing them for the first time. She always recognized my sisters and me, and loved it when we told her stories about our lives and hers. She could be peremptory with the attendants, but they knew how to get along with her. When she regressed for a while to her years at a summer camp where only French was spoken, they actually found someone on staff who could translate.

To pay her bills, we needed to rent her house. But first we had to decide what to do with her possessions. It wouldn't be easy. She was a saver, a Connecticut Yankee who hung on to things, even grocery lists and rough drafts of thank you notes.

I followed Cis into the house, which was empty except for rented tables onto which she and Holly had placed the accumulation of our parents' fifty-year marriage, including travel souvenirs, knickknacks, family heirlooms, and even some wedding presents in the original wrapping. I took in the piles of piano music and musty hardcover books, and paintings leaning against the walls.

"You'll never believe what we found," Holly said as we walked into the living room. In the far corner sat my old, blue camp footlocker. "It was locked, but Frank found the key," Cis said.

I knelt and raised the lid to behold a jumble of papers in utter disorder. Then I saw them: Pete's long-lost letters from Vietnam.

I took in the slender, elongated handwriting—so much like mine—on dozens of letters and thin blue aerograms. Photographs of smiling Vietnamese and cactus- and eucalyptus-studded landscapes peeked from envelopes still bearing their stamps from the now-nonexistent Republic of Vietnam.

Sympathy cards bulged from large brown bags. Carefully, I parted papers that covered reels of eight-millimeter film and spools of audiotape in boxes mailed from overseas. There were road maps of Vietnam, photo albums, Pete's handmade Chinese-language flash cards, and other windows into his world.

I resisted the urge to rifle through the letters. It wasn't hard, because Cis was determined for us to get to work and sort Mom and Dad's possessions in three days. She had been storing many of them at her house and wanted to reclaim the space.

She and Holly agreed to ship the trunk to me once I was home again, knowing that of the three of us, I was the one most determined to learn what had happened to Pete.

Two months later, Pete's personal effects were on their way to California. In anticipation of their arrival, I ordered chocolate éclairs from a bakery. I felt as if Pete were finally coming home, and it seemed only right to have one of his favorite desserts on hand.

I asked a friend to stand by for a phone call when the trunk was delivered. The occasion seemed too important to experience alone. Once the box containing the trunk was on the floor of my carport, we unpacked it and looked inside at the disheveled contents. We shook our heads to think that these papers, so valuable in my sight, had received such careless treatment.

I couldn't resist looking at a few letters, including one addressed to me, but I mostly held off. I wanted to read them in order. Besides, they were fragile and I didn't want to over-handle the aged originals.

Over several days, I organized all the contents of the trunk. I arranged the letters chronologically. Then I took them to the copy store and made three sets of photocopies: one for myself and one for each of my sisters.

Cis, Holly, and I had waited a long time to read these letters—in fact, we had never hoped to see them again. I wasn't going to withhold them now. We had recently lost our father and two fond uncles. Our mother's mental capacity was dimming. Through our losses, my sisters and I had grown closer. We had learned to rely on each other's particular strengths for the many tasks that adult children face as their elders age. I was not going to hoard Pete or his letters, as Mom had. I was determined not to let another day pass before sending my sisters the letters that, finally, I understood belonged to all of us.

On June 25, 2004, I sat down in my living room to read my brother's words forty years after he wrote them. I took my time. I wanted to savor them. In his sense of humor, intelligence, and buoyancy that trumped whatever frustrations he aired, Pete came to life again. Poring over the letters, I encountered the same energetic personality I remembered.

It was evening when midway through my reading I walked into the kitchen for a glass of water. Suddenly it hit me that the stack of letters was getting shorter and I would soon reach the last one. Pete would be dead. I sobbed at the stark reality that his life, so full of promise, had come to an abrupt end.

I resumed my reading the next night. As I put down the last letter, I felt something I have not experienced before or since: I sensed that Pete was in the room. So vivid was this impression, and so specific as to where he was standing, that I reached out my hand. I wondered if the space would feel warm, or cold, or of form. It did not.

Not knowing what to make of this sensation, I asked an Episcopal priest and friend about it. He told me that he had once led a class for widowed spouses, and that when he asked how many of them had sensed their wife's or husband's presence, everyone in the group raised a hand. All had perceived their loved one nearby, on "the other side."

How can you know? I asked. He shrugged. Well then, if it is "real," I pressed, what does it mean? He said that, for some reason, God has permitted the veil between the seen and unseen worlds to be thinner at certain times and certain places, such as around Halloween and at, for example, Machu Picchu and Iona, Scotland. Our loved ones may also draw close when we need them, he said, but they don't stay long.

There was no proving any of this, but it was comforting. Since then, I have felt what I can only describe as a "softening" around All Hallows' Eve.

Along with sixty-four letters Pete wrote to my family, the trunk contained back issues of *Time*, *Life*, and *National Geographic* magazines featuring Vietnam; the "IVS Handbook" and annual reports from 1963 through 1966; the Office of Rural Affairs manual; and articles about the war in general and Pete in particular.

A bag of frayed ribbons, some with small metal or plastic ornaments attached, triggered my memory of a photograph in the lacquer box sent to my parents by Don Luce. Soon I had matched the ribbons to a letter from the IVS office, confirming that they were collected from a dozen floral wreaths at the memorial service in Saigon. Someone had been thoughtful enough to send them to my parents.

When I unfurled a length of white fabric, painted entirely in Vietnamese save for the word "Hunting," I recognized it from a color slide I had seen. It was the dedication banner from the library in Phan Rang.

There were horoscope booklets, the kind sold near cash registers, for Cancer, Pete's astrological sign; Sagittarius, my sisters'; and Scorpio, my father's and mine. In a chapter called "Character Analysis" in the Scorpio book, my mother had darkly underlined the words "inhuman insensibility towards the natural feelings and reactions of others." She had almost obliterated, with a pencil, the sentence "You understand life, its difficulties and problems, and are capable of deep sympathy and true understanding."[1]

In the Cancer booklet, the monthly outlook for the month Pete was killed urged "extra care in travel, especially if you drive your own car. . . . Taking chances is not advisable." The day of his death carried a warning of "unforeseen enmity."[2] My mother had underscored those words and drawn a large exclamation mark in the margin.

A leather album opened to a photograph of Pete in a tuxedo, standing beside a beautiful brunette wearing a black dress and white gloves. Somewhere, years before, I had seen a picture of Margo and knew this was she. On the next pages were school photos of Holly and me.

Cis had sent me a hand-held viewer so I could preview Pete's films. I looked at the fourteen reels he had sent home before I took them to a professional for transfer onto DVD. Although many were blotchy from heat damage, they brought back memories of watching Pete's latest movies from Vietnam with my parents and Holly in Oklahoma City. Tears gathered to my eyes when I came upon the footage of Pete's last homecoming and the two of us standing side by side.

In his address book, I turned to the letter B and found "Margo Bradley." Having heard my parents mention her name long ago but knowing very little about her, I was surprised to see that her parents' home was within twenty miles of my grandmother's. I wondered if I would ever learn what Pete and Margo had meant to each other, let alone meet her.

Reading Pete's letters had been a mostly enjoyable experience, because he came to life on the page. The two hundred sympathy letters and cards stuffed into paper bags were another story. Many were drenched with emotion. Some were beautifully crafted examples of a disappearing literary form.

I grouped them into categories of IVS people, U.S. government employees, Wesleyan contacts, and so on. Pete had made good friends. I wondered what direction their lives had taken in the intervening years.

Kirtland Mead was one friend I wondered about. He had written to my parents from Germany, where he was studying on a Fulbright scholarship:

> I learned of Peter's tragic end only yesterday. A fraternity brother wrote me, knowing that I was Peter's friend and would want to know any news about him, however tragic.

There will be many letters like this. Endowed with unusual personal warmth, he had the rare ability to have many close friends. If our experience at Alpha Delta Phi is any indication, Peter was surely the most popular American in the Delta. . . . The only thing that alleviates the sorrow I feel at this loss is that I know he will always be remembered by all the people he was able to help. . . .

I am among those he helped. . . . I came to college rather achievement-oriented. I worked much too hard freshman year, and thus missed many of the opportunities for development with *people* which were so characteristic of the Wesleyan environment. More than anyone else those early years, Peter taught me these things. Either in the Yacht Club or at night over coffee, he always seemed to have time to listen and to talk. I wish I could say I had given him one-third of what he gave me in the way of attitudes for life. . . . In the midst of deciding what he should do after college, he still had faith that something would come, refused to see life as ruthless or full of tension.

As you may know, he called me at college from Oklahoma City last year when he was home. I was immensely glad to hear he found his work meaningful, a sense of direction was what he needed; I hope I am right in assuming from this call that he had found it before the end. The world would be too cruel if people so good as Peter were denied even the right to personal satisfaction after having given so much. . . .

To go with my sincerest condolences in a time of sorrow, I have taken the liberty of composing a poem in terms of the imagery of sailing, where Peter and I first found common ground for friendship. The quest is for the island which must lie over the horizon. I will always remember your son Peter because he made the voyage so beautiful, because he helped me and so many others along the way, and because in the end he found the island.

He had enclosed a poem called "Sea of Clouds," written in his own hand. Was he now a published poet or a literature professor? On the Internet, I found his name and a telephone number, and guessed it was the same man. I left him a message, asking if he was the Kirtland Mead who had known Pete Hunting. The next day, he called me.

Kirt remembered a drive into Manhattan from his family's home on Long

Island. While he sat in the back seat, his father, who had grown up in China, and Pete "rattled on" in Mandarin.

Pete had visited the Alpha Delta Phi house while he was on home leave, and he and Kirt had stayed up all night talking about Vietnam. "I remember after that discussion telling a friend, 'This guy is more dangerous to the Vietcong than a whole platoon of soldiers,'" he told me. "He was a natural leader."

I asked if he remembered a poem he had enclosed with his letter to my parents and if he would like to have copies of both. After I sent them, he explained the meaning of "Sea of Clouds":

> The poem was first written, if memory serves, in early 1965, as we all realized that our comfortable college world was ending and that we needed to confront the real world. The title came from the Sea of Clouds on the moon, where NASA had landed a probe in preparation for the Apollo manned missions, then in heavy development.
>
> I sent it unchanged to your parents, believing that it symbolized any young man's voyage into the unknown. We must all imagine, as I said in my note, that Peter found an Island of repose somewhere over the horizon. He deserved it.
>
> Peter was that very rare individual who has great dreams and quietly proceeds to make them come true. He was a man of quiet strength and principles who got on with it, living out his destiny. I would have wished to compose the poem directly for him, rather than "repurpose" it as I in fact did. He was not, in my memory, a sailor from birth, as I am, but he liked the sport when I took him along to race Raven sloops in New London at the Coast Guard Academy. He was always up for an adventure and a lark. More than once we got pretty wet riding the rail and screaming downwind under spinnaker. . .
>
> Please keep in touch. Short of having Peter back, it is nevertheless a great consolation to know that he has a baby sister as loving as you so obviously are.

We not only kept in touch, but Kirt and his wife, Susan, visited me in California three years later. By then, Kirt, who was not a poet by profession but an international business consultant, was writing poetry again.

Some letters contained an intriguing detail about Pete's last day, such as the one from an official of the U.S. Operations Mission working in the Mekong

Delta. He stated that for whatever comfort it might offer my parents, Pete's death was not the result of any "foolhardy action." Pete was driving on a road that he knew involved some risk, the man said, but it was a risk many Americans took every day in the performance of their duties. Indications were that Pete was killed "almost instantly." The man offered to send my parents an official report when it was completed.[3] He enclosed a sketch of Pete, assumed to be the work of a Vietnamese friend, which he had found on the seat of Pete's vehicle. It was the same drawing that had sat framed on a shelf in my parents' house when I was in high school.

I studied the current ivs alumni directory and old annual reports to match men and women to sympathy letters identifying the writer as a volunteer. Some were no longer living, such as Harold Kooker, whose chance meeting with Pete outside a barbershop in Vinh Long had made him the last teammate to see Pete alive.

Some ivsers' family members had reached out to my parents. Carl Stockton had begun doctoral studies at Oxford University when he learned of his teammate's death from his sister, Virginia. While still in Vietnam, he had asked Pete to call her while he was home on leave. Carl, Virginia, and their mother had all sent their condolences. I sent him their three letters, for which he was grateful.

I had once believed it was wrong, or at least improper, to ask questions about my brother. When at first I started contacting people who knew him, I had wondered if they would deem my interest in Pete morbid — not unlike the annual visits that the Civil War general Daniel Sickles paid to his amputated leg, which he had lost at Gettysburg, in the Army Medical Museum.

But as one by one I met Pete's friends and found them glad to talk with me, I began to overcome the emotional guardedness I had learned at home. We hadn't discussed Pete, and now I was talking about him with anyone, including complete strangers. The more I did, the more I started to fully inhabit my own life.

Kirt Mead, Carl Stockton, and Frank Wisner were among the many in Pete's circle who had gone on to distinguished careers in the private sector, academics, and public service. They had been shaped by Vietnam. "It makes me sad all over again to think of Peter, maybe more so than when I was so young," the political economist and former Commerce Department official Paul London told me. "He missed a great deal that I have been privileged to have."

They had been shaped, and I was being reshaped. My long journey to retrieve the connection with my brother had put me in touch with something beyond myself. My story of loss and family and war was not merely personal, I was learning, but something I shared with many.

The trunk also contained correspondence between the IVS offices in Washington and Saigon, and my parents. Executive Director Gardiner sent the most specific account of the ambush I had yet uncovered, in the form of a letter Don Luce wrote to the team on November 15, 1965:

> It is difficult to write of the tragic death of Pete Hunting. I do hope a fuller account will make it a little easier in this difficult time.
>
> We received news of Pete's death at 4:00 P.M. November 12. His body was flown immediately by helicopter to Saigon.
>
> He was ambushed fifteen kilometers southwest of Can Tho on his way to Soc Trang at 2:48 P.M. Friday November 12. Five minutes before the ambush, he had passed a military convoy. They reported to have seen two Vietnamese in the car, which one villager later said left with the Viet Cong. The [Associated Press] reported that these two "were believed to have joined the Viet Cong." There seems to be no basis for this statement. It is just as likely that an ambush was set up for the convoy and the two passengers were forced to go with the Viet Cong.
>
> The road which Pete was driving on was driven on a fairly regular basis by Americans including the province representative. Pete had checked one source and had been told it was all right to go. That morning he had informed the regional director of USOM he was driving to Soc Trang.
>
> IVS/Washington was immediately called by military phone. They informed Pete's family. IVS/Washington was requested to send flowers from the IVS members in Vietnam. We also requested that Willi Meyers, a close friend of Pete and a former IVS/Vietnam member, represent us at the funeral....
>
> The loss of Pete Hunting affects us all deeply. I know that Pete would want us to continue our work in the same spirit which he exhibited during his life.

I remembered Gloria Johnson's letter to Don, in which she described him looking more worried after Pete's death than she had ever seen him. She, along with Phyllis and David Colyer, all former team members, had asked Don what would become of IVS now that a volunteer had been killed. I thought of the anxious parents learning of an IVSer's "murder," as it was widely reported, and what little comfort IVS could realistically offer them as to their sons' and daughters' safety. I considered Don's loyalty to his Vietnamese friends and his concern for their future, and what I had heard about his disinclination to believe Vietnamese friends could have led Pete to his death.

For the first time, I grasped the awful position Don had been in, as IVS's in-country director. He was just thirty-one, and not only had he lost a good friend and colleague, but the organization's future and the lives of his team were in his hands.

Don believed that IVS should continue in Vietnam and Pete would want it to, and it did.

Three mysteries remained:

Who were the two passengers in Pete's vehicle?
Why did my mother say that Pete's letters had been destroyed?
Who was Margo?

A single word in a letter led me to the enigmatic person whom I had all but given up on finding. Writing to my mother from Rome, Pete said Margo seemed to have changed since her knew her at "Manhattanville."

I went to the Web site of Manhattanville College and tried to divine, from the list of staff members, whom to approach. In an e-mail I said I hoped to find an alumna who had been a friend of my parents. Assuming the college's policy might prevent the release of her personal information, I offered to write a letter that could be forwarded to her.

Two weeks later, the recipient of my e-mail, who had been on vacation until then, sent me Margo's address and married name.

I composed a note to her: I hoped I hadn't startled her too much by writing. I knew she was important to Pete. Would she be interested in corresponding with me?

A few days later, I came home to find a message waiting on my answering machine:

Hello, Jill. This is Margo. I was absolutely floored to receive your letter. It seems we're on the same wavelength. About six months ago I pulled out

Pete's letters to me and started to edit them with the thought of sharing them with a wider audience. Of course, I wouldn't have done anything without contacting you and your family. But I hadn't had any luck trying to find you on the Internet. I was thrilled to hear from you.

That evening, we spoke for an hour. I asked how she had learned of Pete's death. She was working in an office in Manhattan when a friend called and said she had just heard some terrible news on the radio. Without saying a word to anyone, Margo picked up her purse, left the office, and walked to the friend's home. A call to the radio station confirmed the report. That was a Friday. On Monday she returned to work because, as she said, in those days it was expected.

She had married, but her husband was no longer living. She never told him about the young man who had died in Vietnam.

Were she and Pete engaged, I asked. No, but they had "talked all around it." Pete wanted her to come to Vietnam and teach English, but that had been his dream, not hers. "We thought we would live forever," she said.

She was sorry to hear that my father had passed away and my mother's memory was failing. She had corresponded with them.

I remembered Mom saying that, after a while, she encouraged Margo not to feel bound to our family and to go on and live a full, happy life. The letting-go gesture must have been difficult. My mother had many admirable traits, and one of her best was that she took the high road.

Margo asked if she had been able "to go on with things," because "she seemed to have done that so well." When I said she had shown that persona to the outside world, Margo understood. She recalled her saying, "I keep pushing things back in the closet."

Calling my sisters by the nicknames used only in our family, she asked about "Cissy and Holly." She was happy to hear that they were doing well and we all had children. She had nephews and a niece, but no children of her own. She asked if I was in touch with Pete's friend Gene. I gave her his address.

I inquired about her parents. Her mother was gone now, but her father was in his nineties. He still lived in the house he purchased from my grandfather's estate, she said, and she and her sisters grew up there. Had I stopped to think when I found Pete's address book that relatives of mine in Connecticut still lived in the same house after fifty years, I would have written to Margo at that address right away.

Did I know, she asked, that her father had worked for my grandfather? Having gone through dozens of boxes of Mom's papers, I knew from newspaper clippings that Mr. Bradley succeeded my grandfather as president of the company he founded. One article had a photograph of Mr. Bradley with a few employees and members of my family when they unveiled a plaque in Popeye's honor.

Holly had once heard a relative say that our grandfather had a "mistress," to whom he left a house. I had come across his will and seen the woman's name, so when I saw her in the newspaper photograph, I had put all this together. She worked for my grandfather and probably had an intimate relationship with him. When he died, she stayed with the company as a corporate officer and worked with Margo's father. That explained my grandmother's reaction to the Bradley name. Nana must have been bitterly jealous not to forgive Mr. Bradley for associating with her rival for Popeye's affection. If, having been under Nana's influence, my mother was also a jealous wife, that too made sense.

Speaking with Margo, I detected nothing remotely "controversial" about her. She seemed so genteel, in fact, that I was sure now that I understood why Pete had used that word. The controversy belonged to the past.

Margo said she would like to send Pete's letters and to return a posthumous medal my mother had given her. She felt that the medal belonged in our family. Although I had said nothing about the medal, my sisters and I had wondered why our mother would give away a memento of our brother.

As our conversation came to a close, Margo said Pete had told her not to worry about his safety. He had, however, mentioned dangerous situations he'd been in and close calls he'd had. She asked whether he had said anything to the family about an ominous scene he witnessed shortly before his death. He had not.

One day the sky had suddenly turned dark, she said, then three cranes alighted from a grove of trees. Pete's interpreter started shaking, but when Pete asked him what was wrong, he wouldn't say. Margo received the letter a few days after Pete was killed.

I had been taking notes, because I didn't think I would remember all the details of our conversation and I wanted to tell my sisters about it.

"Premonition?" I wrote.

Four days later, I received three notebooks, each containing forty-two of Pete's letters edited and typed by Margo. I mailed two of the notebooks to my sisters.

A week and a day after that, Sue's scrapbooks with sixty-eight letters arrived.

With the sixty-four letters Pete wrote home and one given to me by John Sommer, I now had 175.

After reading Pete's letters to Margo, I still didn't know how they had met or what their dreams for the future might have been, so I asked if she would write an introduction to the letters. She sent this:

> I was 23 years old, and living and working in New York City when Pete Hunting was ambushed and killed thousands of miles from his loved ones in a country virtually unknown to most Americans at that time. He was the man I had hoped to marry. We thought we had our whole lives ahead of us, but on that terrible November day when death took Pete and all of his personal hopes and dreams for the future, my life, too, changed forever.
>
> In [his letters], written between 1963 and 1965, Pete recounted several "near misses" with the Viet Cong, but he always brushed off concerns for his safety. In hindsight, I believe he refused to let any fear he may have felt drive him away from those he was trying to help. Because of his attitude, I simply didn't fully grasp the dangers he faced working in a war zone, and so his death was all the more unexpected and traumatic.
>
> In difficult times, we must always keep something beautiful in our hearts. For me, that meant getting through those first grief-filled days, weeks, and months by remembering the many good times Pete and I had shared. Our paths first crossed when we were just kids at Lake Sebec in Maine where his family and mine were staying with Pete's maternal grandfather. Back then, Pete delighted in spending hours climbing over rocks, exploring the woods, and swimming in ice-cold water. We were far too young and much too different in our interests to be the slightest bit attracted to one another.
>
> That all changed years later when Pete came East to attend Wesleyan University. By then, he was all grown up, quite handsome, bright, funny,

totally unpretentious, and full of Midwestern charm. I had never met anyone quite like him. For the next four years we dated until he joined IVS and left for his great adventure in Vietnam shortly after graduation. Over the next two years, our letters substituted for dates. I saw him for the last time just four months before his death while he was on home leave between his two tours of service.

In time, I tucked Pete's letters in a desk drawer and pushed memories of him into the farthest recesses of my mind. But we never truly forget those we have loved. Four decades later I retrieved and re-read Pete's letters and decided to share them with his sisters so they would know even more about their remarkable brother. . . .

Pete was a warm-hearted and generous-spirited human being. These personality traits and his inimitable style come across in [his] letters in which he provides lively accounts of the projects he worked on while in Vietnam—from hamlet education and flood relief to the building of windmills, rabbit hutches, and wells. He was passionate about his work, despite frustrating bureaucratic and other obstacles that created delays, and delighted in the Vietnamese people who he had come to love and admire.

I received Pete's last letter a few days after his death. He had just witnessed a scene of awesome beauty that may also have been an omen of how violently his life would end. He had also had a surprising encounter with an elderly man who had been with the Viet Minh during the war against the French. Pete was in soaring spirits. The former freedom fighter had understood and approved of what Pete was doing—as did so many others.

We began corresponding regularly. Margo shared some of her happy memories of "Mr. Russell," the name she used to refer to my grandfather. In Maine, her family and Popeye's employees stayed with him at one of the two hunting camps he owned at Lake Sebec. My family stayed at the other camp. She told me about taking rides around the lake in my grandfather's Chris Craft and waving when they saw us on our dock.

She recalled the all-day drive through New England along rough backroads, the hot dog stand where they always stopped, and the heads that turned as Popeye's eight-passenger black Cadillac sped through small towns. She described the good-natured shouting when a client capsized his canoe and the nightly amusement of someone calling out, after everyone had turned in, that there was a bear in his room. We reminisced about swimming in the frigid lake and roughing it in houses without electricity or running water.

She knew the people and places of my childhood as well as a member of my own family. We were related by two men, my grandfather and Pete.

I suggested that we meet in New York on my return from Italy that fall. When I asked my travel agent to reserve a room for me in the hotel Margo recommended, she advised me, "It's more expensive than the Waldorf. Do you want me to find you something else?" It was all right, I said. If I were to pro-rate the cost over the many years I had waited to meet Margo, the room would seem quite reasonable.

Before the year 2004 closed, Larry Laverentz called to say he had found an address for the intelligence operative who told him a rumor about Pete's killing. I wrote to Mr. O'Connor and asked if he would tell me what he remembered.

I wanted to learn anything I could, so when he called me, I said I had heard the worst of the story by now. I didn't want him to worry about my reaction to whatever he might tell me.

I said I had heard that the road was well traveled and that an ambush there would have been unusual. "It could happen anywhere," he said. "On any road."

I had heard that Pete had started carrying a weapon. I wondered if he had tried to defend himself. "It doesn't matter if you have a gun on the seat," he said. "If someone puts a gun to your ear, you're not going to reach for the gun."

"He was led away. That's what I heard," O'Connor said. "He was very highly regarded. That's what I remember of Pete."

O'Connor starting talking about an explosion he had barely survived. He had feigned death. He remembered the episode vividly, including the man who put his gun to O'Connor's chest and the other who said not to bother shooting him because he was obviously dead.

His story was gripping, but I couldn't get my mind off "He was led away." If that were true, then Pete had not died instantly. He had experienced terror in his final minutes.

"How would they have stopped Pete?" I asked.

"They could block the road, shoot a tire out, or wave him down," he said. "He might think they were friendlies. This is all conjecture. An ambush can mean several things. A roadblock was an ambush then: a tree across the road, you move the tree, a mine blows up. All it takes is that somebody stands out in the road with a weapon and he wears jungle greens or ODs, olive drabs, or they could step out with a weapon and Pete could step out of the vehicle— 'What's the problem?'"

If he had tried to talk to the assailants, wouldn't speaking Vietnamese have looked suspicious and made the situation more dangerous?

"You speak Vietnamese, you're a suspect right from the beginning, you're CIA. He was an effective American. Pete was one of the first of us civilians to go. Civilians were high profile, especially *positively* effective ones. And damaging to their efforts. You don't have to carry a weapon to destroy the enemy. He was loved by the Vietnamese."

After O'Connor was nearly killed, the province chief had mounted an operation to kill the guys that "did" him, he said. "They got all but one. I met him about three years later. I was in the village, and he kept grabbing at my left arm, which was very tender—I had a fourteen- to sixteen-inch gash. He said, 'I'm so happy to see you're alive. If I'd known it was you, I wouldn't have done it.' It took a load off that man's shoulders."

Was it true that the people who killed Pete were executed?

"If I recall correctly, they went and mounted an operation," O'Connor said. "They went after them and reported it was successful."

I asked what the purpose of killing them would have been.

"To say, 'You can't do that to those that are helping us.' To send a message: 'They shouldn't have done this to him, and they shouldn't do it to his successor.'" I remembered an IVSer named Roger Hintze, who came after Pete, saying that someone from a nearby village warned him never to drive on the road south of Can Tho.

O'Connor went back to Vietnam after the war. He met General Vo Nguyen Giap, the North Vietnamese army commander. "We talked one on one as old warriors," he said. "He told me, 'We were ready to give up, but we saw that the [antiwar protests were growing and] you were going to defeat yourselves if we just waited it out.' We're going to get an anti-Iraqi sentiment and defeat ourselves again."

We returned to the subject of Pete. "I remember the total shock throughout the delta," he said. "Anger. Sorrow. Pete was a little wild in certain ways, he took certain risks—'They can't hurt me, I'm wearing a white shirt.' He believed in what he was doing. Better yet, the people believed in him. If he was still alive, Pete would be welcome and people would remember him. They don't forget."

Four years later, O'Connor called me again. He had come across my letter from 2004 and couldn't remember if we had ever spoken.

I reminded him of some of the things he told me—that Pete was "led away," for example. Now he said he'd heard that Pete resisted, that he wasn't "agreeable in going." He added, "A vc hothead would just fire his weapon."

He mentioned the names of several Vietnam hands I should meet. One was a high-ranking foreign service officer who had lived in the Mekong Delta. I knew the man by reputation. It happened that I was on my way to Washington, D.C., where they both lived. O'Connor suggested the three of us have lunch. Nothing came of it.

Since our initial conversation, I had been told he was "a bit of a talker." I thought back to something he said the first time we spoke: "This is all conjecture." Then, and still, I was trying to get at the truth about what happened to Pete, but it wasn't easy sometimes to separate an opinion from a good guess or the facts. In any case, O'Connor told a good story.

FOURTEEN

Darkening Skies

In my hands was Pete's last letter, the one Margo received a few days after his death.

Written sometime early in November 1965, it began, "This job grows on me, although I can't think of any specific reason why."

An old man had expressed approval of his work with youth, and Pete felt good about it. He had been lending a hand to a high school friendship club from the city of Can Tho. The students were young and new to construction work, but they built a road in the hamlet of An Quoi. Their inspiration and stamina for the job had made the project a resounding success.

The road passed by the home of the old man, an artist named Tay-Do, and his wife. They were grateful that their route to town would no longer be muddy. They served lemonade to the hard-working crew.

During a rest break, Tay-Do overheard Pete deliver a pep talk about the students' important role in their country's future:

> I was telling them how they were the hope of Vietnam—that they proba-
> bly didn't realize it, but they were part of the Cach Man Hoa Binh (Peace-
> ful Revolution) of Vietnamese youth. I pointed out that they didn't like
> manual labor, that they were the elite, the rich, but the country is doomed
> if they don't have an appreciation for the needs of the general society,
> etc., etc.

It was the first time they'd heard anything practical and personally relevant to themselves.

Tay-Do was listening. He was with the Viet Minh in his younger days, but dropped it and now hates Communists as "betrayers of the revolution." He's really an old Mandarin type.

I felt good all over for two or three days after that morning. First they are surprised because you're an American and actually working. Second you speak Vietnamese and they start giggling as they try to test your fluency. Then they are triply surprised that you can say such things.

As Pete was about to leave, Tay-Do handed him a sketch, inscribed, "For whom has rendered service for the Vietnamese."

An Quoi was not the first hamlet where Pete had talked with young people about their country's future. Six months earlier, just before he left Vietnam for home leave, he had been a guest at a celebration in Ba Thap, where he had installed a windmill.

The date was May 1, a holiday when Vietcong soldiers could return to their homes. Pete drank beer with two young men whom he had never seen before. Several months later, a writer named George Chuljean recounted their conversation:

Pete wrote in recalling the incident:

"As we drank, the two young men (named Chou and An) were very friendly and asked more than the usual amount of pointed questions, wanting to know about my job, my relation to the Vietnamese and American governments, my opinion of province officials, and, as usual, my appraisal of Vietnamese womanhood. I'd never before had such a thorough grilling at the hands of two young Vietnamese peasants."

When he returned to Ba Thap a few days later Chou and An had gone. Commenting in a report on his activities Pete wrote:

"I'll never know for whose side Chou and An will give their support in the final crucial struggle, but I will always consider myself lucky to have been able to contribute directly and indirectly to Vietnamese understanding of our U.S. role, and of the issues they themselves must decide upon."[1]

Sent to my parents after Pete was killed on November 12, the story stated that Pete's body had been found "slumped alongside his jeep," contradicting Mr. O'Connor's story that he had been walked down the road.

On November 11, Pete drove to Long Xuyen, in An Giang Province, to see how Fred Stone's work was coming along. Fred was helping farmers increase rice and soybean yields, and demonstrating the use of fertilizer and insecticides.

The life of an ivser could be lonesome, Pete knew. Part of his new job as a regional team leader was to boost his team members' morale. Sometimes, a volunteer just needed someone to talk to.

He spent the night at Fred's place. They stayed up late, talking about ivs, the work other volunteers were doing, and their travels. That night, it rained very hard. "Pete was his usual self," Fred remembers. "Very enthusiastic, full of energy and ideas."

The next morning, he left early. He needed to get back to Can Tho, about forty miles away. There, Carey Coulter, another member of Pete's team, was supposed to show him the place he had just rented in a commercial area near the new bus station. It was big enough for both of them. Pete wanted to have a base in Can Tho because the location would make it easier to get around. Together, they would then drive to Soc Trang, down in Ba Xuyen Province, to see Paul Lukitsch.

Pete had recently helped Paul find a new apartment. Now he was going to arrange for a Vietnamese language teacher for him. He might have had someone in mind—a young lady he had met.

But Carey had a last-minute change of plans. A few evenings earlier, while he was having dinner in a little Chinese restaurant, he overheard some Special Forces men talking about a school they wanted to set up for refugees on Phu Quoc, an island off Vietnam's southwestern coast. They complained that they weren't getting anywhere. They needed educational materials. Carey told them he knew the regional education adviser and offered to talk to him. Then, with a USAID man, he went to Saigon and raided a warehouse for school supplies. The USAID man was going to deliver them to the island. But at the eleventh hour, the Special Forces men insisted that Carey come, too.

When Pete reached Can Tho and learned that Carey had gone to the airport, he hurried there to stop him. It was too late. Carey was already on a plane, which was taxiing onto the runway, when he saw Pete pull up in his Scout and get out of the vehicle. He was alone. "I last saw Pete shaking his fist at me," he recalls.

Carey returned from Phu Quoc and ran into an acquaintance who was relieved to see him alive. The man thought he had left with Pete for Soc Trang and been taken prisoner. In the meantime, Pete's Scout had been brought back to Can Tho. Carey watched as U.S. personnel examined the vehicle to determine the angle from which every bullet had been fired. Only one was believed to have struck Pete.

Two days later, on November 14, U.S. forces clashed with North Vietnamese units in the Ia Drang Valley, more than three hundred miles away. It was the first major ground battle of the war. On November 19 *Time* magazine reported, "The toll of Red dead may have reached 600."[2] The number of American casualties in the past four years had just passed the one thousand mark, not counting civilians.

Pete's last letter concluded with a description of an awesome scene:

> I went down to Rach Gia on the far southwest Delta and saw one of the most breathtakingly beautiful scenes in my life. It was as though I'd stepped into a classical Chinese painting come alive.
>
> I was helping our man in Rach Gia distribute cement to a rural hamlet located on the banks of a canal intersection for the construction of pigsties. There was a wooden Y-shaped footbridge connecting the three sections of the hamlet, arched so as to allow boats to pass underneath.
>
> The bank was lined with coconut trees and the houses set back from the trees with their backs to the rice paddies. Looking past the bridge to one end of the hamlet one could see a Khmer temple with a gracefully upward curved spiked roof with coconut trees and cypress trees around the entrance.
>
> Everything was still and dark because heavy black thunderclouds filled the skies. Suddenly there was a flash of lightening and a thunderclap. Three storks or egrets flapped out of the coconut trees on the bank

of the canal and flew over the temple. The interpreter with me started shivering and quaking at such omens, but refused to interpret them for me, saying he wasn't superstitious, yet shuddering and quaking all the time.

Must admit, I shuddered a bit. It was just so beautiful.

From palm readings to subterranean dragons, Pete had come across religious folklore in Vietnam before. He was no stranger to superstition, in fact, having been exposed to it at home. My mother had a predilection for the supernatural. Descended from Puritans and raised in the austerity of New England Congregationalism, she also moved comfortably in their shadow side. She was given to the occasional premonition and would neither kill a white spider, for example, nor allow an umbrella to be opened indoors, because it was bad luck. My father, the son of a Congregational minister, placed his faith in reason. Pete probably had a bit of both in him.

Americans and Vietnamese alike drew on folklore and superstition during the war. In Tim O'Brien's story "Stockings," in *The Things They Carried*, an American soldier wears his girlfriend's pantyhose around his neck for good luck, even after she breaks up with him.

Major General Edward Lansdale studied Vietnamese proverbs and customs, and applied his understanding of traditional beliefs to counterinsurgency strategy. In 1967, he suggested to American Ambassador Ellsworth Bunker that the U.S. mission compile a list of soothsayers who influenced Vietnamese leaders and whose guidance might run counter to American objectives. He took special note of auspicious dates, religious meanings associated with colors, and jokes and nicknames made up about Americans, and sent memos encouraging others to heed them.[3]

Developers of psychological warfare also employed traditional beliefs to gain advantage over the enemy. One psyops, or psychological operations, policy advisory prepared by the Joint U.S. Public Affairs Office in Saigon stated:

Many Vietnamese, particularly in rural areas, are provoked into a fear response if startled at night by the hoot of an owl or the call of a crow. These are considered death omens. The response will not occur, however, if the sound can be detected in any way as originating from an artificial source, such as a loudspeaker.[4]

The advisory noted that enemy superstitions could be manipulated "to achieve results favorable to the friendly [South Vietnamese] forces" if "would-be manipulators" were certain the superstitions were real and powerful.[5]

"Friendly superstitions" were equally important to understand. The same advisory cited a deadly blunder committed by an inexperienced American adviser. Accompanying a South Vietnamese unit on a patrol, he heard sounds that he feared would give away their position. The sounds were coming from stone, wood, and metal amulets worn around the necks of members of the unit. The adviser collected the amulets and had them sent back to the base camp, with tragic consequences. Half of the Vietnamese men were killed. The others were as good as lost, believing it was their time to die because they had lost their protection.[6]

Looking for information about the meaning of coconut trees, birds, temples, and darkening skies in Vietnamese tradition, I scoured Internet sites. I was unable to formulate a cohesive interpretation of Pete's letter. It was then that I turned to a member of the Yale faculty in the Southeast Asia Studies program.

I asked Van Phu Quang if he could help me understand a scene my brother witnessed in Vietnam. He said he would help if he could. He continued:

> Vietnamese, especially people in the countryside, have observed the signs and patterns of the natural environment in order to know what to think, to make decisions, to predict the future, to interpret events of the past and the present, and to act accordingly.
>
> Animals such as birds have an important place in observing the signs of nature. Different birds have different meanings (good or bad, or neutral). In Vietnamese folk tales, many stories involve birds.
>
> Could you elaborate on your question a little, so I can figure out the direction to go?

I sent Pete's description of the scene, adding that he had been killed a day or two later.

After expressing his sympathy, Quang said he would consult a friend whose special interest was Vietnamese folk religion. His own field, he said, was primarily "philosophical questions." In addition to teaching language and literature, he was a lecturer in Eastern philosophy.

A few weeks later he apologetically informed me that his friend, and two of that friend's friends, all agreed that no connection could be made between bad omens and the birds, temple, and storm Pete described. They speculated that the interpreter might have been fearful because of the real danger of violence or the approach of nightfall.

He then moved from the literal to the philosophical:

> From my perspective, I think it was a personal experience, almost like a religious experience. One is so mindful that one has a sense of awareness of everything, including time and oneself. Everything is so transparent and one can see both life and death. You don't have to "see" God but you just experience something so "real."
>
> Existential philosophers talked about the sense of dread (Kierkegaard, Sartre, for example)—the sense of the present, and it's very real. That's my reading.
>
> C. S. Lewis talked about his conversion experience and something that "overtook" him—some power or spirit. Graham Greene also talked about this conversion experience. It's like you came down with the flu and there is nothing you can do to stop it.
>
> Buddhists would use the notion of enlightenment or insight to express this "timelessness of a moment." One experiences both a sense of the finite (death, danger, fear, dread, sorrow, suffering) and the infinite (solitude, peace, God, joy) at the same time. Perhaps at this moment one also feels "the lightness of being."
>
> There are many stories about people who, before they died, experienced or felt things that somehow connected to their death. A Vietnamese man from my church just returned to Vietnam to visit his relatives and children in Saigon. He kept telling them, "This is my last time seeing you." His relatives told him "not to talk like that." He died a few days later.
>
> Vietnamese also believe that if one dreams of losing a tooth (a molar), it's a sign that some member of the family is going to die.
>
> Best wishes, and I hope you will make sense of your brother's omen soon.

At first I was disappointed. I wondered if Quang was too polite to tell me what a terrible outcome the omens had pointed to. I stubbornly felt that the birds and other details must mean something.

Then I remembered that I had written the word "premonition" when Margo described the scene to me. I read Pete's letter again. At first it had seemed to me that he didn't know what to make of the "breathtakingly beautiful" sight. But now, with Quang's wider scope, I saw that I had been too focused on a literal answer. I was missing the more important, philosophical perspective. Quang's interpretation enabled me to relent and understand Pete's words on another plane.

As Margo said, and as Pete had written to me, he didn't want us to worry about his safety. He downplayed the danger he lived with and the risks he took in the performance of his duties. From time to time he expressed the hope that he wouldn't get shot, and relief after a close call. Death had kept its distance. But after he and Ray Gill narrowly escaped being killed on the road to Soc Trang, they had acknowledged that life was not as certain as it seemed.

Then at Rach Gia, Pete witnessed something awesome—long-legged birds flying over a temple, a clap of thunder and a shock of light connecting heaven to earth for an instant—that may have given rise to an awareness, even a foreboding, of death. It seems to me now that he was pressing his interpreter for confirmation, not an explanation. He didn't need to be told what the omens meant. He guessed what they meant.

With the many plans my brother had, I don't think at all that he would have resigned himself to death. I do believe, however, that he was prepared to meet it.

Studying Pete's letter that day, I took comfort, as I do still, in knowing that the last sentence he wrote was about the awesome beauty of all he had seen.

A feeling settled in me that Pete had experienced the timelessness of a moment and the oneness of the infinite and the finite. And in feeling this, I laid down the burden of the question I had borne for so long—What happened to Pete?—not with a thud, but gently, as if someone were helping me.

Pete's desk, with his typewriter, in Vietnam (date unknown).
Photo by Pete Hunting; author's collection.

Dear Jill—

Thanks very much for your letter—it sounds as though the family has had a pleasant summer, especially you and Hall.

My summer has been pretty interesting, although (as you know) it's always summertime over here.

You don't need to worry about my security over here. It sounds much worse in American newspapers than it is in my province. Our province here is quite peaceful, and the people are very friendly, even though we can see guerilla croplands on the mountainsides at the end of our airstrips.

This past month I 1) went to Saigon for a team meeting of IVS Education advisors, and 2) after the meeting I worked with a youth camp with 14 Vietnamese youth. We painted a hamlet school and the hamlet "town hall" which was actually a house, and we repaired the hamlet's road.

I took some movies of the windmill I built and gave to one hamlet, so I'll send those along soon.

Can you please ask Mom or Dad to send me a checkbook for cashiers from my credit account.

On August 25, 1964, Pete wrote to the author, "You don't need to worry about my security over here." Author's collection.

Distribution of surplus U.S. bulgur wheat in a Montagnard hamlet, Ninh Thuan Province (date unknown). Photo by Pete Hunting; author's collection.

Pete with unidentified Vietnamese volunteers and students in Ninh Thuan
Province (December 1964). Pete took visiting Peace Corps volunteer Bob
Goodwin, the photographer, to a strategic hamlet where he planned to
meet with a youth group. Seeing a man wearing a backpack at the gate,
"Pete knew right away that the guard was vc because he had a pack on his
back," Goodwin recalls. "He spun the jeep around and then got out to talk
to the guard. He told him that perhaps it was too late in the day for us to be
visiting. The guard agreed. Pete had gotten the jeep into position so that we
could get out of there fast." Courtesy of Robert C. Goodwin.

Ancient Cham towers on Highway 1 near Ba Thap, photographed by Bob Goodwin during a weeklong stay with Pete and his stationmate Jim Hunt (December 1964). From his station in Thailand, Goodwin went to Vietnam for a vacation. To get to Phan Rang from Saigon he was told, "Just go to the airport and find the Aussie captain of the plane that makes the milk run to Phan Rang, Nha Trang, and Dalat." Courtesy of Robert C. Goodwin.

In this frame, from one of many eight-millimeter films Pete sent home, his vehicle approaches the Cham towers. The author stopped here in 1991 for a photograph, unaware that Pete had installed a windmill nearby. Ninh Thuan Province (1964). Author's collection.

Pete at the wheel of his Land Rover, with a windmill on top, en route to Ba Thap (1964). Author's collection.

Pete unkinks a chain for one of the windmills he built for arid Ninh Thuan Province (1964). When the Joint U.S. Public Affairs Office published this photograph in 1967, the caption stated, "The Viet Cong killed this man of peace." Photographer unknown, U.S. Operations Mission; author's collection.

Pete adjusts the mechanism of a windmill. "It looks like the most significant contributions I'll make as an IVSer will be the things I do on the side while waiting for the Education Program to get moving," he wrote in June 1964. In 1996, after a trip to Vietnam, former IVS Chief-of-Party Don Luce told the author that the irrigation system Pete introduced was still in use.

Photographer unknown, U.S. Operations Mission; author's collection.

"Windmill . . . uh. . . ," Pete, *left*, wrote of surveying the damage from a windstorm with Jim Hunt, *second from left* (1964). Later, the pond dried up, "exposing the bare, bleached, and shattered corpse of a once-glorious machine," Pete said in a letter. "We salvaged the pump and pulleys and retreated to Phan Rang." Author's collection.

ivs hamlet education teammates John Sommer, Pete, Gene Stoltzfus, and Willi Meyers, *left to right* with unidentified child. Vung Tau, Vietnam (March 1965). Author's collection.

Pete with a Cham youth he helped through school. On the back of the photo, Pete described the shirt he was wearing: "Black smock is standard peasant all-duty shirt, known to U.S. military as vc uniform" (February 1965).
Author's collection.

A sketch of Pete found on the seat of his vehicle after he was killed.
It was inscribed "a token of friendship" and signed by the artist, Tay-Do.
Author's collection.

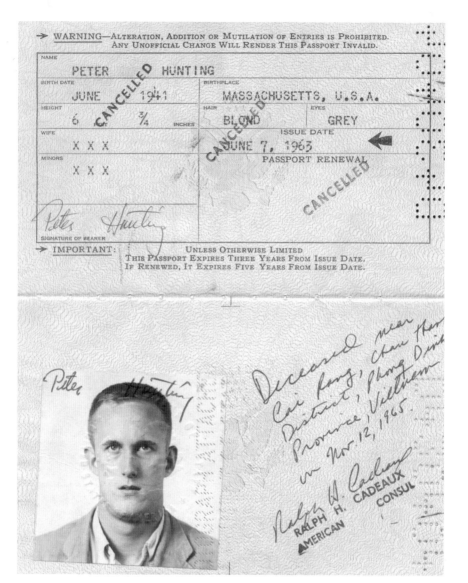

WARNING—ALTERATION, ADDITION OR MUTILATION OF ENTRIES IS PROHIBITED.
ANY UNOFFICIAL CHANGE WILL RENDER THIS PASSPORT INVALID.

NAME
PETER   HUNTING

BIRTH DATE   BIRTHPLACE
JUNE   1941   MASSACHUSETTS, U.S.A.

HEIGHT   HAIR   EYES
6   3/4   INCHES   BLOND   GREY

WIFE   ISSUE DATE
X X X   JUNE 7, 1963

MINORS   PASSPORT RENEWAL
X X X

SIGNATURE OF BEARER

IMPORTANT: UNLESS OTHERWISE LIMITED
THIS PASSPORT EXPIRES THREE YEARS FROM ISSUE DATE.
IF RENEWED, IT EXPIRES FIVE YEARS FROM ISSUE DATE.

CANCELLED
CANCELLED
CANCELLED

Deceased near
Cai Rang, Chau Thanh
District, phong Dinh
Province, Vietnam
on Nov. 12, 1965.

Ralph H. Cadeaux
RALPH H. CADEAUX
AMERICAN   CONSUL

Pete's canceled passport. Author's collection.

Bottom right: After presenting the medal to the author's parents, the vice president fastened a bracelet with the seal of his office on the wrists of the author and her two sisters. When Humphrey was criticized for handing out medals instead of positioning himself for the 1968 presidential campaign, Carl T. Rowan defended him in a syndicated column, referring specifically to Pete. *Left to right:* Humphrey, the author, her mother, and Holly (Cis is not pictured).

Photographer unknown; author's collection.

Vice President Hubert Humphrey received the author's family in his office in the White House on April 27, 1966. In a ceremony at the presidential palace in Saigon, South Vietnamese Premier Ky had recently given Humphrey a posthumous medal awarded to Pete. *Left to right:* Nguyen Phu Duc, minister-consul of the South Vietnamese embassy; Humphrey; and the author's mother and father. Photo a gift of the vice president; photographer unknown; author's collection.

Dedication of the Peter M. Hunting Memorial Library in Phan Rang, Ninh
Thuan Province (June 6, 1968). Author's collection.

Pete's "best buddy" on the IVS team, Gene Stoltzfus, and the
author meet for the first time (1987). Author's collection.

Rice fields, northern Vietnam (1991). Photo by author.

Former U.S. Congressman Chuck Whalen tries out a rice thresher in northern Vietnam (1991). Photo by author.

Left to right: Don Luce, Darlene Fairley, Mike Fairley, the author, and Charles Cable on the afternoon after they were held for questioning near Phan Rang (1991). Author's collection.

The author shows Ninh Thuan Province officials the location of her home during the meeting in which she proposed that Phan Rang and Sonoma, California, become sister cities. *Left to right:* Ho Sy Son and Le Van Binh of the People's Committee; Tran Dinh Song, the author's guide and interpreter; and the author (2006). Courtesy of James Langworthy.

The author with the Cham woman whose parents and grandmother knew Pete. One of her sisters is seated at the family loom. My Nghiep hamlet, Ninh Thuan Province (2006). Courtesy of James Langworthy.

Song and the author honor Pete's memory near the site where he was killed, Phong Dinh Province (2006). Courtesy of Chuck Theusch.

FIFTEEN

"Here Come Blue Eyes!"

S hall we start with champagne?"

From the moment Margo suggested that we begin our weekend in Manhattan with lunch at Jean Georges, I loved her. The Veuve Clicquot sealed it. When it came to appreciating good wine and food, Margo was more like a sister than my own sisters.

During long walks and pauses on park benches, we talked more about our families and ourselves. I could see why Pete said she was easy to talk to. I had to restrain my Midwestern impulse to effuse about meeting her at last and the urge to hug her, a practice common in California and now natural even to me.

We had been exchanging e-mails and letters for several months. In the same period, my sisters began reading Pete's letters to Mom from time to time, and she enjoyed them. They told her I was in touch with Margo and Sue, and she seemed to recognize their names. Cis, Holly, and I knew she was growing weaker and approaching her life's end.

In 2005 my daughter and I went to visit Mom. We pushed her wheelchair through a wooded garden, and she intently watched the birds calling to one another overhead. She cheerfully listened as Cis and I worked on a piano duet we had been trying to master for several years, praising us and enjoying the private concert.

That July, she passed away. Cis and Holly were at her side. They held the phone to her ear while I told her I loved her. Her eyes were closed and she couldn't speak any more, but they said she smiled.

We returned to Connecticut for a service at the cemetery where my father and Pete were buried. An immense yew bush had almost overtaken Pete's headstone. Grass had long since filled in the rectangle where his grave was once dug, but its outline, slim as a finger, had not gone away.

My sisters, our children, and I reflected on my mother's eighty-eight years and her admirable qualities: Her love of beauty. Her easy way with people. Her self-assurance in any social situation. Her depth. Her generosity. Her intellect. Her love for us.

To be sure, her personality had other facets, and my sisters and I remembered those, too. We asked ourselves why she had kept Pete's letters from us.

Did she really think they were destroyed in a basement flood?

Did she not want to share them, and simply lie?

Did she not know what condition they were in, and not want to know until the day she felt ready to look at them again?

We would never know, any more than we would find out how they ended up in my old camp footlocker. What seems most likely is that all three possibilities could have been true at one time or another.

Sadly, she shouldered her loss largely alone. By withholding Pete's letters, if that is what she did, she remained isolated but preserved her singular connection with him. The opposite had been true for me. The connection with others who knew my brother had helped me reestablish my connection with him.

My mother did not pilot our family skillfully through the most difficult of straits, but she ultimately landed me on good ground by doing one thing: she did not throw things away. In the fullness of time I would find a golden lock of her firstborn's hair, tied with a blue satin ribbon; recipes she clipped, hoping my sisters and I would try them even if she hadn't taken an interest in cooking; sixty-four letters mailed from Vietnam; and the condolences of people who one day would befriend a sister manquée.

I forgave my mother and I hope she forgave me.

When Cis, Holly, and I were making plans to meet in Connecticut, I asked them if they would like to meet Margo. They agreed, but it was only as we were on our way to see her that Cis realized, "This is the person who could have been our sister."

We three and Margo, her father, and one of her sisters met for lunch. Mr. Bradley told us about the time when, as a young accountant, he approached my grandfather with some ideas about saving his company money. Not only was Popeye receptive to Mr. Bradley's ideas, he offered him a job. Some time later, the two of them were on a business trip when my grandfather developed a persistent cough. When they got home, he checked into the hospital and died soon afterward of leukemia.

The Bradleys remembered my grandfather fondly. They had all been very fond of Pete, too. Margo's sister recalled his visit when he was home on leave from Vietnam. One morning she, her toddler, and Pete were the only ones up. She remembered Pete following her son around, placing his hand on sharp corners to keep the little one from bumping his head.

Margo showed us the company my grandfather had founded. We drove by the home he had willed to the corporate secretary. Later, when my sisters and I talked about it, we agreed that the "controversy" Pete mentioned in reference to the Bradley name must have derived from my grandmother's resentment of the other woman. The business had prospered with Mr. Bradley as president; sour grapes also may have contributed to Nana's judgment.

After lunch we visited the Bradley home, which my grandfather had originally purchased to lodge clients because there were no hotels close by. The first thing he did was to put in an enormous swimming pool like the one at the farm in Woodbridge.

When Pete arrived in Connecticut to begin his freshman year at Wesleyan, one of our cousins had called Margo to ask if her cousin from Missouri might stop by to see his grandfather's old house. The two of them had spent the day by the pool. Our four parents had enjoyed happy afternoons there, too, and Margo and her sister recalled the sound of their laughter.

It almost seemed to my sisters and me as if we had discovered some long-lost family members. We felt closer to the Bradleys than to some of our own relatives.

Since studying Pete's letters and meeting his friends, I was more curious than ever about the places he had mentioned. Vietnam began to exert a pull on me.

My opportunity to return came in 2006, after I read about an American veteran whose organization had built or was supporting sixteen libraries in Vietnam. I wrote to Chuck Theusch about the library that my parents had helped to establish. I didn't know if it still existed, and Chuck became as curious about it as I was. From the start of our friendship, he accepted me as a sister who was, as he said in one letter, "as much a member of the fraternity of Vietnam veterans as we who wore the olive drab."

He invited me to join his next Library of Vietnam delegation, and I accepted. Two weeks later, he and his wife were my houseguests in California. Three months after that, in August 2006, Chuck and I met again in Hanoi.

Ever since my first trip to Vietnam, I had dreamed of someday linking my home, in Sonoma Valley, with Phan Rang as official sister cities. Sonoma already had this kind of relationship with wine-producing villages in France and Italy. In 1991, I had seen vineyards in Ninh Thuan Province. By now I knew that Vietnam's only commercial grape-growing region was located there.

I proposed to the Sonoma City Council that I explore the possibility of a sister-city relationship when I was in Vietnam. They authorized my doing so and provided me with letters of introduction. I didn't mention it to the council members, but I hoped that these letters of plenipotentiary would discourage any bad actors from confiscating my passport and visa, as on my previous trip. Just to be sure, I asked the city manager to affix his largest, most official-looking sticker to the letters, and he obliged.

My meeting with province authorities in Ninh Thuan was to fall near the end of our trip. Chuck and I began in northern Vietnam and worked our way south, picking up another delegate, Jim Langworthy, and our guide and interpreter, Tran Dinh Song, midway along the journey.

One library was in a village an hour outside of Hanoi. In the car, on the way there, I sat beside our interpreter for the day, Mr. Cuong. At one point he pulled up his pants leg to show me his battle-scarred leg. As a soldier with the North Vietnamese army, he had walked hundreds of miles south to the Mekong Delta. When Chuck told him my brother was a humanitarian volunteer who lost his life there in an ambush, Mr. Cuong brushed off his words and, smiling at me, said, "Blue eyes. All same."

At our destination, we met with a librarian, teachers, and local officials. Afterward, an elaborate lunch was served in the one-room school. Before I had left home, a nurse at the county health department had warned me about avian flu and other health hazards. "You won't be going into the countryside, will you?" she had asked. Avoid contact with animals, especially monkeys, she cautioned. Don't drink anything unless it's in a bottle and you have opened it yourself. If you eat poultry, make sure it has been well cooked.

I stared, I hoped impassively, as a platter of pink-fleshed chicken was placed squarely before me. I watched as my glass was filled with fruit juice and ice cubes. To refuse such hospitality would have been unthinkable.

After lunch Mr. Cuong asked if we would like to meet his aunt and uncle. Understanding the honor his invitation accorded us, we quickly agreed. We left the village, parked the car on a one-lane road, and walked the rest of the way, crossing a dike that separated two ponds. In one, a water buffalo languished near the edge. Chuck insisted I pet it for the camera.

Our hosts showed us their small home, including the family altar and the hardwood bed with no mattress or pillows. They offered us chairs around a tiny table and served us tea. The uncle asked if we would like to smoke from the water pipe in the corner. What would my mother have done?

A photograph of the uncle wearing many medals hung high on the wall. Seeing our interest in it, they led us to another room, where we saw the aunt's picture; she, too, had been a highly decorated Vietminh warrior in the struggle against the French.

As we said our good-byes in the hot afternoon sunshine, the old man told Chuck that he was the first American man ever to visit their home. Then, taking my hand, his wife said that I was the first American woman they had ever seen.

One day we traveled to an orphanage where Chuck was to deliver a donation from an American sponsor. The place was located on a small river and gave new meaning to the word "remote." We parked the car, rode on the back of motorcycles down a path, and traveled the rest of the way in a dugout canoe powered by a small motor. It rode low with our weight, and muddy water lapped at the gunwales. As Chuck and Jim twisted right and left to photograph curious children and women washing clothes along the banks, the vessel rocked precariously. I clung to the rails and studied the water, watching for the snakes I imagined I would be swimming with at any moment. "Pete would be proud of you," Chuck shouted cheerily.

I had not entirely shed the cautiousness of my youth, but I had learned to go ahead and do it anyway, whatever "it" might be.

Another library was located on an island not far from where Pete spent his last night talking with Fred Stone. A motorboat carried us along a waterway bordered by marsh grasses. Song looked intently at them. "vc used to hide in grass like this," he said. "They would breathe under water through bamboo. They could wait there for hours."

He looked uneasy. When I caught his eye, I asked how long after the war he had thought about something like this. "For many years," he said. "And even today I think of it."

The day before we were due in Phan Rang, Chuck, Song, and I mapped out the presentation we would make to the province officials. I would introduce my sister-city proposal in the context of my long-standing interest in Vietnam, dating back to my brother's years as an ivs volunteer. I would show them photographs of Pete working on a windmill and of the library. We would inquire about the library's condition and ask to see it. Chuck would offer his organization's help if it were needed.

At the conclusion of the meeting, I would present the gifts I had brought from home, including maps of California and Sonoma Valley, books about Sonoma, and several products made from locally grown lavender. From some research I had done, I knew that growing conditions in Ninh Thuan were in some ways similar to those of Sonoma and Napa valleys. I thought lavender might be a suitable crop for Vietnam. My interest in the prospect led one friend, a former ivs agriculture volunteer, to quip that I was really an ivser at heart.

The day before our scheduled meeting, I had given away one of the other gifts I brought for the province officials. It was a good bottle of California wine. But we had unexpectedly driven past a viticultural and agricultural research institute that I had read about. My experience in 1991 had made me wary of acting on impulse in Vietnam, but Song said it would be all right to stop and ask if anyone was available for a meeting. A young scientist received us. When he told me that he liked a good Bordeaux, I went to the car, removed the bottle of cabernet sauvignon from my suitcase, and gave it to him. A couple of weeks later, when I was home again, I discovered that the institute's location was the old ivs agriculture station at Nha Ho.

It was not the first or the last coincidence, if you'd call it that.

On the way to Phan Rang, we passed two ancient Cham towers directly beside the main road. They were covered with scaffolding, and laborers were patching the crumbling masonry. We stopped to photograph them. There was something magnetic about the towers. I had also felt drawn to them in 1991, when our breakaway group stopped here and took pictures. At that time, the towers stood isolated like sentinels over the plain. No more: commerce along the highway today requires one to watch for them.

What was striking about the towers was not that shops and houses now encroached on them or that, upgraded to a tourist attraction, they were under renovation, but that I now knew Pete had also stopped at this very place to be photographed. He had been headed in the opposite direction on the day in 1964 when a home movie recorded him delivering a windmill. While someone else held the camera, the Land Rover, with the windmill tied on top, came into view from a distance. Then Pete slowed by the Cham towers and a sign that said Ba Thap, the name of the hamlet he was going to. It was the same hamlet where he had drunk beer with Chou and An, the Vietcong soldiers come home for May Day. Pete wrote about Ba Thap and the windmill installation in a letter:

Province officials considered the hamlet full of Vietcong sympathizers, since it had been moved from a VC-controlled area, and the Vietcong had entered the hamlet unopposed several times. On one such occasion, the rebels had shot holes in the school roof and shot the teacher's wife in both knees. . . .

If the people of the hamlet had not been sympathetic to the VC before relocation, there was good reason for resentment on their part toward the government following their removal to Ba Thap. The new hamlet was set in the middle of a wasteland. The province chief who had determined the site was one of the most hateful and pompous henchmen of Ngo Dinh Nhu that I'd ever seen or heard of. Following the overthrow of Diem, several Vietnamese and Americans with whom I worked in the province agreed to lend support to projects at Ba Thap, hoping to win back the good will of those people. . . .

[I asked several people] to help set up an irrigation windmill in order to grow small gardens within the confines of the hamlet. They agreed.

The project turned out to be more than I bargained for. Available windmills couldn't lift the water to the height required, nor provide enough water. . . . I originally designed it to fit over the top of an open well, but it was placed beside a duck pond. . . .

A short time thereafter, the duck pond dried up, exposing the bare, bleached, and shattered corpse of a once-glorious machine. We salvaged the pump and pulleys and retreated to Phan Rang, the province capital, for another try. . . .

The big day arrived as my Land Rover truck limped into Ba Thap, sagging on the right side under the weight of the wooden beam. It took all afternoon and into the evening to jimmy the beam upright and into the socket in an effort rivaling even the more complicated Cecil B. DeMille productions. Approximately thirty people were pulling on two ropes in the final seconds as the beam swayed and tottered on the lip of the hole; they didn't know whether to drop the ropes and run, risking being caught inside the arc of the falling pole, or whether to hold the rope and gamble that the pole wouldn't fall. Of course, there was never any doubt in *my* mind; a forceful ramming of the beam by the Land Rover did the trick, resulting in joyous ovations from the much-relieved spectators.

I didn't realize in 1991 how close I had come to Pete at the Cham towers. Now I was about to come even closer.

"Ready for the big meeting?" Chuck asked when I found him in the restaurant of our hotel in Phan Rang. It was first light. The previous evening, he and Jim had dared me to try one of the local specialties, sand lizard. After all, they prodded, I had eaten porcupine in Dalat, and if I was proposing a sister city here, I should familiarize myself with the cuisine. On this morning I took just coffee and a bowl of *pho*.

Our driver pulled past a guardhouse and through gates surrounding a large building—the offices of the People's Committee of Phan Rang. A smiling man in his mid-twenties ushered us into a room with a long table and thirty chairs, and half as many microphones. A few minutes later a tall man in his forties entered the room, a high-ranking member of the People's Committee.

I laid out my proposal for the sister-city relationship. I explained what Pete had come here to do as an IVS volunteer. When I finished speaking, the official offered his sympathy for my loss. He opened the gifts I had brought and thanked me for them. He promised to convey my proposal to the next level of decision makers. He offered his young assistant as a guide for anything we wanted to see.

We learned that the old library building was gone but that Phan Rang had a new facility. We drove there and met the librarian. She thought some books from the original building might be in their collections. There were no old people in the library, and no one to ask about the old days.

Outside, we were waiting for our driver and van when I saw across the street a yellow French colonial–style building with dozens of bicycles parked in front. Pete must have come to this school, I realized. Song approached the only elderly person we saw and asked if Phan Rang was his home. The man had come south in 1975 with the liberation, he said. We didn't see anyone else old enough to have remembered a tall, blond American who used to live here. Vietnam is young: in 2007, 57 percent of the population was under the age of thirty.

I had brought along two addresses from Pete's letters. We found that one of the streets had disappeared altogether. The other address was now a shop. The old house was long gone.

A question had been on my mind for two days, ever since we drove down the mountain from Dalat on a road Pete had described vividly. The question was not original, but the one the angel asked Mary Magdalene when she went to the tomb looking for the body of Jesus: Why do you look for the living among the dead? I was looking for Pete, but I had found no library, no house, no tangible evidence whatever of his life in Phan Rang.

Still, my sister-city proposal had been well received, and I felt I had accomplished something worthwhile. Sonoma would get its sister city, even though I would always think of it as a sister-and-brother city.

We had a long day of driving ahead of us, and it was time to leave. But the others had agreed to let me make one more stop in this province. We headed south looking for a hamlet I had read about online, whose Cham women were especially good weavers. I hoped to buy some blankets there and sell them to raise money for the sister-city project. The hamlet's name was My Nghiep.

One of Pete's letters mentioned a Cham woman whose blankets and tablecloths he was helping to sell. She had offered her daughter in marriage, but Pete didn't realize she was serious until she introduced the girl and said she wanted to send him to a palm reader and astrologer.

There were many Cham hamlets in this area. John Sommer had come down from his station, Dalat, to visit Pete, and both of them had filmed a weaver at her loom. I had no way of knowing, however, which hamlet was the home of the "old 'Ba'" and her daughter.

We stopped several times for directions to My Nghiep, turning onto smaller and smaller roads. As we pulled into the sun-baked hamlet, we stopped at a house whose ground floor was open to the street. We could see red, orange, green, and blue weavings draped on dowels lining the walls. A large loom sat out front.

Two young women who appeared to be sisters invited us inside. They began pulling weavings down and unfolding them for our inspection. It was Jim's practice to buy something everywhere we stopped, and though he and the sisters had a limited common vocabulary, a friendly banter commenced. Meanwhile, I admired the weavings one at a time, finding each one lovelier than the last.

Suddenly Chuck realized that he had left a suitcase behind at our hotel in Phan Rang, some twenty minutes back. There was no time to waste, and in an instant he was in the van and the driver was pulling away.

I bought several weavings, and Song and I meandered across the road to the home of another weaver. I purchased a silk runner and took a picture of the woman warping the thread. For no apparent reason, it was much hotter on this side of the road, so Song suggested we go back to the first place and wait there for Chuck. We rejoined Jim to find that the sisters were negotiating a marriage proposal. They had offered him a dowry of five water buffalos. I thought he was worth six, maybe seven.

It was blazing hot and I glanced around for a chair. By now a third, older sister had arrived, who spoke better English. She motioned to a low cot in the shade and offered me a seat. We sat down together. If Chuck had been with us, he would have been in a hurry and what came next would never have happened. But he would not return for a good half hour, and there was nothing to do but bide the time.

Looking toward the weavings inside, I told the young woman that my brother had bought blankets like these forty years ago. I had one at home. He had helped a woman sell her weavings. He had lived in Phan Rang.

She said her mother and grandmother had a good American friend a long time ago. Before the soldiers came. "My mother say he speak our Cham language," she said.

I knew Pete spoke some Cham. My antenna went up.

He was tall, she said, and the way her mother described the color of his hair, it was just like mine. She said he had a "high" nose. Song was standing nearby. She meant a "straight" nose, not flat like some Cham and Vietnamese people's, he corrected. I thought he was too polite to let me think she meant a "big" nose.

He had come here on his motorcycle, she continued. One day he told her mother to put all of the weavings into the biggest basket she had. Then he took her to a Cham temple to sell them. She was afraid to go, but he told her it would be all right. "You come with me," he told her. They rode to Po Klong Garai temple, which Song had shown us the previous day. She sold everything in her basket.

The young woman, whose name I now knew was Cam, told me, "Sometimes my mother say, 'It too dangerous for you.' But he say, 'I don't care. I take you. Come with me.'"

I turned to Song. "Are you listening to this?" Yes, he nodded, clearly amazed.

Cam remembered more of her mother's stories about Pete. Sometimes he brought a live chicken or two with him. When he first started coming to the hamlet, she said, "He very thin!" I thought of his first months when he missed American desserts and McDonald's hamburgers.

When Cam's father saw Pete coming on his motorcycle, he would call out, "Here come blue eyes!"

Then, she said, "He go away, and he never come back." Hearing the question in her voice, I told her Pete had moved to the Mekong Delta and been killed there. She raised her hand to cover her open mouth.

Did I have other brothers? No, I replied, but I had two older sisters. "You are lucky!" she said. In the Cham culture, the youngest daughter inherits the house. She takes care of the parents, while the other children "have to leave" and live with their new families.

Cam's mother, who was now in her mid-seventies, lived too far from My Nghiep for us to visit her that day. Song said I must return, and he would take me to see her.

Chuck and our driver pulled up. I went to the van, opened my suitcase, and removed Pete's picture. When I handed it to Cam, she looked at his face and back to mine. "This is for your mother," I said. "Please tell her Pete's sister came back."

Soon the five of us were on our way again. We all agreed that something extraordinary had just happened. "It is like the Arabian Nights!" Song said. "Like a fairy tale to my ears. It is unbelievable but true! How can you run into this girl? I just told the driver to stop here. Then we went across the street and I said, 'It's too hot. Let's go back.' Unbelievable!"

I wasn't surprised by what had happened in My Nghiep. Granted, it was a miracle. But I was getting used to miracles.

Jim wondered if Pete had been remembered because he was romantically interested in the daughter. Chuck explained, "This isn't an entertainment culture, where people sit around and watch television. They tell stories. Pete was important to that woman, because she has told stories about him for forty years. But that is a reflection of the oral tradition in their culture."

It was lucky, if that was the word, that Chuck had left his suitcase behind, because while no tangible evidence of Pete's life remained in Phan Rang, in an out-of-the-way hamlet, in a weaver's shop chosen at random, I had met someone else to whom my brother was still very real. Ironically, I had traveled to the other side of the world to find a family that, unlike mine, had never stopped talking about him.

Why look for the living among the dead? I suppose it's the way some of us learn that they are not really gone. I used to think, when people said such things, that it was only pabulum. Now, to my surprise, I believed it.

After a long day's drive, my companions and I met for a late dinner in our hotel in Saigon. We ordered french fries, filet mignon, and flan.

Many restaurant menus in southern Vietnam had a "sex" cocktail—a reminder of the sex industry that flourished during the war—and this one was no exception. We had seen Sex on the Beach, Sex on the Pool Table, and now Sex in the Snow. Chuck and Jim were gentlemen, but they never failed to point out the cocktail I should order, since I refused to drink the *vin de pays*.

At five o'clock the next morning, we were bound for the Mekong Delta.

SIXTEEN

"A Wind-Blurred Far Away"

Carey Coulter wasn't supposed to be on an airplane bound for Phu Quoc on the morning of November 12, 1965, but he was. What choice did he have? The school for refugees there needed supplies. If he didn't show up, the Special Forces guys wouldn't be happy.

Pete wouldn't be happy, though, with this last-minute change of plans. But wasn't it the job of an IVS education volunteer to help schools in refugee compounds? And wouldn't his team leader approve of his taking initiative?

They were supposed to look at the new apartment Carey had found in Can Tho. There was no way, however, to reach Pete and ask if they could postpone it. Pete would be back in Can Tho again soon. They could see the place another day.

The pilot of the small plane had already taxied onto the runway when Carey saw Pete's Scout pull up. Pete stepped out. He was alone. He didn't look happy.

As the plane gathered speed and left the ground, Carey saw Pete raise his fist and shake it at him. It was too late. They were airborne. He would just have to explain later.

Les Small, a former IVSer who was now employed as the agriculture representative of the U.S. Operations Mission in the Mekong Delta, was also at the airport that morning. From his base in Can Tho he traveled extensively in sixteen provinces, working with provincial reps, including several ex-IVsers. He went by car if he was headed somewhere relatively safe or a military convoy had secured the road. Otherwise, he hopped a small plane contracted to USOM or one of the military transports making daily milk runs around the provinces. Today, he was on his way to see a prov rep in one of the less secure parts of the delta.

Seeing Les waiting, Pete went over to say hello. He was about to leave for Ba Xuyen Province, he said. Les had never driven that road. He considered it too dangerous. He knew, however, that IVsers were more casual about security than most Americans. In fact, he had driven in some questionable areas himself as a volunteer in Kien Giang Province. Still, he was so surprised to hear Pete say where he was going that he uttered a single word: "Really!"

Pete left the airport and headed southwest on Route 4. In Soc Trang, he needed to arrange for a language teacher for Paul Lukitsch. A member of the ag team, Paul was learning two languages. The farmers in Ba Xuyen were predominantly Cambodian and Chinese-Cambodian, so he needed to speak some Khmer. He also needed to know Vietnamese, and the tones didn't come easily to him.

A young woman Pete had met recently might make a good tutor, and besides, he had been hoping for an opportunity to get to know her better. He and Paul would meet with her, then go to the Cambodian dragon-boat races on the main canal that ran through town.

All of a sudden he remembered the money Paul had given him to pick up a pair of trousers at a dry cleaner's in Vinh Long. Should he turn back and get them? Vinh Long was more than twenty miles in the opposite direction. Turning around would mean crossing the Mekong on the ferry at Can Tho and recrossing it just to get this far again. It would put him well behind schedule.

On the other hand, maybe he should just continue on his way and bring Paul's pants to him next time.

But a promise was a promise.

He wheeled around and headed for Vinh Long.

Since late August, he had been living in a house flanked by a café and a Vespa shop. Jim Linn, an agriculture extension technician on his team, had the room next to his. Jim had done a good job of smoothing things out between local officials and young Vietnamese volunteers who, with his help, were setting up garden plots for refugees to plant fast-growing vegetables.

At the house, Pete went into his room, found Paul's money, and put it in his wallet. On the way out the door he saw Jim. He told him he was on his way to Soc Trang.

He paid for Paul's trousers at the dry cleaner's, which shared the premises with a barbershop. Harold Kooker, another team member, was going in for a haircut. Harold taught English at the normal school in Vinh Long. The job wasn't going so well. First, he had been assigned classes of sixty students each. The principal agreed to divide the classes in half, but that hadn't solved a second problem, which was administrative. English language class was technically an elective, and even though students were required to attend, Harold was not allowed to grade them. When he developed a reputation for giving hard tests, the students threatened to boycott them.

Like other members of Pete's team, Harold appreciated him for the things he did to boost morale. Pete considered it part of his job as a regional team leader to do these things, like stopping to chew the fat with Harold when he saw him at the barbershop. They joked about Pete's receding hairline. Around 1:15 P.M. he left Vinh Long.

The temperature was in the high eighties, with humidity creeping upwards of 80 percent. That morning, it had rained lightly. Now the skies were essentially fair, with only a high, thin layer of cirrus clouds.

Pete reached the river at Can Tho. For the second time that day, he drove his Scout onto the ferry. Always eager to practice his Vietnamese, he struck up a conversation with two people. He hadn't forgotten his years as a hitchhiker and was quick to offer a lift to someone who needed it. He teammates were used to seeing him pull up with passengers in his vehicle.

The two Vietnamese were headed in the same direction. Pete said he could give them a ride.

I am headed south on the highway out of Vinh Long with Song, Chuck, Jim, and our driver. We cross an immense suspension bridge, a joint venture between Vietnam and Australia, that spans the Mekong. It's a clear morning, with blue skies and small puffs of clouds in the east.

When I came to Vietnam in 1991, the country was still recovering from the war and suffering the effects of an economic embargo. It was not unusual then to see three people riding one motorcycle. Today the bikes have only one or two riders. Some wear helmets, but men wearing baseball caps or no head covering at all are more common.

If a woman wears a hat, it is conical. Most women ride in pants. To protect their lungs from pollution and their skin from tanning, many wear a cloth mask that covers their face from the nose down. Some, like Song's wife, also wear gloves to keep their arms pale.

We cross numerous small bridges over rivulets. Bamboo grows right up to the road. I count six pumps at a Mekong gas station and note the heavy black wire strung on telephone poles—more signs of progress since my first trip to Vietnam. A poster bids us good-bye: "Vinh Long—Have a Good Journey!"

Bicycles hauling a kind of surrey with front and back benches, called "pulling taxis," move slowly along. We pull around to pass them. Shops line the road, and in one, red meat is cooking in a large pan on a rack over a table. A man in a baseball cap removes the browned pieces with long chopsticks.

We pass a sign that says we are fifteen kilometers from Can Tho. *Pete has less than an hour left.*

We approach the entrance to the ferry at Can Tho. We will share it with two tourist buses, a few vans like ours, and numerous motorcycles and passenger cars. We wait our turn until a man knocks on the hood, signaling our driver to inch forward so more vehicles can squeeze onto the ferry. Cars and trucks line up three across and seven deep.

The Mekong is one of the world's longest rivers. Six countries share its waters: China, Myanmar, Thailand, Laos, Cambodia, and Vietnam. Here, it gives an impression less of might than of dependability. That so many people earn their livelihood from this river makes clear the connection between "current" and "currency." The ferry transects the river without a struggle, and I gauge our movement only by watching the billboards on the bank recede.

I've been up three hours, since 4:30 A.M., and haven't had coffee yet. I feel a headache coming on. We bump off the ferry and onto the opposite shore. Shops line the road, which is narrower here. Green coconuts dangle overhead from the trees. Some of the bushes have been pruned into popsicle shapes.

Song says we will stop at a hotel to see a man about a horse. He has picked up this expression from Chuck. It sounds funny coming from Song, a man hard to picture on horseback. I like it better than "happy house," the Vietnamese equivalent of "restroom."

In the hotel gift shop I buy a reversible hand-embroidered silk robe. The men I'm with all admire it, especially when they hear I paid nineteen dollars for it. We move on to a coffee garden and my headache lifts, no thanks to the pounding disco music. My companions and I have a good twenty-five years on any of the other customers.

Back in the van, we go through Can Tho, then Cai Rang, which is no longer a village, as in Pete's day, but a city. We rumble across an old metal bridge. Thinking aloud, I speculate that the sound of an approaching convoy must have carried far down the road. Song agrees. I imagine a Vietcong squad waiting to ambush an ARVN, or South Vietnamese army, convoy—alert to the noise of vehicles on the bridge.

Song says we are not far from the X on the map I have given him.

At night, I had heard, the Vietcong dug holes in the roads. They would either bury a mine or dig a hole to make it look as if they had. A driver seeing evidence of digging in the road had three choices: slow down, stop, or speed up and skirt the holes. "At night, the Vietcong dug holes in the road," Song says. "Maybe they buried a land mine, or maybe they only dug a hole. You didn't know if there was a mine, so you had to stop."

I have pieced together a lot of information about the afternoon when Pete took this road for the last time. A hundred details—gathered from more than fifty ivs alumni, papers in the old trunk, my other research, and a word here and a rumor there—have coalesced into a silhouette, if not a complete picture, of that day.

I have learned as much as I can and am reconciled to not knowing everything. I have retrieved my lost connection with my brother and discovered the man he was. I know him better now than when he was alive. I think of him with love and no piercings of sadness.

I always thought someday I would visit this place. Only now, it seems, was I prepared to do it. For years I have imagined this stretch of road. And not correctly, it turns out. Instead of being hemmed in by vegetation, and spooky, it is sunlit and open.

I am no longer searching for information about Pete. I'm here to pay my respects. I feel grateful to have kind companions with me. Even though I am just getting to know them, they want to take part in a ritual of remembering someone they never knew.

At the end of my journey, I have arrived a tenacious, free, more openhearted, more knowledgeable, braver individual. But there is still one thing I need to see.

That's how it will seem, anyway, in retrospect.

At 2:40 P.M., a little more than a mile south of Cai Rang, Pete's Scout comes up behind an ARVN convoy returning from Operation Dan Chi. Two Vietnamese are in the vehicle with him. He passes the convoy.

Hearing the sound of vehicles on the bridge, a Vietcong squad takes up positions on both sides of the road. Concealed by tall grass, they form a V, their semiautomatic weapons trained on the open end.

They see a jeep with a tall, light-haired driver coming down the straightaway. Pete approaches. At the first sound of gunfire, he floors the accelerator pedal. Bullets hit the vehicle from straight on, and on the driver and passenger sides. Pete almost makes it through the hail of fire when a single round goes through the tailgate, through the wallet in his right rear pocket, and into his flesh. With the shock of the pain, his right leg jerks and his foot comes off the gas. He has lost control of the pedal. The Scout comes to a stop. It leaves no skid marks.

The soldiers run up with their weapons drawn. They are screaming and Pete is talking as fast as he can. He tells them he is unarmed.

The sergeant is in a fury, a hothead. Who is this American, speaking Vietnamese? A spy! He has ruined the ambush of the ARVN convoy they have been waiting for! He and one of his men yank Pete out of the vehicle. The rush of adrenaline and the will to live come to Pete's aid as he struggles to remain upright, trying to talk his way out of this. The sergeant grows more enraged. He orders a couple of his men to take the two passengers out of sight.

With great effort, Pete tries to prop himself against the Scout. The sergeant places his weapon against the base of Pete's neck. *TOK-kooo.* Pete slumps to the ground. The sergeant fires four more shots into Pete's head. One of his men sprays ten more rounds into his body.

Five minutes later the convoy comes upon the scene. A radioman informs the duty officer at MACV Command Center J313-1 that a body has been found on the ground beside an American vehicle. It is carrying a lot of identification: Peter M. Hunting, U.S. civilian, regional supervisor of International Voluntary Services, based in Vinh Long. He was killed when his vehicle hit a land mine.

Next, the radio operator reports sniper fire and calls for an air strike and armed helicopter support.

MACV calls the IVS house in Saigon. Don is not there but returns soon and is informed of what has happened. He immediately calls Arthur Gardiner's home in Washington. Gardiner is out of the country. Don calls John Hughes. He tells Hughes that Pete's family must be notified before word gets out and a reporter calls them. He then retreats to his bedroom for a while and loses track of time.

The duty officer enters a correction to the log four pages later. It states that no mining occurred, two tires of the vehicle were blown, and the doors were peppered by small-arms fire. The report adds:

> When convoy arrived at site the VC opened fire. Convoy immediately dismounted and took VC under fire, VC then withdrew. No other friendly casualties occurred. Troops in convoy screened both sides of road. This info furnished by civilians at site and vicinity who were questioned.

Pete's body is flown by helicopter to Saigon. The Scout is returned to Can Tho. Joseph Robinson of the regional USOM office collects Pete's identification papers and a Vietnamese artist's sketch on the seat. No other personal items are found in the vehicle.

Carey Coulter returns from his visit to the refugee school. He is at the airport when someone tells him that Pete has been killed. The only thing that saved his life, he realizes, was the Special Forces guys insisting that he come to Phu Quoc.

Late in the day, around dusk, Les Small arrives back at the airport. An American military officer who saw him talking to Pete that morning comes up to him. "I've got bad news," he says. "Your friend was killed."

What are the chances of finding the exact spot where it happened?

I'm watching the road with Song, wondering where he will tell our driver to pull over. If we have learned anything from our experience in the Cham hamlet yesterday, it is that his choice of stopping places is apparently guided by more than happenstance. We don't know how close we can come to the site of the ambush: A hundred feet? A hundred yards?

We step off the van and into the grass on the roadside. I concentrate on balancing the bunch of long-stemmed flowers under my arm while I hold burning incense sticks in my praying hands. Smoke drifts across my face and into my nostrils.

Addressing Pete, Song prays. He has come to pay respect to his soul. He expresses regret that Pete was killed in an accident of war. He acknowledges his good purpose in coming to Vietnam, the good he accomplished, the help he gave, his goodness as a man. "May you rest in peace," he concludes, "wherever and forever."

I read a passage from the *Book of Common Prayer* for the consecration of a grave: "O God, whose days are without end, and whose mercies cannot be numbered: Make us, we beseech thee, deeply sensible of the shortness and uncertainty of life—"

Because of the traffic at our backs, my voice is inaudible to Song, Chuck, and Jim, and almost to me. I keep going.

"—That, when we shall have served thee in our generation, we may be gathered unto our fathers."

I turn to a sentence from the liturgy for the burial of the dead. I will insert my brother's name. I feel a lump rise in my throat. I read on.

"And grant that, increasing in knowledge and love of thee, Pete may go from strength to strength in the life of perfect service in thy heavenly kingdom."

A forty-two-year-old passerby who has stopped to watch asks Song who I am. She is the sister, he says, of a man who was killed near here in 1965.

The man leads us to the place where there was once a fork in the road. He points to the ground. Song translates. "He says this is where they killed the American. Everyone in the surrounding villages knew about it. His parents told him as a little boy never to come here, because it was very dangerous."

Vietnamese believe that a person who dies violently can linger at the place of death. "But Pete is not here," Song says, "although his spirit seems to be here."

I feel that Pete has led me to the place where he was killed, because I needed to see it with my own eyes.

The man who stopped asks, "Did he come to build a bridge?"

"He came to teach English," I say. Pete had done more, but it was the simplest answer.

He came to teach. And he built a bridge. One measured not by its span, but by what it brought closer: stranger to friend, brother to sister, once to once again, the faraway come near.

Acknowledgments

Some people say that to write a book you have to have faith in yourself. I relied instead on my friends' faith in me. There from the beginning were Robin Kline and Bill Summers, Sandra Day, Antonia Allegra, and others in my "Umbrian family," along with Lois and Jack Chambers. My mentor Patty Johnston and Bill and Caryn Reading stayed close at every turn. There were many.

Thank you to these individuals who helped with the book in specific ways:

My two sisters, who encouraged me to tell our family's personal story.

Margo, Sue, and John for permission to use their letters from Pete.

The International Voluntary Services family, especially Larry Laverentz, Don Luce, Willi Meyers, John Sommer, and Gene Stoltzfus, and dozens of other IVS alumni who answered questions and offered information. Thank you, IVSers, for your service in Vietnam.

Chuck Theusch, founder of the Library of Vietnam project, for inviting me to join his delegation in 2006; Kaeti Bailie, who having pioneered one sister city for Sonoma, California, inspired me to propose another, in Vietnam.

The CBS News Archives Division, for locating a transcript of the November 12, 1965, *Evening News* broadcast; and librarians at Michigan State University, the Library of Michigan, Oberlin College, and UCLA.

Richard Boylan and Daniel Rooney, archivists at the National Archives and Records Administration, for help in locating military information; Jim Henthorn, whose Web site, http://www.nexus.net/~911gfx/vietnam.html, generated the map with the X; and Miles Brown, Jessica Lightburn at the Pentagon, and Mary Claire Murphy, formerly of the Office of the Secretary of Defense, for leading me to Mike Hunsucker of the U.S. Air Force 14th Weather Squadron, who provided weather data for the Mekong Delta.

Doctors Paul Austin and Larry Turley (now a winemaker) helped with medical questions. Mark Brokering, my former boss at HarperCollins, offered sage advice on several occasions. Archivist Lynn Downey of Levi Strauss & Co. organized papers when they threatened to take over my office. Steve Graydon prepared slides and photos, scanned images, provided guidance on technical matters, and kept me from losing my sense of humor.

At the Bread Loaf Writers' Conference in 2006, Paul Austin persuaded me to read from my work. I'm grateful that he did, because Julie Barer happened to be in the audience and subsequently signed me. That such an excellent literary agent had confidence in me and this book was immensely encouraging. My thanks to Julie and to my fellow Bread Loafers, the conference staff, and my teachers, in particular Ted Conover and Scott Russell Sanders, who helped me find the path and provided course correction.

Members of the Wesleyan University Class of 1963 invited me to their forty-fifth reunion and adopted me as an honorary classmate. That same weekend, I met Suzanna Tamminen and felt an immediate rapport with my soft-spoken, smart, tuba-playing editor. With Suzanna, Leslie Starr and Stephanie Elliott at Wesleyan, Ann Brash, and Charlotte Strick formed a dream publishing team.

Someone special created a writer's colony for me, which he named Bagel Loaf, and read chapters with an expert eye.

Other readers on whom I relied were my beloved daughter, May Boeve, who offered many insightful comments, and John Sommer, who brought his knowledge of Vietnam and IVS to the task of vetting the manuscript. George Arack, Jr., Colleen Daly, Larry Laverentz, Caryn and Bill Reading, and Chuck Theusch also read parts or all of the manuscript. Any shortcomings that remain are, however, my doing.

Echoing the words my parents wrote many years ago to the people who helped them when they needed it, to you my door is always open.

NOTES

ONE | The Brunt of It (pages 7–17)

1. "Young City Civilian Slain by Viet Cong," *Oklahoma City Times,* November 12, 1965. Used with permission of the Associated Press, copyright © 2008. All rights reserved. Original copy in the author's collection.
2. Ibid. Used with permission of the Oklahoma Publishing Company, copyright © 1965. All rights reserved. Original copy in the author's collection.
3. The author's mother was a direct descendant of two Yale founders, Noadiah Russell and James Pierpont.
4. John Balaban, *Remembering Heaven's Face,* p. 69 (Athens, Georgia: University of Georgia Press, 1991).
5. Paul A. Rodell, "International Voluntary Services in Vietnam: War and the Birth of Activism, 1958–1967," p. 242, n. 8, in *Peace & Change,* vol. 27, no. 2, April 2002.
6. Le Ly Hayslip, "Sisters and Brothers," *When Heaven and Earth Changed Places,* p. 234 (New York: Doubleday, 1989).

TWO | "Kiss the Sisses Good-bye" (18–34)

1. John Sommer, "Caught in the Middle," in Stuart Rawlings, ed., *The IVS Experience: From Algeria to Viet Nam,* p. 33 (Washington, D.C.: International Voluntary Services, 1992). Author's collection.
2. Richard Holbrooke, Foreword to Harvey Neese and John O'Donnell, eds., *Prelude to Tragedy: Vietnam, 1960–1965,* p. viii (Annapolis, Md.: Naval Institute Press, 2001).
   Tim Weiner, in *Legacy of Ashes: The History of the CIA,* p. 182 (New York: Doubleday, 2007), describes Lansdale as a counterinsurgency specialist whose "trademark was winning third-world hearts and minds with American ingenuity, greenback dollars, and snake oil. He had worked for the CIA and the Pentagon since before the Korean War."
3. Rufe Phillips, "Before We Lost in South Vietnam," in Neese and O'Donnell, eds., *Prelude to Tragedy,* p. 14.

4. Author's interview with Don Luce. Another former IVS volunteer, Willi Meyers, said of Lansdale, "Some of us considered him another CIA/psyops [psychological operations] type." The author corresponded and spent many hours in conversation with dozens of former IVS volunteers. These communications will not be noted unless for amplification or clarification, such as when a source (for example, Don Luce) has been widely interviewed and/or published.

5. "IVS Handbook," p. 7. The publisher and place and year of publication are not listed in part 2 of the handbook that is in the author's collection. Part 2 includes a table of contents and pages 1–35. Part 1 is missing.

6. Ibid., p. 8.

7. Ibid.

8. Don Luce, "IVS Yesterday and Today," in Rawlings, ed., *The IVS Experience*, p. 1. Author's collection.

9. The first IVS volunteers in Vietnam were witnesses to the coming of the war. Paul Sutton remembers seeing two American flag–draped coffins being loaded onto an aircraft. It was the summer of 1959, and he and Don Luce were waiting for a flight to the Philippines. The caskets contained the bodies of U.S. military advisers killed by Vietcong. "Had I thought to photograph it," he said, "it would have been one of the first photographs of casualties in the Vietnam conflict."

10. This explanation of the Strategic Hamlet Program draws on the description of Rufus Phillips's deputy, Bert Fraleigh, in his "Counterinsurgency in South Vietnam," in Neese and O'Donnell, eds., *Prelude to Tragedy*, pp. 98–103.

11. Weiner, in *Legacy of Ashes*, p. 211, refers to Lansdale's associate as "the CIA's Rufus Phillips."

12. Fraleigh, "Counterinsurgency in South Vietnam," p. 104.

13. Luce, "IVS Yesterday and Today," p. 1.

14. From John F. Kennedy's inaugural address, January 21, 1961.

15. Dang Nguyen, in remarks at the 2005 IVS alumni reunion in Santa Fe, New Mexico, attended by the author.

16. Paul Sutton recalled that, in the late 1950s, American military advisers in Ninh Thuan Province, where he was assigned, kept a low profile. On some occasions they wore khaki pants, T-shirts, and baseball caps while on duty, instead of uniforms.

17. *International Voluntary Services in the Republic of Vietnam, Annual Report, 1963–1964: Annual Report of IVS Participation in the Financial Assistance Program (Agriculture, Education, Health Improvement and Development) Sponsored Jointly by the Agricultural, Education and Health Agencies of Vietnam and the United States Agency for International Development*, p. 6 (Washington, D.C.: International Voluntary Services, 1964). Author's collection.

18. "IVS Handbook," p. 33.

THREE | Sand Between My Toes (35–47)

1. Willi Meyers's appointment was reported in "Friend Takes over Hunting's Viet Nam Job," *Daily Oklahoman*, July 4, 1966. Original copy in the author's collection. Later, when many college campuses were rife with antiwar protests, some IVS recruiters found themselves heckled or harassed by students and professors who believed that IVS was supporting the U.S. war effort. According to IVS alumnus John Esser, protesters held a former teammate hostage for a day in a college placement office.

2. "Russell, General William Huntington," *Genealogical and Family History of the State of Connecticut: A Record of the Achievements of Her People in the Making of a Commonwealth and the Founding of a Nation* (4 vols.), vol. 1, p. 430, edited by William Richard Cutter, Edward Henry Clement, Samuel Hart, Mary Kingsbury Talcott, Frederick Bostwick, and Ezra Scollay Stearns (New York: Lewis Historical Publishing Company, 1911). Author's collection. The Wikipedia entry on General Russell (wikipedia.org/wiki/William_Huntington_Russell, last accessed November 29, 2008) suggests, right or wrong, that the financial hardship story is likely untrue because his cousin, Samuel Russell, was a wealthy opium trader.

3. Allan Cromley, Washington Bureau, "Medals, Praise Go to City Family," *Oklahoma City Times*, April 27, 1966. See also Allan Cromley, "Hubert Charms Away Tears," *Daily Oklahoman*, April 28, 1966. Used with permission of the Oklahoma Publishing Company, copyright © 1966. All rights reserved. Original copies in the author's collection.

4. Carl T. Rowan, "A Letter to the Vice President," *Washington Star*, May 6, 1966. Original copy in the author's collection.

FOUR | "Just Heard over the Radio" (48–64)

1. In correspondence with the author, several IVS alumni expressed mistrust of some American journalists who served in Vietnam. Paul Lukitsch, for example, stated, "Some reporters went out into the countryside to gather the news while others stayed in Saigon, enjoying the comforts of the Continental Hotel, etc., and just repeated to their media whatever the daily MACV briefing had told them. When a reporter sent the story back to his or her newspaper or whatever, the editor or subeditors could, and usually would, make changes to suit their own editorial or political slant."

2. "IVS Handbook," pp. 10, 11.

3. See "Places of Interest," in Ann Caddell Crawford, *Customs and Culture of Vietnam*, ch. 11 (www.militaryliving.com/vietnam2/index.html), for a description of François' and its reputation for serving both American and Vietcong clientele.

   If a rumor the author heard from a former IVSer doing business in Vietnam is true, François died in 1975. It is said he attempted to cling to the landing gear of one of the last American airplanes to leave South Vietnam.

4. Chuck Fields and other IVS volunteers were instrumental in carrying out the Pig-Corn Program, a USAID self-help project. According to Harvey Neese, a former IVSer who returned to Vietnam in 1962 as a Rural Affairs employee, the program was "high on the list of counterinsurgency activities to show that the Vietnamese government was interested in helping the rural people in the countryside." See Neese, "Destination South Vietnam, 1959," in Neese and O'Donnell, eds., *Prelude to Tragedy*, p. 258.

   As Neese explains, the program allowed villagers to purchase three Yorkshire piglets and U.S. surplus feed corn on credit. Sheets of metal roofing and bags of cement for constructing a pigsty floor were also provided. Fifteen thousand pigs were distributed.

5. Holbrooke, Foreword, p. viii.

6. Phillips, "Before We Lost in South Vietnam," p. 53.

7. Ibid., p. 57, n. 6.

8. Ibid.

9. "IVS Handbook," p. 34. Ping-pong and billiards were popular sports, the handbook stated, adding, "If you enjoy these . . . , you will be able to find some real sharp competition among the Vietnamese."

10. Neese, "Destination South Vietnam, 1959," p. 275; on p. 278 is a photo of the occasion.

11. Don Luce and John Sommer, *Viet Nam: The Unheard Voices*, p. 44 (Ithaca, N.Y.: Cornell University Press, 1969); foreword by Edward M. Kennedy.

12. Included in a letter from John Hughes in the Washington, D.C., IVS office, dated November 14, 1963. Author's collection.

13. Ibid.

FIVE | "A Peaceful Sleep Forever" (65–84)

1. Author's collection.

2. The source of these verses is unknown.

3. In time, Wisner would attain the highest rank in the U.S. Foreign Service, that of career ambassador.

4. Jay Turk, "Eulogies Pour in to Parents of Peter Hunting, Extraordinary Ordinary Kid," *Sunday Oklahoman*, December 19, 1965. Original copy in the author's collection.

5. Pete was the first IVS volunteer to be killed during his term of service. Ten others would die in Southeast Asia either during or soon after their tour. See the dedication in Rawlings, ed., *The IVS Experience*, pp. 2–3.

6. Beryl Darrah's account of his work on the Peter M. Hunting Memorial Library and other experiences in Vietnam is posted on his Web site, www.bdarrah.com/VietnamYears, last accessed November 18, 2008.

7. Ibid. Another former volunteer, Roger Montgomery, echoed Darrah's sentiments in correspondence with the author: "Both sides thought we were spies for some group or the other, largely because we spoke Vietnamese and walked around without guns. It was just no use telling them that we were not spies; only confirmed their beliefs."

8. From "A Library in Phan Rang Was Named After an IVser," a Vietnamese newspaper clipping without name or date sent to the author's parents by Jay Scarborough. English translation courtesy of Kim Nguyen Tang. Author's collection.

   CORDS, the Office of Civil Operations and Rural Development Support, was formed in 1967 to coordinate U.S. military and civilian pacification programs, including those of the State Department, USAID, U.S. Information Agency, and CIA. The head of CORDS, Robert W. Komer, reported to General William Westmoreland.

   The author's mother originally sent a check for $1,252.00, representing the combined contributions of family and friends. Additional contributions were made directly to IVS.

9. "Survivors of Lost GIs Urge War Step-Up," *Oklahoma City Times*, October 19, 1967. Used with permission of the Oklahoma Publishing Company, copyright © 1967. All rights reserved. Original copy in the author's collection.

SIX | Mr. Tall American (85–100)

1. *International Voluntary Services in the Republic of Vietnam, 1963–1964*, pp. 50–51.

2. Ibid, p. 49.

3. Ibid., p. 45.

4. "Would You Like to Have All of the Fish You Can Eat All of Your Life at No Cost Whatever?" in *Helping People Help Themselves: A Guide to Self-Help*, page unnumbered (n.p.: Office for Rural Affairs: United States Operations Mission/Vietnam, Publications and Graphics Division, 1963); published in Vietnamese and English. Author's collection.

5. "Smoking Meat, Fish and Poultry," in ibid., p. 2.

6. Lt. Gen. Phillip B. Davidson, *Vietnam at War: The History, 1946–1975*, pp. 314–16 (Novato, Calif.: Presidio Press, 1988).

7. "IVS Handbook," p. 32.

SEVEN | Never "Very Good at the 'Why'" (101–117)

1. For this anecdote and others that illustrate the evolution of ivs leaders Don Luce, Gene Stoltzfus, and Willi Meyers, see Rodell, "International Voluntary Services in Vietnam," p. 229.
2. Ibid., p. 230.
3. Ibid., p. 229. Winburn T. Thomas, in *The Vietnam Story of International Voluntary Services, Inc.*, pp. 69–70, states that the early ivser (who was male) was effective because he "recognized and was content to work within the definition of his assignment, which was to execute 'on the lowest level . . . the objectives of us foreign policy that the American Embassy and usaid were executing at the national level.'" Three additional reasons were a volunteer's idealism, will, and energy; his (and later her) willingness to live on the same level as Vietnamese and speak their language, and to avoid identification with other American entities/ organizations; and his (or her) supervision by peers who had held the same job before being promoted to ivs leadership positions. On page 41 of the same publication, Pete is referred to as "the ivs martyr." Document available at the usaid Development Experience Clearinghouse Web site, www.dec.usaid.gov, last accessed November 18, 2008.
4. Luce and Sommer, *Viet Nam: The Unheard Voices*, p. 12.
5. Author's interview with Gene Stoltzfus, July 12, 2008.
6. Rodell, "International Voluntary Services in Vietnam," p. 237.
7. Author's interview with Gene Stoltzfus, July 12, 2008.
8. Ibid.
9. For the full text of the letter, see Luce and Sommer, *Viet Nam: The Unheard Voices*, pp. 315–21.
10. Ibid., p. 20. Don Luce's account of releasing the letter is based on his experience alone, although he and John Sommer wrote in the first person plural. Though of one mind with his former teammates, John had returned to the United States before the letter was released.
11. Ibid., p. 20.
12. *New York Times*, September 25, 1967.
13. Luce and Sommer, *Viet Nam: The Unheard Voices*, p. 21.
14. Don Luce, "The Tiger Cages of Vietnam," p. 1, www.historiansagainstwar.org/ resources/torture/luce.html, last accessed November 28, 2008.
15. Ibid., p. 1.
16. This quotation and others from John Sommer are from an interview with the author.
17. Rodell, "International Voluntary Services in Vietnam," p. 232.
18. Ibid., p. 236.

19. This quotation and others from Gene Stoltzfus are from an interview with the author.

EIGHT | "At War in Another Year" (118–134)

1. From "Jet Well Drilling," in *Helping People Help Themselves: A Guide to Self-Help,* pp. 1, 2.
2. Harkins stated, "I am an optimist, and I am not going to allow my staff to be pessimistic." In Stanley Karnow, *Vietnam: A History,* p. 258 (New York: Penguin, 1984).
3. Ibid., p. 345.
4. The Central Lowlands region is the long, narrow band that lies between Vietnam's coast and mountains.

NINE | Trip to Vietnam (136–153)

1. Recounted in Linda James, "Vietnam Is Disorganized but Hospitable," *San Diego Union,* Knight-Ridder News Service, June 2, 1991.
2. "It's the Birthday Season," *Sonoma Index-Tribune,* Staff Notebook, November 12, 1993. Original copy in the author's collection.

TEN | "A Promise Is a Promise" (154–170)

1. "Dependents Withdrawing!" in "The Cyclo," published by USOM to Vietnam, February 10, 1965, issue no. 2, p. 1. Author's collection.
2. "The Lone American," *Time,* April 23, 1965, www.time.com, last accessed August 5, 2008. The article states that the secretary, Barbara Robbins, was the first American civilian killed in Vietnam.
3. Pauline Kael, *Kiss Kiss Bang Bang,* pp. 177–78 (Boston: Atlantic–Little Brown), 1968.
4. It is unclear whether Pete meant that the war would end soon or that it would create conditions under which IVS would be unable to function.
5. "Airborne" is probably a reference to the U.S. 183rd Airborne Division.

ELEVEN | "An Open Question" (171–182)

1. Pete and Larry took their Vietnamese language study seriously, but learning the proper inflections took time. At a reunion of IVS alumni in 2007 at Sea Ranch, California, attended by the author, Larry related that for weeks as a newcomer to Vietnam he thought he was telling people, "I have a headache," only to learn he had been saying, "I have syphilis."

2. Mike Chilton, a former IVS agriculture team leader, recalled in a conversation with the author that the situation eventually led to a discussion about weapons. "If you had to work in an area where a handgun was necessary, your effectiveness was probably already diminished," he explained, "and if you were picked up, chances were that [if you were carrying a weapon] you would have lost credibility."

3. The countries IVS served in were Algeria, Bangladesh, Bolivia, Botswana, Cambodia, Cape Verde, Caribbean (various locations), Colombia, Ecuador, Egypt, Ghana, Honduras, Iraq, Jordan, Laos, Liberia, Libya, Madagascar, Mali, Mauritania, Morocco, Nepal, Papua New Guinea, Sudan, Syria, Thailand, Vietnam, Yemen, Zaire, and Zimbabwe.

4. In disputing the claim of former Defense Secretary Robert McNamara in his *In Retrospect: The Tragedy and Lessons of Vietnam*, former IVS volunteer Harvey Neese has written: "There were literally hundreds of Americans in South Vietnam who had worked and lived in the provinces many years before 1965. Many of them could speak Vietnamese. Although they knew the situation in the rural areas where the war was to be fought by American troops, no one wanted to tap their knowledge. It was an arrogant and stupid attitude by American officials that led America into the Vietnam morass with little chance of winning. If political and military leaders had bothered to ask those who knew the situation on the level where the war was to be fought and then took their advice, America might never have blundered into the unwinnable situation." See Neese, "Destination South Vietnam," p. 279.

TWELVE | "Too Much Talk about Danger" (183–198)

1. Whether the author's parents took Pete's article to the newspaper or what an editor might have thought about it is not known. No evidence of publication has been found.

2. Luce and Sommer, *Viet Nam: The Unheard Voices*, p. 246.

3. Ibid., pp. 246–47.

4. *International Voluntary Services in the Republic of Vietnam for the Year of June 1965–June 1966*, p. 33 (Washington, D.C.: International Voluntary Services, 1966). Author's collection.

5. Ibid., p. 24.

6. As Ray Gill told the author, Air America planes were targets because they transported Americans, notably CIA personnel.

7. Luce and Sommer, *Viet Nam: The Unheard Voices*, p. 189.

8. This and other interesting anecdotes about Lane, including her trip to South Vietnam, are related by William T. Anderson in *Laura's Rose: The Story of Rose Wilder Lane, Daughter of Laura Ingalls Wilder* (centennial edition), pp. 19, 33, 35, and 41–42 (De Smet, S.D.: Laura Ingalls Wilder Memorial Society, 1976).

9. Rose Wilder Lane, "August in Vietnam," *Woman's Day*, December 1965, pp. 33–94. Original copy in the author's collection.

THIRTEEN | Pete's Long-Lost Letters Surface (199–216)

1. *Scorpio*, p. 8 (New York: Zodiac International, 1964). Author's collection.
2. *Cancer*, p. 73 (New York: Zodiac International, 1964). Author's collection.
3. Despite the author's inquiries under provisions of the Freedom of Information Act and the able assistance of staff members at the National Archives and Records Administration, in College Park, Maryland, no copy of this report has turned up.

FOURTEEN | Darkening Skies (217–224)

1. The story was sent to the author's parents by Don Luce with an undated note signed by Robin Pell, a public relations officer with USAID in Vietnam. He indicated that a George Chuljean, otherwise unidentified, wrote the story. No evidence of its publication has been found.
2. "The War: Deeper & Wider," *Time*, November 19, 1965, vol. 86, no. 21, p. 35. Original copy in the author's collection.
3. Lydia M. Fish, "General Edward G. Lansdale and the Folksongs of Americans in the Vietnam War," *Journal of the American Folklore Society*, October–December 1989, vol. 102, no. 406, http://faculty.buffalostate.edu/fishlm/folksongs/lansdale .pdf, last accessed July 29, 2005.
4. Joint United States Public Affairs Office (JUSPAO) Psyop Policy no. 36, May 10, 1967, www.psywarrior.com/superstition.html, last accessed Dec. 7, 2005.
5. Ibid.
6. Ibid.

INDEX

ABOUT THE AUTHOR

Jill Hunting was on a writing retreat in Umbria, Italy, when she set aside a book about food and wine to take up a more personal story: barely fifteen when her older brother, Pete, was killed in Vietnam, she had wondered for years if reports were true that friends led him to his death.

That afternoon in the Italian countryside, she turned to the story of the brother who died and the family that didn't talk about it. The writing of *Finding Pete* became a bridge from the past to the future, leading the author to initiate a sister-city relationship between her home in California's wine country and her brother's in Ninh Thuan Province, and to launch a feasibility study of lavender farming in Vietnam. She proposed the *Book of Remembrance,* a sculpture honoring civilians killed in war, for the new headquarters of the U.S. Institute of Peace, on the War and Peace corner of the National Mall in Washington, D.C.

She lives in Sonoma, California.

A READING GROUP GUIDE TO *FINDING PETE*

According to a 2005 United Nations report, conventional warfare has decreased in recent decades and the nature of violent conflict has changed. Increasingly, civilians are at risk, either deliberately targeted or caught in crossfires. In the "Author's Note" to her book, Jill Hunting says that some survivors of civilians killed in war go forward with "a chamber deep within sealed up." What does this description evoke? What benefits can we anticipate from opening up such chambers?

Finding Pete is a researched memoir. Half of the book is about the author's quest to learn what happened to Pete. The alternating chapters are the story of his life in Vietnam as reconstructed from his letters. The book is structured like a detective story. In your opinion, what was the most important discovery that the author made in the course of her research? How does the author change or evolve throughout the course of the story? What events trigger such changes? In Jill's journey of healing, what was the "tipping point"?

What event in the book was most moving for you? What was the most powerful scene in the book?

After graduating from Wesleyan University, Pete Hunting joined International Voluntary Services (IVS), an NGO on which the Peace Corps was modeled. In college, he had studied Chinese and government. He thought his job in Vietnam would be to teach English. What might have motivated young men and women to join IVS? What were some of the risks for IVSers in Vietnam? How might these have been similar to, or different from risks faced by other Americans there?

If you had been faced, as Pete was, with the decision to extend your IVS contract, join USAID, join the military, or return to the U.S., what would you have done?

The book features Jill Hunting and her family, along with Pete's co-workers in Vietnam, and his girlfriends in the States. Who in the book do you relate to? Why?

The author's reserved New England family didn't talk about Pete's death. Her mother tells her that all of Pete's letters have been destroyed in a basement flood. How do you feel about the author's mother? What would you have done in her shoes? Has she unwittingly closed out the rest of the family, or do you think she has consciously chosen to shut them out? Did you find yourself criticizing her, empathizing with her, or both?

Pete didn't know it, but his letters were eyewitness accounts of U.S. policy in the making. Reading them, you can feel the war coming closer. Has this book had an impact on your view of the Vietnam War or war in general? Was Pete a "typical" or an "atypical" American? True or false: Pete personifies what the U.S. lost in Vietnam.

The subject of Vietnam touches people deeply, even after all these years. How is this book like other books or movies about the Vietnam War, or war in general? How is it different? What are some ways that war can divide families?

What is the significance of the image that closes the book?